PROSE STYLE: A HANDBOOK FOR WRITERS

STONE & BELL
PROSE STYLE:
A HANDBOOK
FOR WRITERS

WILFRED STONE

Stanford University

J. G. BELL

Stanford University Press

McGRAW-HILL BOOK COMPANY

New York, St. Louis, San Francisco, Toronto, London, Sydney

Library of Congress Catalog Card Number 68–14762

1 2 3 4 5 6 7 8 9 0   BABA   7 5 4 3 2 1 0 6 9 8

CREDITS FOR EXCERPTS

Harold A. Abramson, excerpt from *The New York Times Book Review,*
January 3, 1965. © 1965 by The New York Times Company. Reprinted
by permission.

James Baldwin, excerpt from "What It Means To Be An American," *The
New York Times Book Review,* January 25, 1959. © 1959 by The New
York Times Company. Reprinted by permission.

Patricia Blake, excerpt from "A Bargain with the Devil," *The New York
Times Book Review,* October 22, 1967. © 1967 by The New York Times
Company. Reprinted by permission.

J. Bronowski, excerpt from *Science and Human Values,* Julian Messner,
Inc., 1956.

Herb Caen, excerpt from his column in the *San Francisco Chronicle,* February 16, 1964.

Bruce Catton, excerpt from *A Stillness at Appomattox,* Doubleday & Company, Inc.

Loren Eiseley, excerpt from *The Immense Journey,* Random House, Inc.,
1946.

H. W. and F. G. Fowler, excerpt from *The King's English,* Oxford University Press, 3rd ed. 1930. By permission of The Clarendon Press, Oxford.

Henry Watson Fowler, excerpt from *Modern English Usage,* Oxford University Press, rev. ed. 1965. By permission of The Clarendon Press, Oxford.

Sir Ernest Gowers, excerpt from *Plain Words,* Alfred A. Knopf, Inc., 1954.

Julian Huxley, excerpt from *Man Stands Alone,* Harper & Row, Publishers,
Inc.

James Joyce, excerpt from *A Portrait of the Artist as a Young Man* by James
Joyce. Copyright 1916 by B. W. Huebsch, 1944 by Nora Joyce; copyright
© 1964 by the Estate of James Joyce. All Rights Reserved. Reprinted by
permission of The Viking Press, Inc., the Executors of the James Joyce
Estate, and Jonathan Cape Ltd., publishers.

Weston La Barre, excerpt from *American Anthropologist,* 67:595, April, 1965.

PREFACE

The freshman of today is a more sophisticated individual than his counterpart of ten years ago. He has been exposed to more information, has met more academic competition, has watched more TV, has had more of what the Victorians called "experience," and—the point here—has had more training in the fundamentals of English composition. Freshman English in college is still a going concern, perhaps more so than ever, but it has increasingly left its remedial aspect behind and gone on to more sophisticated concerns. For the student in such a course, or in any of the various other courses involving writing that Freshman English has splintered into during the last few years, a new kind of handbook is needed. We think this book is the proper kind.

First of all, it is short. It makes no attempt to be encyclopedic, or to provide lists of all the pitfalls that the beginning writer might possibly encounter. We have assumed that in fundamental matters the student needs to be reminded, not taught from the ground up, and that so far as possible the old rules and caveats should be not merely repeated but related organically to the writer's purposes. We have written a shortwinded book, partly to keep it interesting, but mostly to focus students' attention on what we think is most important to their development as writers.

Second, it is designed to be read and not just referred to. Most teachers of Freshman English will remember that semester or quarter when they never did get around to using the old-fashioned handbook—except perhaps for occasional reference. It was too mechanical, too heavy, too removed from what a good Freshman English class is all about. Such a book is like a fire extinguisher on the wall: there in case it is needed, but often dusty from disuse. We have tried to write a different sort of book, one that a teacher can hand his students early in the course and say: "Read this through, learn what you can from it, try to practice what it preaches, and keep it handy when you are writing."

Third, it ranges far beyond such basic matters as syntax, diction, and usage. It is also a guidebook to style, to research strategies, and even to the kind of person the writer ought to be. We present writing as a three-way relationship between writer, reader, and written work—as a liaison among all three elements, not a mechanical operation. We have made much of questions of tone, style, and imagery for these are important parts of the "voice" that readers hear in a writer's work and to which they fundamentally respond.

Finally, the book is the combined effort of a college teacher and a professional editor: the first, an authority of sorts on what students need and want in their early maturity as writers; the second, an authority on writing as such. As we point out more than once in the text, the college writer must be both writer and editor. How very different the two talents are, and how they complement each other, we have discovered only in the course of writing this book.

WILFRED STONE
J. G. BELL

CONTENTS

PART 3 THE RESEARCH PAPER

PART 1
THE WRITER
AND HIS MESSAGE

1
ABOUT WRITING

Often the beginning writer thinks of good writing as something he must imitate rather than something he can create. Surrounded as he is by handbooks and anthologies—those weighty repositories of precept and example—he feels frustrated, even a little humiliated. In the face of all those established rules and models, the work of experts and professionals, he concludes that rote learning and imitation are his best hope. To be a writer, he feels, he must become someone other than himself; he must set aside the Joe Smith he is and write like some Joseph R. Smith he is not, never was, but vaguely supposes he ought to be. From this point of view, writing is not saying what one thinks, but more like acting in a play written by others.

This point of view is quite mistaken. Moreover, it makes the job of learning to write more difficult and less rewarding than it ought to be. Writing should be a matter of finding your own voice and using it—*your* voice, not someone else's. If Joe Smith is who you are, then Joe Smith is the one your reader wants to hear from. A writer should put himself into the act, write his own part. Nothing less, in the long run, makes writing worth reading.

But the act of writing is never entirely a private performance; it is a three-way relationship between writer, reader, and written work. These three aspects are the basis of the following discussion.

THE WRITER

Writing begins with the writer. He must have something to say, must want to say it, and must learn how to say it clearly and well. The easiest of these three requirements is the last: the rules and conventions of good writing. They can be learned, and a good part of this book is given over to teaching them. What cannot be learned (at least in the same way) is self-confidence, belief in yourself and the validity and interest of what you write. Many students look at a blank sheet of paper and then despair. How can I have anything to say that the teacher or anybody else will want to hear? What do I know about history, psychology, ethics, science? I am young, yet I am supposed to write from personal experience. I am a beginner, yet I am supposed to write like a professional. How can I?

The answer is: Don't try so hard. Don't try to be professional; try to be honest with yourself, with your own feelings and thoughts, and with the ideas you encounter in your reading. There is nearly always some point where you and your experience do intersect with those ideas, some point where you can speak with authority. The point may be only a tiny corner of a large issue, and may take some searching and pondering to find; but authority is none the less real for being asserted in a small matter. Writing about World War II is inherently no more interesting than writing about your roommate. The interest depends not on the size of the subject, but on what you have to say.

Let us assume that you have been assigned a paper on two well-known essays on American dating practices, Margaret Mead's "Trends in Personal Life" and Geoffrey Gorer's "Love and Friendship." You are no anthropologist or sociologist, but you have had dates, and to this extent you are an expert. You cannot pass final judgment on Mead's or Gorer's argument, perhaps, but you can respond to some part of it that pleases you, annoys you, or evokes some lively sense of recognition. These reactions—pleasure, annoyance, recognition—are part of you; no one else on earth can react in exactly the same way. In a certain sense, these responses say who you are.

Maybe the following passage from Margaret Mead interests you:

> Beginning with the date, significantly an occasion in time rather than a relationship to a person, boys and girls practice a style of social intercourse whose content is personal and sexual but whose form is impersonal and asexual. Each date stands alone, one incident in a series whose number and character determine one's popularity rating. One has dates because it is the thing to do. The popular boy goes with the popular girl, because by so doing each enhances his own popularity. The evening is spent in a conversational and postural game as patterned as a minuet, in which the boy claims the girl's favors as his right, and she refuses them, because she is secure enough in her popularity to do so. All refusals lie with her, and she learns to discipline her responsiveness so that she will never go farther than she wishes.

Or the following passage from Gorer:

> Because every American man has a feminine component in his personality, there is always a deeply hidden doubt concerning his own masculinity; and any person or situation which might bring this into question is seen as a drastic threat to a man's integrity and reacted to with violence and panic.

The wealth of ideas here is enough for several themes; but it is your job to concentrate on whatever it was that aroused your interest in one of these passages. Ask yourself why you responded to it. Search your experience for evidence to support it, prove it wrong, or add important qualifications to it. Ask yourself questions that have answers, that you can meet from your own experience: not general questions like "Is dating really foolish?" but specific questions like "When I dated Kathy in high school, did she behave like that?" Only in this way can you find ground where you can stand with confidence and speak with authority. The young writer's inclination is all the other way, to make the whole world his province. But mature writers know that an intelligent statement about a fragment of experience carries far more weight than a dozen unsupported generalizations.

Generalizations are of course important; they represent the end products of thought and one of its rewards. But one does not start there; one starts with the evidence, the concrete data and details out of which generalizations are made. Our advice, then, for the dating paper is not to worry about abstractions like "popularity" and "masculinity," but to concentrate on a small incident that might illuminate what Mead and Gorer are writing about: a date that went wrong, a response that puzzled you, a relationship that does not fit the pattern.

Let us say that you, a girl, are interested in the question of popularity raised in the Mead quotation. You are a popular girl yourself, though you had never defined yourself that way before. In class discussion someone suggested that whether a popular girl accepts or refuses a date depends more on her sense of status than on whether or not she likes the man involved. The idea seemed radical and bothered you. Another member of the class complained that most student politicians thoroughly confused popularity and leadership, could not tell the difference between leading the crowd and giving it what it wants. This bothered you even more; the class president is a good friend of yours. Then one boy backed up Mead by saying that the typical college girl, in his experience, was or was not popular according to whether or not she was sexually generous. This struck you as a disgusting idea. You have always been popular, you like parties, you are going with a football player, you don't pretend to be an intellectual; but you don't see why such qualities should make you an object of suspicion or stir this kind of discussion. Is being popular un-American or something? Those anthropologists and the students siding with them seem to think that unless you're against everything you're not healthy. You think there's something to be said on the other side. You start to write.

You write a couple of paragraphs, and then stop. Until now you have been writing in the clear, sharp accents of righteous indignation. But caution rears its head. It occurs to you that the teacher seemed to *like* those essays. Why risk offending him? After all, you want to graduate from this school, not die trying. So you talk yourself out of your indignation—in this case your true subject—and decide to play it safe. You develop a case against popularity as a value, and you bow out of the act yourself by making another person—a high school acquaintance named Eloise—the butt of your criticism. Here is a sample of your theme:

> Eloise was a pretty girl, much prettier than I was, and always had dates on weekends while often I stayed home. She was a very sweet girl, too, but all this attention went to her head. When I first knew her in Kansas City, she liked to come over to my house on weekends and we would listen to records or talk, but after she started going out with boys this sort of thing was no fun to her any longer. She went from bad to worse. At first she was contented with two or three dates a month, but at the end of that year she just *had* to go out about every night. Popularity had become all she lived for. All she could talk about—on those rare occasions when she still talked with me—were clothes and dancing and boy friends. The lust for popularity had turned a nice girl into a tramp.

Although the "you" of this story is our invention, the paragraph is from a real theme. Because it was tidy and relatively error-free, the theme was graded C+. Why so low a mark?

First, the theme is boring. Eloise is a cardboard figure. We never see her, never learn whether she smiles or not, whether she is short or tall, what her voice sounds like, what kind of clothes she wears. You may not have room for all the details, but there should be room for some. Without them, a reader cannot get up much interest in Eloise one way or the other—and there is very little else in the theme to arouse his interest.

Second, the theme is superficial: it does not begin to come to grips with any of the substantive issues raised by Mead and Gorer. It is full of personal experience at the "I said . . . she said" level, but it does not use this experience to support any particular idea or argument. To write about personal experience is the whole point of the assignment, but the personal experience must be relevant. The writer must show that she has taken in what Mead and Gorer have to say; she can endorse it, oppose it, or suggest modifications in it, but she cannot ignore it. Mead and Gorer see the dating system as a specifically American problem. Our writer never questions the system; she apparently sees it as natural, universal, and eternal. Though she has a hard word for Eloise, it is not for excessive attachment to the system but for violating its standards of discipline and decorum. Had the writer elected to defend the system, as in our reconstruction she started out to do, she might have used Eloise effectively. As it is, Eloise is simply irrelevant.

Finally, and most important, the theme is poor because the writer is not on the level. She hides too much; she wears a mask. The question she asks is "What should I say?" not "What do I think?" and this attempt to please destroys the theme. Not only is her writing proper without conviction, lighthearted without real validity, but it fails even to achieve its goal of disguising her true feelings. It takes no trained psychiatrist to see envy in her words, even before the giveaway word *tramp* at the end. Clearly Eloise's sexual behavior bothered the writer. Could it be that in the race for popularity Eloise beat her out by having fewer scruples? Then why doesn't she come out and talk about it? There is a good subject there, and a relevant one; it should be discussed not indirectly, but directly, perhaps along the lines of the writer's initial inspiration. Here is a girl of real intelligence, with something to say, who for prudential reasons kills off her real self in favor of a fraudulent self. Nothing is gained by this kind of self-murder, not even a good grade; and an opportunity for learning is lost.

Good writing, in short, begins in self-knowledge (or some degree of it) and helps provoke further self-knowledge. The act of writing is an act of self-commitment. "How do I know what I mean till I see what I say?" said the old lady, and she has a point. We are not saying that all good writing consists of forthright confessions of weakness, confusion, fear, or sin. In writing, as in talking, you are under no obligation to reveal matters that you would rather keep to yourself. What we are saying is that what you do write should be true to your experience, true to your vision of the way things are—not your mother's vision, not your teacher's vision, *your* vision. The reader usually knows when you are saying what you mean. He also usually knows when you are saying what you think you ought to say, or what you hope somebody will think is profound. When you say what you mean, he will keep on reading; when your mind turns off, so will his.

But what about subjects more distant from the student's personal experience—a political or literary issue, for example, or a historical question? The situation is not basically different. The student may be obliged to do more research, to gather knowledge from books and other sources, before he begins to write; but still his writing will begin where his research crosses some private nerve that relates it to his own concerns. He may be more at home comparing the road performance of Fords and Chevrolets than comparing the statesmanship of Jefferson and Hamilton, but the problems are different only in degree. That difference of degree, that widening of horizons, is part of what growing up and getting educated means.

THE AUDIENCE

Without an audience or the hope of an audience, most writers would have no motive for writing. Writing is a medium of communication. It carries your thoughts not only out from you, but in to someone else. How you write will depend on who that someone else is: you write one way in a letter to a child, another way in a business letter, still another way in a love letter. The differences are not only in what you want to say, but in what will interest your reader, and in what ideas and words you think he can grasp.

What is true of a letter is equally true of a theme or a report. If you are a scientist writing for scientists, a clergyman for clergymen, a labor leader for union members, you will feel free to use terms that a lay audience would not understand without an explanation. The same assumptions about the educational and intellectual level of your readers will govern other decisions as well. For example, they may determine the length of your sentences and paragraphs (inexperienced readers like them short), the complexity of your syntax, the level of detail.

If you are addressing a general audience—as, let us say, a writer for *Life* or *Harper's*—you will adjust your writing to the presumed capacities of a much wider range of readers. If you use technical language, you will be sure to explain what it means; if you deal with complex issues, you will state them in clear and simple terms; if you take a position on a controversial topic, you will be concerned with how readers may react to what you say. If, by contrast, you ignore your readers' capacities, or even if you overestimate or underestimate them, your words will be imperfectly understood at best, and probably will go unread.

To say that a writer must think constantly of his readers, must anticipate their confusions and choose his words accordingly, is not to contradict what we said earlier about the need for honesty and courage. The purpose of writing is to say something, not to get published. If you temporize or compromise your principles, if you oversimplify to the point of misrepresenting, if you pander to the prejudices of an editor or a teacher, you will not be the kind of writer that we are talking about. Your integrity as a writer comes first. When we define attention to your readers' capacities as a very close second, it is only because a writer's integrity has no meaning if his writing is ignored.

We have spoken here in terms of publication, and of a wide range of readers. Though you are not literally writing for publication, you should imagine that you are—and that your teacher is not your audience so much as your editor, receiving and judging a manuscript you have sent him at his request. If the manuscript is something that he thinks would interest the readers of his magazine, he will accept it; if not, he will send it back. Your teacher, to be sure, is an audience, too, and since he may be your most attentive and critical reader, you can hardly be indifferent to his reactions. But his personal reactions are secondary to his views on how your imaginary audience will react, and on what revisions might make its reaction more favorable. In short, you should think of him as an editor helping you to ask wise and honest questions about the effect of your words.

From this point of view, consider the following excerpts from a student theme on the Mead and Gorer essays:

> I had my first date with a college woman (?) before I had ever heard of Mead and Gorer, but the experience showed me how much a guy can learn from books (or es-

says). I showed up at Sally's dorm wearing my green pants and black shirt, and as she got in the machine I wondered what in hell she was doing in a black cocktail dress and heels a foot high. Did she think we were going to Trader Vic's or something? Before we were halfway to the drive-in I realized she was straight from goonsville. I heard a shrieking noise and had already pulled over to the side and had my license out when I realized it was only Sally singing something from *Carmen....*

Later I went through the rest of the ritual. I drove off into a dark road, turned off the ignition, and jumped over to her side of the seat. She hit me with her 14-pound handbag, which only goes to show—as Margaret Mead says—that the woman makes the moral decisions in the dating dance. Moral, hell. She didn't even pay for my missing teeth.

This writer is addressing that most narrow and parochial audience, his own classmates. His motive is to make them laugh, or perhaps to get a rise out of his teacher. These aims, though not wrong in themselves, are here too low and too limited. Like the girl who wrote about Eloise, this writer is not discussing the issues raised by Mead and Gorer but evading them.

What would an editor who had asked for a serious article on dating think of this effort? Not much. A funny anecdote is always welcome when it makes a point, but this particular anecdote is so obviously faked that it is useless as evidence: we simply don't believe that anything like this happened, that a singing voice was mistaken for a police siren, that a handbag weighed fourteen pounds. By indulging his desire to clown, the writer treats his audience with contempt. Exaggerations can be funny, but they are out of place when you are presumably seeking or relating the truth.

Finally, the tone of the paragraph is wrong. The author is playing the adolescent in a place where maturity is expected, and the reader is irritated, just as you might be irritated by your little brother's pranks when you are trying to study. The inappropriate use of slang, the crude exaggeration, the question mark after *woman* all strike the wrong note. The writer has misjudged his audience. Though he shows admirable energy and no little talent, and though he has clearly grasped the "ritual" and "dating dance" issue (as our earlier writer did not), he has failed to focus on his readers and their needs.

THE WRITING

We come finally to the third element in our three-way relationship, writing itself. Much of this book is given over to the rules or conventions that make for clear writing, but conventions are only part of the story. To approach the task of writing only through rules—through learning what is proper and improper, grammatical and ungrammatical, conventional and vulgar—is, we feel, a dead end. The rules are important, but there is a big difference between knowing the rules and knowing how to write, and an even bigger difference between writing "correctly" and writing well. The best writers tend to be people with something on their minds that they want to get off; curious people who want to discover things, or think things through, and tell others what they have come up with. They may be well organized or not, they may or may not get good grades; there seems to be no correlation between the various standard forms of academic excellence and the instinct for expressing oneself in writing. The heart of writing is not rules but this instinct or motivation. If the writer is not motivated, what he writes will not be worth reading; if he is, he will find out where to put his commas and how to write good paragraphs almost as a by-product of his motivation.

There are many varieties of writing, ranging from formal through informal and colloquial to slangy, varieties that reflect both the writer's approach and his assumptions about his audience. There is nothing "wrong" or "right" about any of these varieties as such; each has its place, each its charm. Our concern in this book will be with so-called Standard English, the kind that most educated people write for publication, or public attention, on subjects they are serious about. This definition obviously covers a lot of ground, from the smooth professional journalism of *Time* and *Newsweek* to the academese of *Classical Philology*, from the bright, empty cadences of a television commercial to the earnest exhortations of a Sunday sermon.

Standard English is a variety of usage, not an indication of quality; Standard English is not necessarily good English. Indeed, a great deal of what passes for Standard English in American writing, even at the most exalted levels, is graceless and unclear. That is one reason why books like this one are necessary. These days the writing of business executives, government officials, engineers, social scientists, and educationists is particularly awful. Here, for example, is a communiqué written by an elementary school principal to inform parents of a proposed curriculum change:

> The highly structured nature of grade level standards is well recognized. While a majority of pupils may be operating on what is defined as average or standard, the very fact that material is so identified tends to lead to conformity. Pupils in this school tend, traditionally, to operate above these standards. The teacher usually groups to handle the variation found in the verbal and performance operations of the class. To us, therefore, it was more logical to relate the child to his success and mastery of the subject area sequence rather than to the number on the textbook.

Here is a fair rendering of the same paragraph in Standard English, without the bewildering passives, the elusive abstractions, and the pseudoscientific jargon:

> Most of you parents have had firsthand experience with the old-fashioned grading system, in which children stay with other children of the same age from first grade through sixth regardless of differences in ability. I feel (and the teachers agree) that this system has flaws and needs changing. At present, when a student shows special ability, he is put in a special group within his grade. Under the new system, a child would advance beyond his grade in subjects he is especially good at and stay with his grade in other subjects. If, for example, a third-grade child were good at mathematics and reading, he could do fourth-, fifth-, or even sixth-grade work in these subjects as his talents permitted, while remaining at the third-grade level for his other subjects.

In the rewritten piece we know who is doing the speaking (or writing), we know who is responsible for the ideas being proposed, and we can understand what is being said. The double-talk and the ambiguity of the original were entirely unnecessary. What seemed hard to understand was in fact extremely simple.

Not everything can be made simple, but most things—even the most complicated things—can be said clearly. In fact, the more complicated the message, the greater the writer's responsibility to make it clear. Good writing is a matter of communication, of getting something across. Our school principal's failure to communicate is only one of many possible kinds. Another is what teachers ironically call "fine writing," which comes from the notion that writing to be good must be flowery, or polysyllabic, or larded with quotations or foreign words. Fine writing is the kind of prose that says "Joseph traversed the path to his domicile" instead of "Joe went home." At best this style sets up a kind of static between the sender and the receiver; at worst it has to be translated to be understood.

In the pages that follow, we will have a lot to say about tone, imagery, grammar, sentence structure, and diction. We will invoke rules and conventions. But it should not be forgotten that these rules and conventions are means, not ends. The aim of writing may be defined as follows: to spare your reader the error of misunderstanding your message, and the pain of translating it, by making it as clear as possible from the outset. Rules and conventions are useful only to the extent that they serve this end.

SUBJECT AND THEME

Your first practical step in doing a piece of writing is to choose your subject; your second is to decide what you are going to say about that subject, or what your "theme" will be. For example, the subject of George Orwell's well-known essay "Politics and the English Language" is stated in the title. The theme is established in the first few paragraphs, and can be paraphrased as follows: "When a civilization is decadent, as ours is, the language of that civilization becomes decadent, too. By cleaning up the language —ridding it of its bad habits—we can reverse the process of political decay." Behind all of Orwell's examples of stale language lies this theme; indeed, this theme is the point of his essay, its *raison d'être*. In a formal argument the theme is the proposition or contention to be proved. In an informal essay proof as such may not be called for, but the theme must be backed up by example and reasoning.

Choosing a Subject

In choosing a subject, look for something that you care about, that you respond to, that hits you where you live. If your teacher offers a choice of subjects none of which interests you, or one broad subject on which you feel you have nothing to say, the problem is a little harder. In this situation, two words of advice. First, take your time deciding: a quick, what-the-hell decision may lead to hours of anguish or tedium, whereas another ten minutes' thought might turn up an angle or aspect of the subject that you would enjoy exploring. Second, use your imagination. The fact that A. E. Housman's poetry bores you is not necessarily a reason to avoid writing about it. Why not write about *why* Housman bores you, why you like some other poet better, or even why you don't like poetry at all (if you don't), giving examples from Housman? If your essay is up to standard in other respects, your teacher will not object to this slight departure from the assigned topic.

Just as there is probably no such thing as an inherently dull human being, so there is probably no such thing as an inherently dull subject, if, that is, we get far enough below the surface to reach that point of intimacy where affection and sympathy come into play. A girl may not be interested in politics. Then let her choose a politician whose looks she likes, listen to him, read about him, write about her reaction to what he says. Everybody is interested in people; and this girl might even end up interested in politics after all. A boy may have no taste for classical music. Then let him read a biography of Mozart, think about Mozart's amazing career and the universal acclaim for his works today, and write whatever comes to mind. Somewhere along the way he will certainly want to listen to a few records, if only to hear what it was that made such a stir in 1769 or 1787. He may end up liking classical music better; people often dislike things only because they know nothing about them. If one aspect of a subject bores you, look for another that does not. If all aspects bore you, try another subject. If all subjects bore you, you had better see a psychiatrist. The extremes of boredom are a condition in the writer rather than in his subjects.

Choosing a Theme

Choosing a theme is a much more difficult task. Finding a theme in a subject means finding a point of view toward it. Some people bring to serious subjects a built-in point of view: that of a Christian, a Communist, a self-made man, or whatever. But most college students are not so endowed. For them, finding a point of view is part of a hard, even harrowing, search for moral, spiritual, and intellectual values.

Where this search will take a student he does not know and we do not know; nor do we have any basis, in the circumstances, for recommending one point of view over another. Our Mozart man may end up writing that he does not see what the fuss over Mozart is all about, that for his part he prefers Charlie Parker or rock 'n' roll. Our politics girl may end up by coming out with flags flying for some fool with nothing more above his ears than a handsome head of hair. Well and good. Say what you think. If you don't know what you think, try arguing both ways—Mozart is terrible, Mozart is wonderful—and see which argument you feel more comfortable with, which one you feel readier to defend.

You will be "wrong" sometimes, maybe often; no matter, that is part of getting educated. In particular, your teacher's opinion of Mozart, or of politics, is irrelevant to what you write. You are writing not to please him, or spite him, or flatter him, but to make a reasoned presentation of your own views to a wider, if hypothetical, audience. He will grade you not on the degree to which you manage to say what he thinks, but on how well you have said what you yourself think.

Writing, as a transaction between writer, subject matter, and audience, begins and ends with the writer. His integrity, his perception, his tact—in short, his qualities of character—are what finally make the difference between worthwhile writing and junk. Intelligence, education, and maturity help. But what is needed most of all is that the writer seek to understand and honestly express his understanding of that most vital of all subjects, himself.

2

LOGIC AND EVIDENCE

A sound argument is not the automatic result of being right or well intentioned. If a child says he knows that the moon revolves around the earth because it is there at night and not in the daytime, he is right about what the moon does but his reasoning is unsound. When Mother says Johnny was bad to hit his sister, she is saying what she honestly thinks; but is her reasoning sound? If she knew the whole story, she might have congratulated him on his restraint.

An important part of Aristotle's pioneering study of logic in the fourth century B.C. was his naming of logical fallacies, those errors in reasoning that he found common enough to classify. Since then, logicians have refined and qualified this list, but all the fallacies Artistotle identified are still in evidence, and many of his names and definitions are still used. No matter how well an argument is researched, no matter how well it is written, a logical fallacy or error of reasoning will weaken it. The writer who has a fine style but cannot think straight is not a good writer. Style and logic are inseparable parts of the written fabric, and in the best prose become virtually one and the same thing.

Most of us have an instinctive sense for logical error, even when we cannot put our finger on what is wrong. After a disappointing lecture, we may say nothing more profound than "What a lot of hot air!"—yet our reaction probably indicates that the speaker has been guilty of one or more of Aristotle's logical fallacies. You're arguing in a circle! My bad habits are not the point! But that doesn't follow! These familiar phrases point to the presence of the classical fallacies known respectively as *petitio principii, tu quoque,* and *non sequitur.* We shall pay only passing attention to these ancient terms, and almost no attention to these three fallacies in particular; indeed, we make no pretense to exhaustiveness of any sort in this chapter. Our intention is merely to warn against logical fallacies in general, and to illustrate and discuss ten logical fallacies that we have encountered frequently in student writing.[1]

A fallacy is an erroneous or unjustified inference. An inference is a logical relationship expressible by the formula *if P, then Q*: if this statement (P) is true, then it follows that this other statement (Q) must be true. This relationship can be expressed more completely as a syllogism, a three-term relationship consisting of a premise (major premise), a middle term (minor premise), and a conclusion:

Premise
    All men are mortal.
Middle term P
    Socrates is a man.
Conclusion
    Therefore Socrates is mortal. Q

This classic syllogism contains no fallacy; the premises are sound and lead inexorably to the sound conclusion. In a fallacious argu-

---

[1] Those who are interested in fallacies not touched on in this chapter, or in the Latin names of those for which we use English terms, should consult a good elementary logic text, e.g. Monroe C. Beardsley, *Thinking Straight,* 3d ed. (New York, 1966). An excellent chapter on logic, geared to the use of words in writing, is Chapter 3 of Richard D. Altick, *Preface to Critical Reading,* 3d ed. (New York, 1956).

ment, by contrast, either the premise or the path from the premise to the conclusion is erroneous; either *P* is wrong, or the statement *if P, then Q* is wrong, or both.

Most noninductive arguments, if labored over long enough, can be reduced to syllogistic form, but for writers this exercise is not very helpful. Modern logicians tend to substitute letter and number symbols for words and sentences, and with good reason: the written language is not as precise an instrument as they require. The statement "I intend to pay my bills on time after this" seems simple enough at first; yet when we ask just what "I" means in this context, or whether the speaker is making a moral commitment or expressing mere future purpose, we get into profound philosophical problems. This book is not concerned with such tangles, but the beginning writer should be aware that they exist. Words are symbols, imperfect symbols invented and used for the most part by nonlogicians. A large part of the writer's job is fashioning clear and logically sound statements out of these imperfect materials. It is not an easy job.

But neither—given some basic common sense and a little care and thought—is it an impossible job. These qualities, alas, are missing in the following essay, which is an only slightly modified version of a paper actually submitted in an English class. The superscript numbers, indicating various logical fallacies committed by the writer, are keyed to the numbered headings in the subsequent discussion.

An American Myth

One of the most persistent American myths[1] I know is that all the poor people in the world,[1] the people to whom we shell out billions in aid every year, are unhappy[1] just because they are poor. Sitting where we are on our mountain of luxury, we feel that if people do not have television sets, two cars in the garage, paid vacations, and a nice house in the suburbs, they are unhappy.[9] It just is not so. I can say with absolute assurance—from personal observation in Turkey, Syria, Egypt, Lebanon, Greece, and Mexico[3]—that the poor are not unhappy if we leave them alone.[9] They do not enjoy themselves in the same way we do, but their lives are nevertheless full of pleasure. They have their own holidays and dances and rituals—which are entirely different from ours—but this is their own culture and they like it. Nor do the poor suffer or feel pain in the same way we would under similar conditions;[9] they have grown used to their lot and are happy in it if left alone. We forget that often the loveliest flowers grow on manure[4] heaps.[8]

To prove my thesis, look at what happened last year after we sent millions of tons of wheat to India during the famine.[3] Instead of making the country contented, there were food riots all over North India and some fighting with Pakistan.[5] The people were more ungrateful, not less. And the same thing some years ago in Egypt; after all our help, Egypt let the Russians build the Aswan Dam and the country was overrun with "Yankee Go Home" signs.[5] We stirred the people up with our aid, with a vision of luxury to which they were not accustomed, and then nothing would satisfy them.

The same thesis applies to the poor at home. Our relief rolls are filled on the one hand with deadbeats[2] too lazy to work and on the other with beatniks[2] who won't work on principle. Why do we go on subsidizing whores[2] who have a child a year—each one by a different father? If we cut off the supplies, then these people would straighten out and join the same civilized society that the rest of us live in and pay taxes in.[5] Why do we do it? Because we are infected[2] by the sentimental idea that these people cannot help themselves, and that if we do not help them we will be Bad Samaritans. Actually we are Bad Samaritans doing what we do now, for these people—once they get used to living on handouts—lose all pride and self-respect, like zoo animals.[8]

How many of our policy makers have actually been in a slum? They think it is terrible because it is so unlike the place *they* live. But my father has worked in embassies all over the Middle East and I have had plenty of opportunity to see slums. Actually slums are no worse than any other place once you get used to them; they are just different.[9] There's no place like home applies there just as much as anywhere. Instead of getting people out of slums, we should get the slums out of people.[4]

Jesus said "Blessed are the poor," and "The poor shall never cease out of the land." Yet here we are engaged in the absurd[2] effort of trying to eliminate what cannot be eliminated.[7] More-over, it should *not* be eliminated, for the presence of those less fortunate than ourselves in this world brings out the best in us. When we give to our favorite charity, we are sharing part of our best selves. But we should not ever forget that charity begins at home.

1. Undefined Terms

No clear communication is possible if we do not know what our words mean. Since words, unlike mathematical symbols, are not fixed in value but constantly changing, a writer who hopes to be understood must frequently pause to define his terms. A complete definition may be impossible (such a simple, everyday word as *property*, for example, is subject enough for a book), but the writer should at least provide a working definition—some indication of which of a word's various possible meanings he is using. In the essay under discussion, for example, the word *myth* seems to be used in its secondary and derivative sense of "something untrue," but it could also have that richer meaning suggested by Mark Schorer: "Myths are the instruments by which we continually struggle to make our experience intelligible to ourselves. A myth is a large, controlling image that gives philosophical meaning to the facts of ordinary life; that is, which has organizing value for experience." Does the writer have this meaning in mind as well as the more obvious meaning? We cannot know, for he has not told us.

Other problems of definition occur throughout this essay. Just what is meant by "poor people," and in particular by the phrase "all the poor people in the world"? That's a large number of poor people, and of different kinds of poor people—people with plenty of food and no money as well as people in danger of starvation, young people with big debts but bright prospects as well as old people with no debts but no prospects either. Which of these people is the writer talking about? All of them? But surely some are happy, some unhappy; some interested in help from abroad, some not. Is he talking about only some of them? Then which ones?

And what about that word *unhappy*? It is hard enough to define happiness in the abstract; it is far harder to say with assurance whether someone else is or is not "happy." Is happiness the same as pleasure? Then what about those Christian martyrs who claimed to find ecstasy in their self-sacrifice—so much so that the early church inveighed against the seeking of martyrdom? Are brides happy, as the greeting cards say? If so, are the fainting fits, cold sweats, and hysteria that often accompany a bride to the altar part of her happiness? To see the concept in these terms is to see the word *unhappy* as mixed and relative, connected to the human condition, and not as absolute.

What should our writer have done? Probably he should have said, early in the paper, something like this: "By happiness I do not mean bliss or uninterrupted satisfaction, but simply a condition of contentment relative to the possibilities of a given culture." This is no formal definition of happiness, but it is a good working definition for our writer's purposes. It will make his argument clearer to his readers, and his competence to expound it more apparent.

Obviously, most of the words in any essay have more than one possible meaning, and no one stops to define them all. How far should a writer go in defining terms? He should define all key words in his argument whose definition is not self-evident—words like *unhappy*, on which the argument of "An American Myth" pivots. He should define any other abstract terms—*myth, the poor*—that are not clear in context. He should define or explain all strange words. In the interests of style, he should present his definitions as gracefully and unobtrusively as possible; but if the claims of precision and the claims of grace conflict, the former should prevail.

2. Name-calling

Name-calling is an appeal to prejudice by false or invidious labeling. Words have connotations; some are neutral, some favorable, some unfavorable. A few years ago there was a popular parlor game in which people were asked to describe a given condition successively in the first, second, and third persons with increasing acerbity as the focus shifted away from themselves: "I am intelligent, you are clever, he is a smart aleck"; "I am enjoying myself, you should slow down, he is dead drunk." It is an old trick to place what you dislike in a class of things that all respectable people dislike, and the writer of this essay has indulged it freely. Obvious examples are his use of the words *deadbeats* and *beatniks* to describe people on relief. Are there no old women, no cripples, no unemployed who would work if they could? Three other instances of name-calling in the essay, not all of them nouns, are indicated by the same number.

3. Inadequate Sampling

One of the commonest errors in amateur argument is that of generalizing from too small a sample. The writer of "An American Myth" claims to "prove" his thesis by citing what happened during one year in India. But it does not follow from that one instance (see 5 below) that the poor are happy if left alone or even that they riot and start wars whenever anyone gives them a little wheat. Even the one instance itself leaves something to be desired. What part of India are we talking about, for example, and what was the connection between the wheat and the outbreaks of violence? Not only is this instance no proof of the general case; it is itself unacceptable as evidence.

Another error in sampling appears in the list of countries—Turkey, Syria, Egypt, and so on—that the author provides. At first glance this list seems impressive; the author has been around and seen things. But then doubts creep in. Has he seen enough to make generalizations about "all poor people"? Has he even really *seen* what he says he has seen? Looking and seeing are two different things, as different as tourism and research. "Personal observation" could mean occasional glances out the back window of the embassy limousine. Is that a big enough sampling to make generalizations about the poor in the Middle East and Mexico? Few would think it was.

4. Equivocation

To equivocate is to use a term in two or more senses without making the shift in sense clear. In "An American Myth" the most obvious equivocation is the play on the word *slums* in the next-to-last paragraph: "Instead of getting people out of slums, we should get the slums out of people." This sounds fine, but what does it mean? The argument rests on our equating run-down areas like Harlem or Watts with an internal psychological condition of which we know only that it is offensive to the writer. Can such disparate things be equated? Almost certainly not. But they are equated here anyway by the equivocal use of the word *slums.* Similarly, the word *manure* in the first paragraph is used simultaneously to mean filth and fertilizer.

There is also another and opposite kind of equivocation, in which different words are used for essentially the same thing, so that what is one thing in nature is made to appear two. A clever mystery novel was once published in which everything depended on the identity of one narrator, "I," with a "Mr. Taylor" frequently mentioned by another narrator; the reader was allowed to infer the twoness of this onesome right up to the last sentence of the book. Most such equivocations, however, are less deliberate. Thus the writer of "An American Myth" distinguishes between *aid,* which is no good, and *charity,* which is good. But what is foreign aid except charity on a large scale? If our writer objects to one and supports the other, let him speak of small-scale and large-scale charity, or of public and private aid. To do otherwise is to transform a difference in degree into a difference in kind.

5. Post Hoc Reasoning

If one of two associated events happened before the other, it may be wrongly argued that the first caused the second: *post hoc ergo propter hoc,* "after this, therefore because of this." Thus Philip Wylie writes of the effect of giving the vote to women: "Mom's first gracious presence at the ballot-box was roughly concomitant with the start toward a new all-time low in political scurviness, hoodlumism, gangsterism, labor strife, monopolistic thuggery, moral degeneration, civic corruption, smuggling, bribery, theft, murder, homosexuality, drunkenness, financial depression, chaos, and war." The implied assumption is that votes for women caused all the trouble. Wylie's facetious intent is plain, but this same fallacy is frequently found in more serious arguments. In "An American Myth," for example, the appearance of riots in India and "Yankee Go Home" signs in Egypt after these countries received American aid shipments does not prove that the aid *caused* the riots and the signs. Maybe it did, but the case is yet to be proved; our author provides no evidence.

Post hoc is closely related to a more general fallacy known as *non sequitur*, "it does not follow." It is a good idea to be careful in using words like *because, since, thus,* and *therefore.* "I bought Lucy a Christmas present because I like her better than Eileen" is a *non sequitur* unless it has been established that you were in a position to buy only one present. When the author of "An American Myth" claims that cutting off American aid would be a boon to its present recipients, he is voicing another variety of this fallacy. How can he predict so simple and universal an outcome from so complex a set of conditions?

6. False Disjunction

To be caught on the horns of a dilemma is to be forced to choose between two equally undesirable alternatives. A dilemma is an either-or situation. If we take the highway, we will encounter traffic; if we take the bypass, we will be on a rough road. If we vote Republican, we will get a reactionary; if we vote Democratic, we will get a leftist. We must choose—or so at least we are told. But are these the only alternatives, and are they accurately and honestly defined? Often they are not. In "An American Myth," for example, we are told that everyone on relief is either a deadbeat or a beatnik. A moment's thought will demolish this assertion. Elsewhere we have a subtler disjunction: between leaving the poor alone and trying to give every poor family television sets, two cars, and a house in the suburbs. If this is the choice we must make, there is much to be said for the author's recommendation that we leave the poor alone. But are these really the only alternatives? Surely the most starry-eyed dreamer favors more modest and realistic benefits for the roadless and suburbless peasant farmers of India.

The worst disjunction of all in this essay is the persistent separation of the poor ("they" or "these people") from the writer and his audience ("we" or "the rest of us"). This kind of simplification is one of the ways of prejudice; if one can somehow regard another person as a thing or a statistic, one is relieved of the necessity of understanding him, sympathizing with him, treating him with respect. According to the United States government, a family of four with an income of under $3,100 a year is poor. According to our writer, such a family is not only poor but radically different, as if the $2 difference between $3,099 and $3,101 were some sort of unbridgeable chasm. F. Scott Fitzgerald was experimenting with the same distinction in reverse when he remarked to Ernest Hemingway, "The very rich are different from you and me." We like Hemingway's answer: "Yes," he replied. "They have more money."

7. Argument to Authority

Writers who have no evidence for their views often resort to citing some authority whose pronouncements they assume the reader will accept as sufficient. How do you know there is no serious smog problem in the city? Mayor Schultz says so. How do you know that the Chinese Communists are evil? General Baker says so, and he has spent over 30 years in the Far East. This is all very well if the so-called authority does in fact know what he is talking about, but he may not. Especially in matters as complex and controversial as the smog problem and the future behavior of China, a discriminating reader is likely to want something more convincing than the opinion of Mayor Schultz or General Baker.

The all-time champion in the list of authorities cited, ranking just above Aristotle and J. Edgar Hoover, is the Bible. If the Bible says something, it must be true, or so millions of Christians have believed. Thus, in "An American Myth," we find Jesus cited to support the argument that it is pointless to talk about eliminating poverty. A deeply religious person might be swayed by this argument; but most people today would find the use of Jesus's name here a way of removing the discussion of poverty from the rational to the emotional level.

8. False Analogy

The writer of "An American Myth" is particularly addicted to the fallacy of false analogy. Consider, for example, his claim that some of the loveliest flowers grow on manure heaps. This is intended to suggest not only that some of the loveliest people come from slums, which may be true, but (as is clear from the context) that these people are lovely *because* they live in slums, which is doubtful. The intended analogy may be stated as follows: Slums are to the growth of lovely people as manure is to the growth of lovely flowers. As we have seen, the force of this metaphor depends heavily on equivocation in the use of the word *manure*.

The analogy between poor people on welfare and zoo animals is equally false. Basically it asserts that poor people and zoo animals are the same in one particular: if they are given the necessities of life and not forced to work for them, they will grow lazy and decadent. But zoo animals have no choice; they cannot hunt their food, they must eat what they are brought or starve. And as for people, some of the most energetic people in history, from Plato to John F. Kennedy, have not been deterred from achievement by having the necessities of life assured them from birth. The writer might reply that the very poor are different from John F. Kennedy, but that, as we have seen, remains to be proved. It would seem more likely on the face of it that they are very different from zoo animals.

A further discussion of false analogy will be found in Chapter 4, pp. 48–49.

9. Undocumented Assertion

The essay is full of undocumented assertions. We must again and again ask this writer questions. How do you *know* what you say you know? How do you *know* that the poor in Egypt and those other countries don't feel pain the same way you do? How do you *know* what our policy makers think about slums? These generalizations appear here sometimes as premises and sometimes as conclusions, but in either case they are for the most part inadmissible. This writer has not learned much about evidence or its use. Slums are no worse than any other place once you get used to them, he says. How close has he been to one? We gather that he has frequented embassies, not slums. If he knows nothing about them from this kind of experience, then what other kind of experience is he drawing on: interviews, polls, books, other authorities? He does not tell us.

Bacon once wrote, "If we begin with certainties, we shall end in doubts; but if we begin with doubts, and we are patient with them, we shall end in certainties." A serious inquirer may take either path and find truth at the end, but not our writer. Beginning with certainties, and heedless of the most obvious objections, he proves (to himself) what he wants to prove and ends where he began. Whatever appeal this method may have, there is no truth in it, and less learning. Truth is a matter of keeping your mind open and adjusting what you think to accord with what you learn, a matter of weighing all the evidence you can find before deciding where you stand. The more evidence you have, no matter which way it points, the better your decision is likely to be.

10. Argument ad Hominem and ad Populum

An argument that directs its appeal to the emotions rather than to the mind—to the pride, prejudice, cupidity, or private interests of the audience rather than to its reason—is called an argument *ad hominem* (to the man) or *ad populum* (to the people). One of the great *ad populum* arguments in our literature is Antony's funeral oration in *Julius Caesar;* such twentieth-century demagogues as Lenin, Hitler, and Senator Joseph McCarthy have done almost as well. The *ad hominem* argument is a staple of the television commercial: you, being a man of taste and discrimination, will of course want to smoke *our* brand of cigarette or use *our* soap. Indeed, it is a soft-soap argument, the appeal of flattery to our soft spots or blind spots. In "An American Myth" the reader is repeatedly invited to see himself as part of an elite "we" who send wheat to India, who subsidize the poor, who pay the country's taxes. The writer instinctively feels, and he is right, that to the extent his readers identify with this "we," they will accept the separation between "we" and "they" on which his argument depends.

One flaw in "An American Myth" that has not been explicitly singled out for comment is the suppression of contrary evidence. This is not so much a logical fallacy as a moral failing, and perhaps not so much a moral failing as a strategic error. In writing exposition, there is no purpose in being dishonest; the whole point of writing an essay is to determine what is relevant to your subject and discuss it to the degree that its relevance warrants. The writer of "An American Myth" did not so much knowingly suppress facts as choose to ignore facts that would not support his case. The resulting argument was (and usually is) less effective than it would have been if the writer had introduced and discussed the evidence he ignored.

The ten fallacies enumerated in this chapter, and the dozen-odd others discussed in books on logic, have a peculiar characteristic: they tend to merge into each other. Thus the manure-heap image is an instance not only of false analogy and equivocation, but of name-calling, false disjunction, and undocumented assertion. The appeal to Jesus is not only an argument to authority but an *ad populum* argument, not to mention an instance of "poisoning the wells," a logical fallacy in which the other party, though not demonstrably dishonorable, is deprived of all opportunity to reply with honor, as in the celebrated question "Have you stopped beating your wife?" It is also a fair case of suppressed evidence, since Jesus had a few remarks on the other side of the question as well, notably "Go and sell that thou hast, and give to the poor."

Most of the other examples discussed above could also be classified under two or more of the fallacy headings. What does this mean? It means, as we might expect, that illogicality is more a general state of mind than a series of particular fallacies with neat little names. Far from being the monster of unreason that our bill of particulars makes him out, the author of "An American Myth" is just a slightly more than ordinarily sloppy thinker, a slightly more than ordinarily hasty writer, and a slightly more than ordinarily passionate partisan. The way to avoid logical fallacies is to stop and think. Are you telling the reader no more than you can prove? Are you telling him everything he has to know if he is to judge matters for himself? Have you used words unequivocally and defined your terms? Are your premises clearly related to each other and to your conclusion? In a word, have you been honest and thorough? If you have, you have probably also been logical.

3
TONE

Tone is the quality that conveys a writer's attitude, and perhaps something of his intentions. "When you say that, smile!" said Owen Wister's cowboy to the stranger; unless the words came with the right tone, they were fighting words. Our culture hangs together partly because we know its idiom, know what tone to adopt in given situations. It also hangs together because at least some of us have an ear for tones that lie below the surface: the malarkey in the politician's promises, the hostility in the peace lover's sermon, the lie in the advertiser's "truth."

What is true of speaking is equally true of writing. In every written statement there is an implied voice, a tonal quality that reveals the writer's attitude toward his subject matter and toward his audience. Is he objective, angry, contemptuous, indifferent, amused, cynical, ironic, sentimental? The list of possible tones is almost endless. Indeed, a one-word description can rarely do justice to the tone of a piece of writing, for the tone can be as subtle and complex as the personality of the writer.

Here is a scientist writing for fellow scientists: "Proteins are long-chain molecules built up of hundreds of molecular subunits:

the 20 amino acids." The tone is calm, unimpassioned, neutral; the writer's purpose is not to urge or persuade, but simply to put known quantities together into an objective description, and that purpose governs his attitude both toward his subject and toward his audience. If the same scientist were addressing a lay audience, his tone might be quite different. Here is the biologist Loren Eiseley writing for a popular audience on "How Flowers Changed the World":

> Before the coming of the flowering plants our own ancestral stock, the warm-blooded mammals, consisted of a few mousy little creatures hidden in trees and underbrush. A few lizard-like birds with carnivorous teeth flapped awkwardly on ill-aimed flights among archaic shrubbery. None of these insignificant creatures gave evidence of any remarkable talents. The mammals in particular had been around for some millions of years, but had remained well lost in the shadow of the mighty reptiles. Truth to tell, man was still, like the genie in the bottle, encased in the body of a creature about the size of a rat.

What makes the difference in tone? The fact that Eiseley, though objective in the sense that he never departs from what biologists accept as true, has another motive as well: the desire to be vivid and entertaining. Adjectives with immediate visual appeal like *mousy* and *lizard-like*, familiar turns of speech like *some millions of years*, familiar analogies like the genie in the bottle, all indicate that this author is writing to stimulate the interest and imagination of readers who know little about his subject. If he had addressed a professional audience in such terms, he would have seemed patronizing if not ridiculous.

KINDS OF TONE

It is impossible, as we have indicated, to list all the possible tones of voice a writer might use. They are as various as human temperaments and moods. But some tones are frequent enough in student writing, and give enough trouble, to be worth a few words.

Invective

Invective is name-calling, the expression of undisguised anger or passion in writing. Here is a letter to a college newspaper, lamenting the treatment a speaker received at the hands of a crowd:

> In any community—even an academic community, I suppose—there will always be those fearful, ignorant, sadistic people who feel their smelly little existence to be somehow threatened by ideas different from their own. Usually, though, the university tradition of free inquiry manages to keep their neurotic tendencies toward anti-intellectual, sheep-like orthodoxy and violence in check, at least until they get out of college.
>
> But now I watched a mob of these mental pygmies whose sick and unpatriotic intolerance had found a seemingly "legitimate" outlet in two-bit patriotism. They threw various objects at ——— and then ducked behind each other (that's the old American way for you!).

Writers of invective in no way disguise their righteous indignation; they are not calm analysts but passionate partisans indulging (with apparent relish) their moral outrage. This kind of writing is rarely effective. An angry writer usually has one of two effects on his readers. If they agree with him, his lack of restraint embarrasses them: all right, they think, but why carry on so? If they do not agree, his lack of restraint confirms them in their disagreement: loudmouths, after all, are never right. A soft answer turneth away wrath; a loud answer incurreth contempt. Be wary of invective. Even if people happen to be "mental pygmies," they will not thank you for telling them so.

Exhortation

Exhortation can be close to invective. It is the voice of the preacher or the moralist, hammering home his values and opinions; its intention is to convince. The exhorter does not use the language of indirection, but editorializes openly and frankly. Here is Philip Wylie on the subject of war:

> There is no other way to look at war than as the final proof of the infantilism of man—the revelation of his inherent lack of civilization, his serfdom to his instincts, and, therefore, his failure to achieve adulthood. War proves how wholly dependent we are upon the instinctual plane for our motives and what a thin tissue our repressive brain—our reason—has stretched between us and other animals.

Although a step beyond mere invective, this passionately opinionated statement contains as much heat as it does light. Note the unqualified assertions ("there is *no other way* to look at war," "war *proves*") and the denunciatory tone ("infantilism," "serfdom to his instincts"). This writer is not sitting down to reason with you; he is letting you know what's what. As the reader, you are placed in the irritating position of being talked at: Wylie is doing all the speaking and you all the listening. A writer's tone says a great deal about what he thinks of his readers—whether he considers them intellectuals or boobs, reasonable men or fanatics, friends or enemies. Be careful not to insult your readers unless that is your intention.

Exhortation need not be so strident. In "The Moral Equivalent of War," William James took an antiwar position in many ways similar to Wylie's, but listen to the difference in tone:

> It is plain that on this subject civilized man has developed a sort of double personality. If we take European nations, no legitimate interest of any one of them would seem to justify the tremendous destructions which a war to compass it would necessarily entail. It would seem as though common sense and reason ought to find a way to reach agreement in every conflict of honest interests. I myself think it our bounden duty to believe in such international rationality as possible.

We are here a long way from invective; James keeps his temper, does not raise his voice. He is practicing some of the reasonableness he preaches, and in doing so he is tacitly saying to the reader, "You are the kind of person who can be reached by reason." Note the qualifications ("it would seem," "reason ought to"); our assent is invited, not commanded or presumed. Such language tells us that we are being regarded as ladies and gentlemen, not as people who have to be browbeaten or yelled at. Is James's approach as effective as Wylie's? Probably more so. When James's article appeared in 1910, some thirty thousand copies were distributed, and it has been often reprinted since. It has had an enormous influence on world opinion if not on world behavior, and is still one of the most honored arguments against war in our literature.

Narrative

Narrative does not overtly argue or editorialize, but simply presents a set of events or conditions. Consider the following paragraphs from Edward Loomis's story "Wounds":

> A rifle bullet striking bone hits with a fine hardness, followed instantly by a numbing shock; and then down you go.
> When it happened to me, I felt my left leg for blood, thinking to gauge the wound, but could not do it, for the blood was running imperceptibly in my heavy trousers already soaked with the rain. I moved the knee, where the bullet had hit, and said to the man ahead of me: "I think maybe I'm hit, by God! Now what do you think of that?"

There is no editorializing here, save in the selection and arrangement of details. If any argument against war is implied, that argument must be put into words by the reader. In effect, the writer of narrative creates a kind of vacuum for the reader's emotions to fill. "How awful!" the reader might exclaim, precisely because the author has not so exclaimed, has not taken the words out of the reader's mouth. The tactic of dispassionately presenting material that speaks for itself is one of the most powerful at the writer's command. It is perhaps particularly successful with American readers, who tend to equate objectivity with honesty and to associate emotion with weakness or hysteria. That these associations are not necessarily valid makes no difference; you write for readers as they are, not as you think they ought to be.

Satire

Satire is a form of ridicule aimed at correcting some folly or abuse. Here, for example, is part of a satirical book review by Thomas Reed Powell. After lamenting that most books on the Constitution of the United States "are very hard to read" and make you "think very hard all the time," Powell goes on to say:

> The new book which Mr. Beck has written about the Constitution is a very different kind of book. You can read it without thinking. If you have got tired trying to read the other kind of books, you will be glad of the nice restful book that Mr. Beck has written. It runs along like a story in a very interesting way. Most of the story is about how the Constitution got made. This is really history, but it is written in a very lively way like a novel, with a great many characters, almost all male, and plenty of conversation and a very exciting plot. . . . Besides the story there are many quotations from Shakespeare, Beethoven, Horace, Isaiah, Euripides, Beard, and other famous men. Many of these quotations are quite old, but some of them seem fairly new.

The book is made ridiculous. Why? Because by pretending to be a fool who admires it, Powell persuades us that no one but a fool *could* admire it, and hence that it must be a foolish book. As his satirical device, Powell has adopted the tone and tastes of a twelve-year-old. Note the incidence of the schoolboy word *very*, the jumbled chronology that puts Isaiah after Shakespeare and the historian Beard cheek by jowl with Euripides, the writer's simpleminded taste in novels (which he reads because they are lively, have exciting plots, and are above all easy), and the devastatingly feeble "seem fairly new." The writer is clearly immature, half-educated, and uninteresting; a book he likes must be awful.

Satire requires of a writer not so much a tone of his own as a sensitivity to the tone of others. Indeed, in parody, which is what

Powell is writing, the satirist actually takes the tone of the person or piece of writing that he is satirizing—pompous, childish, inarticulate, or whatever. Although satire can be biting, it is more often gentle: fun to write and fun to read. Unlike invective, satire invites the reader in, asks him to join the fun.

Irony

The dictionary defines irony as "a sort of humor, ridicule, or light sarcasm, the intended implication of which is the opposite of the literal sense of the word." This is an imperfect definition. Irony is by no means always funny, nor is it the same as sarcasm; sarcasm comes from a Greek word meaning "to tear flesh," a kind of direct assault, as when one says, "You think you're pretty damned smart, don't you?" One thing is said and another meant, but there is no real deception. Irony, by contrast, is oblique, subtle, and indirect in its working; the deception is not just a gimmick, but is usually an essential part of the writer's message.

It is the last part of the dictionary definition that gets to the heart of the matter. Irony always sets up a tension between opposites: between the ideal and the real, the seen and the unseen, the literal and the implied, the achieved and the intended. This duality must always exist. A fairly low form of it was displayed some years ago by a San Francisco entrepreneur who marketed 29-cent cans of "fresh air" to be sent as gifts to people in Los Angeles. The directions on the can went something like this: "Punch a small hole in the top and inhale slowly. Do not gulp the air; breathing air can be habit-forming. Increase your intake by degrees. Ten cans a day can be safely consumed. If excessive euphoria is experienced, see your doctor." Where is the irony? In the contrast between the giver's ostensible motivation, benevolence, and his actual motivation, self-congratulation; and in the receiver's awareness of that contrast.

This is a low form of the genre, hardly more than a practical joke. At the other extreme is Jonathan Swift's famous "Modest Proposal," which sets forth in sober, businesslike language a proposal that the children of Ireland be slaughtered and used as a source of food for that starving land. The irony here comes from

Swift's implied message: that even the most outrageous brutalities must now seem commonplace alongside the horrors wrought by England's exploitation of Ireland. He is ostensibly saying to the English "As a conscientious student of English administrative practice, I have come up with a plan that I think you will admire." He is in effect saying "You are monsters." The tension between the literal proposal and its implied meaning generates a terrific heat.

In desperate situations, irony sometimes seems the only possible mode of redress. Most Negro jazz has irony at its base; Louis Armstrong's classic "What Did I Do to Be So Black and Blue?" plays profound changes on the cliché "black and blue." Lenny Bruce's quip "Toilet, you're lucky you're white!" evokes the Negro problem in five words. In the following exchange reported in the *New York Times* between a South African judge and a political prisoner up for retrial, the prisoner is aware that any expression of dissatisfaction with his lot will be taken as evidence of criminal revolutionary sentiment:

"You have no objection to being ordered around by whites?"
"I have become satisfied to such an extent that my health keeps improving."
"Are you satisfied with your wages?"
"I have never complained—not on a single day."
"Do you want better wages?"
"No, your worship."
"Are you satisfied with your house?"
"It's a very beautiful house."
"Are you satisfied with the pass laws?"
"Yes, entirely."

Who could be taken in by this irony? Perhaps the judge was, perhaps he was not; either way he looks a little foolish.

Similar circumstances evoked a celebrated piece of irony from Sigmund Freud. In May 1938, after intense harassment by the notorious Nazi secret police unit known as the Gestapo, the 82-year-old Freud was at last granted an exit visa from Vienna on the condition that he sign a document attesting that his treatment by the Germans had been irreproachable. He asked permission to add a few words below his signature, and this being granted, he wrote: "I can heartily recommend the Gestapo to anyone."

Irony can take many forms. There is dramatic irony (where a theater audience or a reader knows something a character does not know), there is Socratic irony (the pose of ignorance that Socrates assumed to bait his opponents), and there is verbal irony —some forms of which we have illustrated. Irony is one of the sharpest instruments of criticism available; thanks to its unique balance between intelligence and feeling, it can probe into the deepest aspects of existence. The ironic tone is not easy to master, but it is worth the effort.

ERRORS IN TONE

Tone is what establishes the rapport between writer and reader, the emotional premises of their relationship. But often a writer, without intending to adopt any particular tone, alienates his reader through sheer inadvertence, clumsiness, or even excess of high spirits. In our remarks on invective and exhortation we pointed out some pitfalls to be avoided; in the following pages we discuss some others.

Sentimentality

If irony is difficult for the beginning writer to master, sentimentality is difficult for him to avoid. By sentimentality we mean not just maudlin or gushy writing, but the whole range of counterfeit emotions. Here is a football player describing a visit to a hospital for crippled children:

> When I held Gracie in my arms, I knew then the meaning of the phrase "Strong legs run that weak legs may walk." She was about seven years old, and when I picked her up and held her close to me I could hear her heart beat, and when she smiled she brought tears to my eyes in spite of myself. I somehow knew, as I held her, that this was the happiest moment of her life. And seeing her suffering, I was filled with rage at all those ungrateful bums in Harlem and Watts and

Berkeley who were out rioting and raising hell because they didn't think they were getting enough for nothing out of this life.

In a class discussion of this paragraph, one student put her finger on something puzzling: "I don't see how the writer could be so full of love in the first part of the paragraph and so full of hate in the last." When asked if the hate in any way discredited the love, made it seem fake or insincere, the class was almost unanimous in saying yes. What the class detected was the presence of sentimentality.

Sentimentality is often defined as "emotion in excess of the fact," the fact being a human situation—the death of a loved one, the election of a president, the birth of a baby—that legitimately evokes emotion. The sentimentalist squeezes more emotion out of such an occasion than discriminating people regard as proper or decent. He enjoys the emotion for its own sake, as a kind of narcotic, and he does not shrink from the stalest clichés when the fit is upon him. He invokes the patter of tiny feet, the love of a good woman, silver threads among the gold—all those prefabricated phrases that evoke stock emotional responses. During a recent political campaign a commentator reported a candidate's speech in these terms:

> He got his first rafter-ringing response by coming out four-square for the Declaration of Independence and the Constitution. He rated another salvo for saying he would not bend before the breeze or run with the tide. . . . And [he] talked tough about sending out the Marines to win back our respect. "History shows us what happens to appeasers," he said as the militant ladies in the audience beat their white gloves together.

That candidate knows the tricks of the sentimentalists. He is talking from the emotions to the emotions with no mediation from the mind. Sentimental clichés defeat the possibility of thought. What specific policies does our candidate believe in? He does not tell us, and those ladies with the white gloves, being sentimentalists themselves, do not ask him.

Sentimentality is a way of not facing reality; it prettifies things rather than seeing them as they are. The sentimentalist believes not in love, but in "true love," an ideal absolute that exists only as a fantasy and has nothing to do with real relations between real people. What he hates above all else is the complexity, ambiguity, and mess of actual life. "All idealization makes life poorer," wrote the novelist Joseph Conrad. "To beautify it is to take away its character of complexity—it is to destroy it." This insight is beyond the sentimentalist's comprehension. He will say, with Edgar Guest, that "It takes a heap o' livin' to make a house a home," but he will not include in that "livin'" the dirty diapers, the family quarrels, or Grandpa's addiction to bourbon. He does not care about "livin'" in any real sense; he lives in a world of wish fulfillment and sees what he wants to see. What he sees is not necessarily hearts and flowers; it may be violence, brutality, sadism. The point is that he sees life partially, not whole.

Henry Fielding has one of his heroines declare: "I love a tender sensation and would pay the price of a tear for one any time." She is a sentimentalist, but she knows her weakness and makes a game of it. Most sentimentalists, by contrast, do not know their own condition and confuse their tender sensations with moral sensitivity. Holden Caulfield, in *The Catcher in the Rye*, describes the classic type as he observes a woman sitting next to him in the movies. Although the film is (to use one of Holden's favorite words) hopelessly "phoney," the woman is crying her eyes out; and the phonier the film gets the more she cries. This action would seem to indicate a kindhearted woman, whatever one might think about her taste. But Holden wasn't fooled; for sitting next to her was a small boy who, throughout the show, was bored and had to go to the bathroom. She wouldn't take him, but told him to shut up and behave himself. Comments Holden: "She was about as kindhearted as a goddam wolf. You take somebody that cries their goddam eyes out over phoney stuff in the movies, and nine times out of ten they're mean bastards at heart. I'm not kidding."

Holden is perfectly right; moved by the suffering on the screen but indifferent to her boy's distress, this woman is a mean bastard without even knowing it. So is Françoise, the cook of Proust's

Swann's Way, who weeps over the childbirth symptoms she reads about in a medical book while ignoring a fellow servant in the agony of labor. Proust supplies a telling comment: "The sufferings of humanity inspired in her a pity which increased in direct ratio to the distance separating the sufferers from herself." Scratch a sentimentalist and you will usually find a person capable of cruelty, or at least an unlovely indifference to the distress of others.

This brings us to the illustration we began with. It was probably not just chance that brought hate and love into such uneasy juxtaposition in that football player's theme, but something more fundamental in his life, some deep-lying feeling of resentment or insecurity. His words described what he wished he felt or thought he ought to feel, not what he did feel. Sentimentality is a pretense, a masquerade, a protective device; it pretends to be full, but it is empty. As John Galsworthy said, "Sentimentalism is the working off on yourself of feelings you haven't really got."

Pomposity

The following passage is from an address given by a dean at an American university. He is welcoming the freshman class:

> I would like to welcome you to X—— University and to express the hope that your educational work will be most productive and rewarding. I am sure you will find that members of the University community are most willing to help you receive the maximum benefit from the curriculum and to have an enjoyable and satisfying learning experience at X——. . . .
>
> This program, which is designed to facilitate learning, involves the imparting of knowledge through research. To maximize learning, the University has made provision for small classes, close student-faculty contacts, high-quality instruction, and personalized education.

What is wrong with this passage? Simply that when we hear language like this we don't believe a word of it, and we don't believe the speaker believes a word of it either. The dean is welcoming the freshmen, but he doesn't say so: he says he "would like to welcome" them. He presumably hopes they will get a lot out of their work, but he doesn't say so: he says he "would like . . . to express the hope." This formal double-talk, this reluctance to be simple and straightforward, is the antithesis of communication. What sort of welcome or helpfulness is there in words like *program* and *personalized education* and *learning experience*? This is language for computers, not people.

Anybody trying to be friendly or personal or even human in language like this is fighting a losing game. It is a language insisting that one *not* be personal; it is remote, it translates personal relations into abstractions. So when someone talks or writes in this language, we dismiss him as not only boring but insincere. A sincere writer would care more about whether we were able to understand him.

Young people are less given to pompous writing than older people, except perhaps to the extent that they seek to gain their seniors' esteem. For one reason or another, many young writers have a desperate fear of being themselves in their writing. In conversation or in personal letters they may be relaxed, but when they go before a wider audience they put on a mask. Here is part of a report by an education student on an experiment in which music was piped into the corridors of a high school:

> The hypothesis, therefore, is that music can reduce the intensity dimension of the student so that he remains in the range of the effectiveness along the continuum. By remaining within the range of his greatest effectiveness he should be able to maximize his rewards and thus possess a positive attitude toward school.

Language like this cannot be read; it must be translated. What this seems to mean is: "Students seem calmer and happier when the music is on, and do better work." But one cannot be sure.

Highbrowism

Highbrowism is close to pomposity as an error in tone, but it is usually more deliberate. The pompous writer indulges in "fine writing" out of insecurity, which leads him to a false notion of his own dignity and the dignity of the written word. The highbrow writer has a different motivation: he wants to show off. He cannot resist letting his teacher and classmates know that he is up on the latest avant-garde play or the latest theory of history. His theme may begin as follows:

> "The Love Song of J. Alfred Prufrock" is a vision of the relativism of our time. "I should have been a pair of ragged claws" is but a distant paraphrase of Rilke's "Der Panther" and its "weiche Gang geschmeidig starker Schritte." To understand both works one profits immensely by an acquaintance with the Existentialist vision of Jean-Paul Sartre in "The Root of the Chestnut Tree" and Camus in "The Myth of Sisyphus."

What is wrong with this passage is not that Rilke, Camus, and Sartre are irrelevant, but that they are dragged in by the ears, introduced for self-advertising reasons rather than for what they contribute to the discussion.

The writer who cares about his readers will either suppress allusions of this sort or take care to explain them fully; he will be interested less in impressing than in instructing. To revert to our image of distance, the good writer does not widen, but narrows, the distance between himself and his readers. The heavy use of unexplained allusions is a manifest error in tone.

Flippancy

Flippant writing is writing that takes a serious subject lightly. Flippancy is a fault comparable to whistling in church or making jokes about wooden legs to a cripple; it can be forgiven in the very young, but it is seldom appreciated. Here is a sample from a freshman theme:

> I thought themes on what I did last summer went out with model T's, but since they didn't, I'll dig right in, for there's no point in flunking out of this school before I've given it a

> whirl (or vice versa). I'll tell you what I did last summer: I worked in a canning factory. And I'll tell you what I did in that canning factory every chance I got (which wasn't often): I sat on my can.

Most teachers will react to themes like this with bored tolerance. Sometimes, by accident, writing like this can be funny, but usually it fails of its own ingenuousness. Good writing takes time and effort. Flippant themes usually come from an unwillingness to accept the challenge of an assignment, and they are judged accordingly. This is a pity in the case of our young canner, who clearly has a way with words. A little more effort, a little more restraint, and he might have written something effective and genuinely amusing.

Some writers seem to think that whatever emerges from their gut is sacred and should be recorded without modification for posterity to ponder. Their teachers rarely agree, and hence a conflict arises—one only partly related, to be sure, to the question of tone. Here is the beginning of a theme on the assignment "Is it ever permissible to break a law?"

> I started to think. I thought, questions like that don't turn me on. I mean, how do you answer questions like that, when those questions don't really exist? I moved on to what was important. What was important was the music, and the music told me all about law that I needed to know. I just took the hand of that music and it led me right between the cliffs of right and wrong. It led me out, man, and it didn't matter whether the law said it was right or wrong.

Flippancy aside, this kind of psychedelic free-associating, probably fake, is of no use to anyone. Writing should be intelligible to as many people as possible. This writing is in a private lingo; it may mean something to the writer's friends, but it says nothing to anyone else. Did the writer have a meaningful experience involving music and the law? Then let him describe it. A writer's job, let us repeat, is to communicate, to share something, not to hint at what he could tell you if he would.

Tone is an expression of the relationship that exists between writer and reader, of the assumptions they share. The tone we use in discourse is a reminder of the kind of people we are, at least at the moment of speaking. If a conversation begins with "Listen, you son of a bitch," it is one sort of conversation; if it begins with "Is there anything I can do to help?" it is another sort. The same thing happens in writing. No matter how sure we are of our opinions, it is elementary courtesy and good sense to acknowledge the reader's existence, the possibility of his disagreement, the potential value of his criticism. No matter how indifferent we may be to our readers, it is elementary courtesy to put them at their ease. Unless we are bent on mayhem, it is elementary good sense to establish a basis for mutual respect.

4

IMAGERY

The comedian Shelley Berman once described a hangover in these terms: "My left eyeball has a headache, my tongue's asleep, and my teeth itch." The effect of this sentence depends upon images, in this case bizarre images. By attributing familiar sensations to unlikely parts of the body, Berman obtains some surprising effects. He not only makes us laugh, he gives us a new sensory experience (or the memory of an old one); we are not just told about the hangover, we feel it. Our response to this image is not the same as the actual physical experience, any more than grief felt in reading a story is the same as real grief; but it is a good approximation of reality. In imagination, we have had a hangover.

Images can do such things. They invite us into experience; they do not keep us at a distance, as mere descriptions or explanations often do. They communicate the sounds, tastes, smells, sights, colors, and tactile feelings of life. Images are not just figures of speech, though they usually appear in this form; they are all those means whereby sensory experience is conveyed in language. Our senses do not report to us on "justice" or "beauty" or "the gross national product"; these abstract concepts are products of thought, or ratiocination, rather than of direct experience. Images tell us about the smell of a flower, the beauty of a woman, the sound of music, the fear of death. They refer to that immediacy of experience where we live and move and have our being.

Not that imagery is unconnected with abstract thought; on the contrary, it is often the best possible way to make difficult abstractions clear, especially to a lay audience. Thus an atomic physicist will say: "Just as a coal fire needs oxygen to keep it going, a nuclear fire needs the neutrons to maintain it." A biologist explaining spectroscopy to lay readers: "Just as in a crystal chandelier the sunlight is shattered to a rainbow, so in the spectroscope light is spread out in colored bands." A political analyst: "It is as sensible to combat communism by military means as to combat malaria by swatting mosquitoes." A great poet and moralist: "No man is an island entire of itself; every man is a piece of the continent, a part of the main."

The greatest of all English poets, seeking to convey the patriotism of the venerable John of Gaunt in *Richard II*, does so almost entirely in images. Gaunt, near death, speaks of the country he loves:

> This royal throne of kings, this scepter'd isle,
> This earth of majesty, this seat of Mars,
> This other Eden, demi-Paradise;
> This fortress built by Nature for herself
> Against infection and the hand of war;
> This happy breed of men, this little world;
> This precious stone set in the silver sea,
> Which serves it in the office of a wall,
> Or as a moat defensive to a house,
> Against the envy of less happier lands;
> This blessed plot, this earth, this realm, this England.

COMPARISON AND ANALOGY

Definition and Examples

Imagery evokes comparisons, implied or explicit. "He wormed his way into her good graces" sets up an implicit comparison between a man's insinuating tactics and the movements of a worm. "The recent escalation of the war" compares a political event to the steady mechanical rising of an escalator. "The batter fanned" compares the batter's futile swing to the motion of a fan, which touches only air. And so it is with the salesman's *broad-brush* categories, the data that are *fed in* to a computer, the ship that *plows* the sea, the football team's *draw* play, the market that *nose-dives*, the housewife who is *snowed under*, the business that stays *above water*, the effort that gets *sandbagged*, the timid man who is *cowed*. All evoke comparisons with familiar acts or things.

It is useful here to distinguish between analogy and true comparison. "That man is a rat" is an analogy; "Hitler was a greater tyrant than Mussolini" is a comparison. In the first, two dissimilar things, a man and an animal, are being compared; in the second, two men are being compared. Analogies ask our emotional assent to similarities between two wholes: a man and a rat, war and hell, love and death. Comparisons ask our intellectual attention to literal and particular similarities or differences. If I compare John F. Kennedy and Lyndon B. Johnson as statesmen, I will compare specific and parallel aspects of their statesmanship, such as their success in handling international affairs or in protecting civil liberties. But when Shakespeare asks in a sonnet "Shall I compare thee to a summer's day?" he has no literal or intellectual comparison in mind: to compliment his lady he wants us to think of the beauty, warmth, and luxuriance of summer, and to ignore the mosquitoes and the sunburn. The poet asks our indulgence and we grant it.

Analogies that are just and fresh not only delight but clarify, emphasize, instruct—even win arguments. The best are unanswerable. Mrs. Thrale once remarked to Samuel Johnson that a certain young woman would be terribly unhappy to hear of a friend's losing an estate she had long expected to receive. "She will suffer as much, perhaps," replied Dr. Johnson, "as your horse did when your cow miscarried." Montaigne quotes the witty reply of a Roman Stoic who was asked why Stoics sometimes became Epicureans but Epicureans never Stoics: "Plenty of capons are made out of cocks, but cocks are never made out of capons."

Misuses of Analogy

But analogy can be as tricky as it is useful. The Vietnam war, for example, was at one time widely justified by the so-called domino theory, which held that unless Chinese expansionism were stopped in Vietnam, the other countries of Southeast Asia would fall to the Communists like a row of standing dominoes when the first one is knocked into the second. "Domino theory" is a striking phrase, simple and visual; it reduces a most complex issue to terms a child can understand. But is the analogy true? Are nations really comparable to dominoes? Will they fall in the same mechanical way when pushed? Why didn't Yugoslavia or Greece fall like a domino before Russian pressure after World War II? If the analogy is false, the argument is false.

Does this matter? It depends on how the analogy is used. Literal truth is not always an issue. Shakespeare's sonnet is no less effective for the omission of mosquitoes, Dr. Johnson's remark no less compelling for his ignorance of the lady's true thoughts. A lawyer can be an "ambulance chaser"—that is, someone who makes capital of other people's disasters—without having ever chased an ambulance. And it would be pointless to reproach the man who defined a camel as "a horse designed by a committee" for being harder on committees than they deserve.

The trouble comes when an analogy is presented as part of a logical argument, as the domino theory often was in the mid-1960's. If you use an analogy this way, as a building stone in a larger argument, you forgo the poet's right to indulgence; the analogy must be demonstrably sound on all relevant points, the stone able to bear the weight you put on it. Many faulty analogies pass for true, usually by suggesting that their two elements are literally comparable when they are not. Uncle Harry may be a rat, but it does not follow that he can live on an ounce of cheese a day. The only defense against this sort of thinking is the kind of dogged scrutiny illustrated in the following argument, where Julian Huxley is examining the assertion that God rules the universe:

> I believe this fundamental postulate to be nothing more than the result of asking a wrong question: "Who or what rules the universe?" So far as we can see, it rules itself, and indeed the whole analogy with a country and its ruler is false. Even if a god does exist behind or above the universe as we experience it, we can have no knowledge of such a power; the actual gods of historical religions are only the personifications of impersonal facts of nature and of facts of our inner mental life.

SIMILE AND METAPHOR
Simile

Most figures of speech, and most of the examples given so far in this chapter, are either similes or metaphors. On a superficial level it is easy to distinguish between these two categories. A simile is an explicit comparison or analogy using *like, as, compared with,* or the equivalent. Here are some examples:

> The gray chill seeped into him like water into sand.
>
> WILLIAM FAULKNER

> Almost without exception, the men with whom I worked on the assembly line . . . felt like trapped animals.
>
> HARVEY SWADOS

> Yet, when the mind looks out for the first time into this manifold spiritual world, it is just as much confused and dazzled and distracted as are the eyes of the blind when they first begin to see.
>
> CARDINAL NEWMAN

> She plays bridge with the stupid voracity of a hammerhead shark.
>
> PHILIP WYLIE

> The female body, even at its best, is very defective in form; it has harsh curves and very clumsily distributed masses; compared to it the average milk-jug, or even cuspidor, is a thing of intelligent and gratifying design.
>
> H. L. MENCKEN

These similes serve in various ways to clarify, to give emphasis, to control the tone, and to support arguments. Faulkner's visual image makes us feel the penetration of the chill; one sensory impression is used to emphasize another. Swados and Newman use similes to clarify and back up arguments. Wylie and Mencken use them mainly for dramatic effect, to underscore their semicomic invective. All these similes, and 99 percent of all successful similes, are short, simple, and clear. They make their point without straining, and are free from self-contradiction.

Beginning writers sometimes have trouble on this last point. The following examples from student themes show how one can go wrong:

Macbeth struggled like a man in a whirlpool formed partly by nature, partly by the witches, and partly by his wife.

The radio quiz show is like a vast technical jungle that is intent on making itself a pleasant form of gambling.

Linda was beautiful, he thought, like a Spitfire or a DC-3.

The first two sentences show the imprecise and clumsy thinking characteristic of this kind of error: the idea is lost in the strained and overcomplex image. In the third sentence, the intended analogy between a girl's beauty and the beauty of two classic airplanes is destroyed by the connotations of *spitfire* (is beautiful Linda a shrew?), and perhaps, at least among readers not familiar with the DC-3, by connotations of great weight as well (is beautiful Linda a *fat* shrew?). However clear and just these three images may have seemed in the writers' minds, they appeared out of focus on the written page.

Metaphor

In metaphor, *like* and *as* are omitted and the comparison is asserted as an identity; the gap between the things compared is virtually closed. Instead of saying "He's like a jackass," we say "He's a jackass." Instead of saying "The raindrops are coming down *like* pitchforks," we say "It's raining pitchforks." George Orwell, in reviewing Salvador Dali's *Life*, writes: "Dali is even by his own diagnosis narcissistic, and his autobiography is simply a strip-tease act conducted in pink limelight." "*Like* a strip-tease act" would have been far less forceful.

A remark of James Baldwin, "I have discovered the weight of white people in the world," is a more complicated metaphor, one that works partly as a literal statement and partly as a play on words. White people, the oppressors, are *like* a weight on the Negro's back; but Baldwin is also using *weight* in the sense of weighty people who make weighty decisions, people with the power to push other people around. When Shakespeare wrote "the hearts that spaniel'd me at heels," he condensed what otherwise would have been a clause with a simile ("that followed me as spaniels follow their masters") to a single verb, and in so doing not only snapped our imaginations to attention, but voiced at the same time Antony's controlled contempt for his fickle followers. When Jesus spoke to the crowd in the Sermon on the Mount, he spoke almost entirely in metaphors, drawing upon their enormous dramatic power to drive home his meaning:

> Ye are the salt of the earth: but if the salt have lost his savour, wherewith shall it be salted? . . . Ye are the light of the world. A city that is set on an hill cannot be hid.

But metaphor is more than a way of decorating or enlivening language. It is a way of thought as well. Comparisons—not just between things as alike as Ann's hair and Sally's, but above all between things as unlike as rain and pitchforks, as wind and time, as men and salt—are part of the unending human effort to find unity in a universe of bits and pieces. "Like and like and like— but what is the thing that lies beneath the semblance of things?" asks Virginia Woolf. Whatever that ineffable "thing" may be, it will be expressed (if it is expressible at all) as a metaphor.

Poetry is especially devoted to this search for unity in diversity, and poets constantly use metaphor to probe into reality. "I can hear light on a dry day," says the poet Theodore Roethke. And again, as he recovers from an illness that is both physical and mental, "I'm sweating out the will to die." In the first metaphor, two senses, sight and hearing, are fused into one. In the second, two levels of meaning are joined: the physical "sweating" of the poet's fever and the figurative "sweating out" of his psychological crisis. "How can we know the dancer from the dance?" asks William Butler Yeats in the poem "Among School Children." The question gives us an unforgettable glimpse of the poet's vision of unity behind, and within, all experience.

The poet is not the only one who takes metaphor seriously. The "bandwagon approach" in advertising, the "Iron Curtain" in political thinking, the "Oedipus complex" in psychology—all these terms are metaphors used as shorthand for more or less complex ideas. The distinguished scientist J. Bronowski asserts the value of metaphor for scientific thinking as well:

> All science is the search for unity in hidden likenesses. The search may be on a grand scale, as in the modern theories which try to link the fields of gravitation and electromagne-

tism. But we do not need to be browbeaten by the scale of science. There are discoveries to be made by snatching a small likeness from the air, too, if it is bold enough. In 1932 the Japanese physicist Yukawa wrote a paper which can still give heart to a young scientist. He took as his starting point the known fact that waves of light can sometimes behave as if they were separate pellets. . . . A schoolboy can see how thin Yukawa's analogy is, and his teacher would be severe with it. Yet Yukawa without a blush calculated the mass of the pellet he expected to see, and waited. He was right; his meson was found, and a range of other mesons, neither the existence nor the nature of which had been suspected before. The likeness had borne fruit.

As a beginning writer, you may find it hard to think of yourself as in the same class with these poets, scientists, and professional writers. But you, too, will use metaphors, and for comparable purposes. They are virtually inescapable in any writing that strives seriously for clarity, vividness, or depth. It is therefore important that you employ the device properly. When metaphor is used well, it calls attention less to itself than to the meaning it carries. When it is misused, it is conspicuous and often absurd.

MISUSES OF METAPHOR

Three errors in particular should be avoided: stale metaphor, mixed metaphor, and inappropriate metaphor. By stale metaphor we mean tired or dead images; by mixed metaphor, combinations of incompatible images; by inappropriate metaphor, images that are likely to make readers uncomfortable.

Stale Metaphor

Imagery, as we have seen, should evoke comparisons in which one element helps to clarify the meaning of the other. Some images, however, no longer have this power. "The field of medicine," for example, no longer calls to mind a piece of land. What was once a living image is now moribund, a cliché without grace or force. Yet such images hang on, and in thoughtless hands yield sentences like this: "My eventual area of specialization attracted my attention before I was seduced by a larger field." The writer of this sentence has lost sight not only of what a field is but of what seduction is. Our language is full of such stock comparisons: "His mind is like a steel trap," "We got down to brass tacks," "Moving to Florida gave them a new lease on life." Some of these images have more force left than others, but they are all more dead than quick. Writers who habitually rely on such hoary phrases are letting dead people do their thinking for them.

Even worse are those weary old saws that many people confuse with wisdom. Take, for example, the old standby "Where there's smoke, there's fire." When Senator Joseph McCarthy claimed in 1950 that there were 205 Communists in the State Department, many people swore that there was truth in his assertion because —naturally—"Where there's smoke, there's fire." Yet in this instance it would have been truer to say "Where there's smoke, there's a smoke screen."

Mixed Metaphor

The trouble with old saws, as with dead images, is that they tend to become a substitute for thought. This leads to two dangers. One is that their relative truth tends increasingly to be seen as absolute. A moment's thought dispels this illusion. If "Virtue is its own reward" and "Honesty is the best policy," why all the proverbs about prudence and discretion? If "A bird in the hand is worth two in the bush," what are we to make of "Nothing ventured, nothing gained"? If "Haste makes waste," why is it that "He who hesitates is lost"? The second danger is that the residual force of a stale image will clash ludicrously with its context. Thus we find sentences like "When he pulled up stakes, you could have knocked me over with a feather."

A person who writes this way has lost touch with what his words mean; he has used metaphors without remembering the pictures they were created to evoke. "The sole aim of a metaphor," writes George Orwell, "is to call up a visual image." He was wrong to exclude the other senses, but right to insist on the importance of the visual. The man who wrote "The house system must be geared into the whole teaching arm of the university" was not seeing straight, and consequently not thinking straight. Gears do not mesh into arms. A similar blindness afflicted Secretary of State Dean Rusk in this comment on Vietnam: "When all the frosting is off the cake, it boils down to this—when they keep coming at you, do you get out of the way or meet them?" Nor was the general superintendent of the Chicago public schools at his best when he wrote: "With limited resources at his command, each youth must meet and conquer his own Achilles' heel."

Alas, these are not rare specimens to be chuckled at and forgotten. Here is a sampling of comparable howlers from one year's student themes and exams:

Since Kafka was imbedded in the ice of many frustrations, he naturally formulated ideas for dynamiting the ice.

The big question, which has been in the background for so long, has finally come to the surface.

The West was not a stable enough place even to have its pulse taken.

I have come to the point where I must cease casting anxious eyes about, wondering which path in life will be presented to me on a silver platter.

The desire is monomaniacal, reaping, if not suicide, at least the stagnant, self-polluting backwaters of nihilism.

What is a young man to do in this day and age, with the octopus of Communism spreading its testicles all over the face of the earth?

But as soon as we draw back to define our own conclusions about these novels, a gnawing dissatisfaction, a vague worm of discontent, peeks its head above the back of the tapestry.

Grammar can be made palatable if only the teacher will hold out the plum of fresh vistas in literature.

Sometimes, of course, metaphors can be deliberately mixed for purposes of humor or other special effects. The student who wrote "Jane Austen is intent on carving her little piece of ivory until the blood runs" mixed a metaphor with happy results. And in *The Heart of Midlothian*, Sir Walter Scott has Reuben Butler,

a dour old puritan, mix a metaphor with spectacular effect. Butler is referring to his son's fitness for the ministry:

> I will make it my business to procure a license when he is fit
> for the same, trusting he will be a shaft cleanly polished, and
> meet to be used in the body of the kirk; and that he shall
> not turn again, like the sow, to wallow in the mire of heret-
> ical extremes and defections, but shall have the wings of a
> dove, though he hath lain among the pots.

Wyndham Lewis in *The Apes of God* got a suitably ironic effect
by describing a character as possessing "fountains of energy,
of the sort that do not grow on every tree"; and we are indebted
to a newscaster (who may not have been trying to be funny) for
"The United Steelworkers will get down to brass tacks today."

Sometimes, too, well-known metaphors can be turned inside out
to good effect. It has been said of Henry James, for example,
that in writing at great length about small matters "he chewed
more than he bit off." And Oscar Wilde once threw new light
on the old biblical injunction by saying, "If a man smite thee, turn
the other face."

Inappropriate Metaphor

Finally, there is the question of taste. As Keats once said, we
hate writing that seems to have a "palpable design" upon us. We
dislike the hard sell; we turn away from writing marked by excess, by too much spilling of emotion; we are annoyed, or pro-
voked to laughter, by signs that the writer is working too hard.
The excessive or tasteless use of metaphor can give this effect.
Take this sentence: "The conscience of man takes precedence in
the logistics of American action; it is the silk thread shining
through the hair-shirt of our native literary search." Military
images and images of sin vie for our attention; the metaphor is
not exactly mixed, but it is too rich to swallow. In rejecting a
metaphor of this kind, of course, a reader rejects the message as
well.

Another kind of error in taste may be illustrated by the following horrendous sermon, which was reprinted in the *New Yorker:*

At a meeting in the Benson Hotel to promote the Portland Open golf tournament, the following invocation was given by Rev. Lester Harnish, pastor of the First Baptist Church:

"Oh God, in the game of life you know that though most of us are duffers, we all aspire to be champions with plenty of birdies or eagles.

"Help us, we pray, to be grateful for the course—including both the fairways and the rough.

"Thank you for those who have made it possible for us to tee off. Thank you for the thrill of a solid soaring drive, the challenge of the dog leg, the trial of the trap, the discipline of the water hazard, the beauty of a cloudless sky and the exquisite misery of rain and cold.

"Thank you, O God, for Jesus Christ our pro, who shows us how to get the right grip on life, to slow down in our back swing, to correct our crazy hooks and slices, to keep our head down in humility and to follow through in self-control.

"May He teach us also to be good sports who will accept the rub of the green, the penalty for being out-of-bounds, the reality of lost balls, the relevancy of par, the dangers of the 19th hole and the authority of our special rule book, the Bible.

"And Lord, when the last putt has dropped into the cup; the light of our last day has faded into the darkness of death; though our trophies be few, our handicap still too low and that hole-in-one still only a dream; may we be able to turn in to You, our tournament director, at the great clubhouse, an honest scorecard.

"Through Jesus Christ we pray, Amen."

No student would be guilty of such an effort. Yet it is not entirely unlike what many beginning writers try to do—or get caught in doing. It is easy, once a metaphor gets started, to keep it rolling; and it is almost always a mistake. Metaphor is like a beautiful motif in a symphony. Used with restraint, it gives the work meaning and depth. Used grossly or too frequently, or sustained too long, it cloys. Taste in these matters cannot be legislated or dictated; it must be felt. But when in doubt, remember the Reverend Lester Harnish and keep your metaphors short.

PART 2
THE TECHNIQUE OF WRITING

5

ABOUT TECHNIQUE

Before you start to write, you must know your subject and your audience, you must have your material ready, and you must make your basic strategic decisions. But all this is not enough: you must also develop a talent for writing itself, an ability to reach and hold your readers. That is where technique comes in. Technique may be defined as a mastery of the psychology and the mechanics of good writing; it is what clears the static off the line from writer to reader. Always there is the reader to think of— the elusive reader with his unknown capacities and incapacities, his sophistication and his ignorance, his prejudices and his susceptibility to distraction. The pitfalls are many. Make what you write too long, and he will be bored; make it too short, and he will be confused by your omissions; add a comma, choose a word carelessly, and he may misunderstand you; get a fact wrong, misspell a word, and he may write you off as an ignoramus.

There is still another pitfall: make him work too hard, and he will give you up for the boob tube. The educated American today is accustomed to skillful writing—in newspaper stories and magazine articles, in national advertising, and even on network television, where scarcely a sentence is uttered that has not first been written down and revised to exacting standards by a professional writer. To be sure, much of this writing is slick, shallow, unmemorable, devoted to conveying news or selling hair oil; but for better or for worse it has taught the educated American reader to expect economy, clarity, and directness in what he reads. To get a hearing from readers so conditioned, you must not only say what you mean, but say it well.

Learning to write is essentially a process of modifying the spoken language, with its natural redundancies and imprecisions, to meet the requirements of another medium. Our first serious efforts to write yield a kind of written talk, charming enough no doubt, but needing to be reconsidered, revised, perhaps condensed or expanded, if its full meaning is to come through. If the revising is left undone, or done badly, the result is mere writing, mere brushstrokes on the canvas. If the revising is done well—whether in the mind before writing, or after writing a first draft, or more commonly both—the result is good prose. In this chapter we will illustrate and describe these two classes of writing, mere writing and good prose, and discuss the gap between them. The next seven chapters are concerned with specific ways of narrowing this gap.

GOOD PROSE
Some Examples

Good prose comes in hundreds of varieties, from the long, rolling periods of Milton to the short, spare, mannered sentences of Ernest Hemingway; from the sturdy, measured narrative of Defoe to the antic cadenzas of H. L. Mencken. Even in the more modest realm of serviceable expository prose, on which we shall concentrate in this chapter, excellence takes many forms. Four passages follow, all in the first person, all expository (though two are from fiction), all different in tone and technique, all good prose.

Here is the novelist William Styron:

> For without knowing the white man at close hand, without having submitted to his wanton and arrogant kindnesses, without having smelled the smell of his bedsheets and his dirty underdrawers and the inside of his privy, and felt the casual yet insolent touch of his women's fingers upon his

own black arm, without seeing him at sport and at ease and at his hypocrite's worship and at his drunken vileness and at his lustful and adulterous couplings in the hayfield— without having known all these cozy and familial truths, I say, a Negro can only *pretend* hatred. Such hatred is an abstraction and a delusion. . . . Such a Negro, unacquainted with white men and their smell and their blanched and bloodless actuality and their evil, will perhaps hate but with a hatred which is all sullenness and impotent resentment, like the helpless, resigned fury one feels toward indifferent Nature throughout long days of relentless heat or after periods of unceasing rain.

The drama critic Kenneth Tynan:

Let me court peril with a generalization: that good drama, of whatever kind, has but one mainspring—the human being reduced by ineluctable process to a state of desperation. Desperate are the cornered giants of Sophocles; desperate, too, as they huddle in their summer-houses, the becalmed gentry of Chekhov; and the husband of French farce, with a wife in one bedroom and a mistress in another, is he not, though we smile at his agony, definably desperate? The clown in the haunted house and the prince on the haunted battlements have this in common, that their drama heightens as they are driven to the last ditch of their souls. How, in this extremity, will they comport themselves? It is to find out that we go to theaters.

The poet Yvor Winters:

At the church I sat with the family, in a private room to the side of the pulpit. After the sermon I looked once more into the casket. The black hair seemed not to have stirred. The face was not heavily wrinkled, but there were a few small wrinkles about the mouth and eyes. The skin was preternaturally and evenly white, and in the wrinkles there seemed a trace as of an underlying darkness, even and impenetrable. At the grave, a mile and a half outside of town, the ceremonies were brief, for a vile sleet had set in. The coffin was lowered; the last prayer was read; and the grave was filled with stones and mud. As we drove away, I looked back to see a huge mound of hot-house flowers, dark heavy green, and clear hard white and yellow, lying as if murdered in the colorless air, beneath driving sleet.

The journalist Dwight Macdonald:

I remember when Franco's planes bombed Barcelona for the first time what a thrill of unbelieving horror and indignation went through our nerves at the idea of hundreds—yes, *hundreds*—of civilians being killed. It seems impossible that that was less than ten years ago. Franco's air force was a toy compared to the sky-filling bombing fleets deployed in this war, and the hundreds killed in Barcelona have become the thousands killed in Rotterdam and Warsaw, the tens of thousands in Hamburg and Cologne, the hundreds of thousands in Dresden, and the millions in Tokyo. A month ago, the papers reported that over one million Japanese men, women, and children had perished in the fires set by a single B-29 raid on Tokyo. One million. I saw no expression of horror or indignation in any American newspaper or magazine of sizable circulation. We have grown calloused to massacre, and the concept of guilt has spread to include whole populations. Our hearts are hardened, our nerves steady, our imaginations under control as we read the morning paper. King Mithridates is said to have immunized himself against poison by taking small doses which he increased slowly. So the gradually increasing horrors of the last decade have made each of us to some extent a moral Mithridates, immunized against human sympathy.

Characteristics of Good Prose

What makes these passages good prose? In the first place, authority. A good writer knows what he wants to say, how to say it clearly, and how to make us listen when he talks. Even when his subject does not essentially interest us, or when we disagree with him, he will keep our attention.

In the second place, detail. Not just flowers, but hothouse flowers of two specific colors; not just European cities, but Rotterdam and Warsaw, Hamburg and Cologne. Detail is a tricky quality, to be sure. Too many details make for tiresome reading, and a wrong or obtrusive detail may be worse than no detail at all. But the impulse to precision is central to good prose. The telling detail is the essence of descriptive writing.

In the third place, brevity. A good writer pares away unnecessary blubber: abstract nouns like *situation* and *circumstances,* mechanical intensifiers like *very* and *really,* flabby phrases like *in such a way as to* and *in view of the fact that.* Our examples contain next to no excess words of this sort. Tynan does not say, "It is to find out *the answer to this question* that we go to theaters"; the italicized words are unnecessary, hence burdensome, all weight and no substance. Good writing is the right length for its content. What can be said in 80 words is said in 80 words, not in 100.

Finally, variety, in the rhythmic sense. There is something in the human mind—in the reader's inner ear—that calls for a short sentence after several long ones, or a longer one after several short ones. Too many simple sentences set us to wishing for a complex sentence, and vice versa. The rhythms of prose are not the rhythms of popular music; steady repetition of the same beat after a point is not pleasing but irritating, and in the end stupefying. Without knowing why, the reader wearies of his reading and puts it aside.

MERE WRITING

An Example

Let us now sample some mere writing, where we shall find the same truths illustrated in reverse. Here is the substance of the Winters passage as an unskilled writer might render it:

> Sitting there with the family in the church, in a private room on the left side of the pulpit, was one of the most frustrating experiences of my life. After the sermon for some reason—though I didn't want to—I looked into the casket again. This was my first funeral, and I guess I was in a state of shock or something. His black hair looked just the way it did in real life, and so did the wrinkles on his face, but

what especially got me was the chalky whiteness of the face. During the services at the grave, it began to sleet, and everybody hurried to get the ceremony over with. The coffin was lowered into the open grave, the last prayer was read by the minister, the grave was filled, and everybody hurried to drive away. Afterward, as I looked back at the grave, I saw some frozen flowers with the sleet pelting down on them.

This is not exactly bad. It is free of the errors in grammar and spelling that mar much undergraduate writing, and it conveys a reasonably clear message. But the writing is mere writing. Why? Basically because it lacks the qualities we have just discussed: authority, detail, brevity, and variety.

What authority the passage has is that of the recorder: this happened, then that happened; I felt this way, I felt that way. Gone are the tight control and rhythm that made the Winters passage eloquent, gone the complex vision that likened the "underlying darkness" in the dead man's face to the vivid image of the murdered flowers. What are we to make of the present account? The writer does not tell us. He offers no point of view, only some facts about the funeral and a confused and incomplete effort to describe how it affected him.

In the matter of detail, we miss several of the particulars that gave the original much of its power. The grave is no longer a mile and a half outside of town; it may be inside the city limits for all we are told, or in the churchyard itself, and in either event a distinctly different sort of place from Winters's dreary heath. The flowers are no longer hothouse flowers, no longer a "clear hard white and yellow" with foliage of "dark heavy green"; no longer, in short, Winters's pathetic gladioli, florist-forced and chosen by family and friends in the traditional pale funeral colors, but flowers of no special kind or color. The loss of detail is one no reader can be expected to make up on his own. Details are important: they give a message form and impact. Only poor writers shun them, whether from caution, ignorance, or the mistaken belief that it is more impressive to be general than specific.

As for brevity, Winters's passage has 152 words, and every word counts. Our second version is no longer, but some 30 of its words could be omitted without the least loss. Do we really need the third sentence, which seems to lead nowhere? In the next-to-last sentence, do we really need "into the open grave" and "by the minister," and in the last sentence do we need "Afterward"? Good writing does not waste words establishing routine connections like this; it suggests them or leaves them to inference. Poor writing, by contrast, typically spells out connections at unnecessary length.

Of variety the new version offers less than it should. Four of its seven sentences are compound sentences in *and* and *but*, a form whose allure for the unskilled writer often leads to its excessive use. The word *looked* is used three times in close succession, *grave* occurs four times in the space of only 48 words, and the unattractive *everybody hurried* is used twice.

In short, the passage, though unassailable on grammatical grounds and easy enough to understand, lacks style. Style is not easily defined. It is not the same thing as technique, though the two are closely related. Authority, detail, brevity, and variety are some of its components, but it has others as well. One is a linguistic verve or daring: whatever it was that led Styron to write that powerful mounting period, or Tynan to invert the construction of his second sentence. Another is a sense of words: the sense that one particular word or arrangement of words is right for one's purpose, and that no other will serve as well. A third, and perhaps the most important of all, is the impress of the writer's personality. A good writer sounds a certain way and not any other way. Macdonald is earnest and impersonal; Styron eloquent, moving, and rhetorical; Tynan ingratiating; Winters remote, almost magisterial. Even on the evidence of the brief passages before us, the four styles cannot be confused. Each man has his own voice.

That is all very well, you may say, but where does it leave less gifted people? You may feel that you are being asked to learn writing techniques before you have anything much to say, and indeed to write paper after paper before you have even learned writing techniques! But writing is like playing tennis or playing the piano: doing it badly is the necessary first step to doing it well. You may not write like Winters or Styron or Shakespeare today, or next week, or ever; but that is not the point. The point is to find your own voice and write like yourself—or rather like yourself at your best.

Another Example

As a start, let's have a look at something rather less than your best. Here is a paragraph from a freshman theme about an essay by George Orwell:

> The descriptions in this essay are incredibly graphic. I was carried along from one beautifully written paragraph to the next, and I was horrified by some, disgusted by others, but I was always amazed by how close the writer's experience had been to mine. After I had finished reading this essay, though, I was in an exceedingly dismal state of mind, recalling how bleak my own childhood had been and realizing that others were the same.

One finishes this paragraph with irritation. Its adverbs are too frequent and intense, its two long sentences are poorly constructed, it lacks detail, and its messages conflict. The writer seems simultaneously impressed with Orwell's writing ability, disgusted and horrified by the incidents Orwell describes, amazed at the parallel with his own experience, and plunged into gloom by recalling that experience. Nonsense, says the reader: the mind is no such three-ring circus. One of these emotions we might have believed, or two in sequence; but not all four at once. Either the writer does not know what he thinks about Orwell's essay, or he dislikes it but thinks he had better pretend otherwise.

Let's get rid of these difficulties and see what happens. Let's bring on the circus acts one at a time, and leave the main act on longest. Let's cut down on the adverbs, tighten up the rambling sentences, and replace empty general words like *descriptions* and *experience* with specifics. With these changes made, our paragraph might look like this:

> Orwell's essay helped me to see my own boarding-school days in perspective. Crossgates and my school were very similar: the snobbery, the concern with money, the sexual anxiety, the obsession with sports. Perhaps all boarding schools are like that; at all events, Orwell helped me to see for the first time that I had been one of many. Others were

just as timid, just as withdrawn. Dozens of my schoolmates must have suffered as I did, and for as little reason.

This paragraph is not perfect prose, but it has risen above mere writing. It has authority: the writer has clearly understood Orwell's experience and related it to his own. It is spare: there are no gratuitous intensifiers like *incredibly* and *always,* no functionless words like *reading,* no ambiguous words like *others.* It offers details: not "the writer's experience," but snobbery, money, sexual anxiety, sports; not mere bleakness, but persecution for being timid and withdrawn. Finally, it has a rhythm or pace that puts the rambling original to shame.

On this last point, a word of advice: reading aloud can help. In matters of rhythm, or even in matters only tenuously connected with rhythm, the ear can sometimes hear what the eye cannot see—that a sentence is too complicated for a reader to take in, or too feebly related to another sentence, or ugly or pompous-sounding or just plain silly. If our freshman had read his Orwell paragraph aloud and listened to himself as he read, he might have rewritten his long, shapeless first sentence into something more easily grasped; and he might have toned down such overintense words as *disgusted* and *amazed.*

Reading aloud works best with a listener or two, since most of us are sensitive to criticism from others, including unspoken criticism, and since such criticism is likely to tell us more than our own biased promptings. Alternatively, of course, you can read the work aloud to yourself, or read it silently but try to sound the words in your mind. Whatever you do, if something sounds wrong—even if you don't know why—throw it out, replace it, edit it. Conversely, what your ear tells you is good probably *is* good. If something sounds exactly right when you say it, it will usually pass muster on paper.

EDITING

The Nature and Functions of Editing

The process by which you convert mere writing to good prose is called editing. All book publishers and magazines assign editors to manuscripts, and newspapers have editors to edit the raw writing of reporters for clarity and style. College students, having no such help available, must be both author and editor, both writer and rewrite man.

In our formula for good writing—authority, detail, brevity, variety—the strictly editorial elements are brevity and variety. Editing cannot supply authority, though it can bring out what authority the writer commands. Nor can it usually supply detail not already present; all it can do is select whatever details seem most effective and arrange them to the best possible advantage. Authority and detail are ultimately matters of the author's knowledge of his subject. But brevity and variety are the editor's precinct.

Editing takes time. If you leave yourself only two hours to write a paper and spend two hours writing it, you have a first draft, not a paper. You are better off if you leave yourself three hours and spend the third editing what you have written in the first two. Another thing editing takes is perspective: it is best done after an interval. Ideally, this interval should be several days or more—the Roman poet Horace recommended nine years—and should include time for pondering or researching the main troubles revealed in the first draft. If your schedule allows no time for such luxuries, shorten the interval, but try not to eliminate it. If you can separate writing and editing by as little as a night's sleep, or even a meal or a game of tennis, you will do a better job of editing than you would after no interval at all.

Finally, editing cannot be done well under pressure. You can sometimes bat out a first draft in hot haste; some people even write more fluently that way. But editing is another matter. In editing you have to ask yourself how well a sentence or a paragraph works, whether its meaning comes through, whether it can be made clearer and stronger, what kind of change might help. If you are not pressed for time or distracted, whatever you do will probably improve things.

Editing has two functions: to correct and to improve. The first function has to do with errors of grammar, syntax, diction, and so on, and with basic clarity and consistency; these matters will be discussed in the following chapters. In this chapter we are concerned with the second function: with ways of making writing generally more effective. Mere writing, first-draft writing, may be errorless; it may also be clear. What it usually is not, and what editing seeks to make it, is readable. Mere writing can often be understood, but only good writing can be enjoyed.

An Example

In the previous section we discussed and illustrated the editing of a few sentences from a student theme about George Orwell. Another example of editing may be helpful. We begin with a paragraph from a first draft:

> There is not very much to be said in favor of the argument that the right to vote in elections should be dependent on residence in a community for a period of at least six months. The living patterns of the American people at the present time are not the same as those of fifty or a hundred years ago, at the time of the passage of the laws that established the six-month residence requirement. There is more changing of residence today from one community to another; for example, some men are transferred from one city to another by the companies they work for, and many old people move to California or Florida when they reach retirement age. It does not seem fair that people who move to new communities should have their right to vote taken away from them, and especially that they should be deprived of the right to vote in national elections.

In editing dull writing like this, the first thing to look for is what some professional editors call "fat": long phrases that can be cut out altogether, or replaced by a shorter phrase or a single word, with no loss of meaning. Consider the first sentence. Its first thirteen words can be replaced by the shorter and more direct phrase "It seems unjust," and two later phrases—"in elections" and "a period of at least"—can be simply deleted. The second sentence is just as overweight. "The living patterns of the American people" can be cut down to "American living patterns"; "at the present time" can be deleted altogether, since the time is perfectly clear from the context; and the sixteen-word final phrase can be cut to "when the residence requirement was established." Analogous changes elsewhere make the paragraph much leaner:

It seems unjust that the right to vote should depend on residence in a community for six months. American living patterns have changed in the hundred years since the residence requirement was first established. People change residence more frequently today: for example, executives are transferred and old people move to California and Florida. It seems especially unfair that people who move should lose the right to vote in national elections.

This is much better, but still rather flat. Some further changes, to bolster the argument and introduce variety into the sentence pattern, make it better still:

Why should the right to vote depend on six months' residence in a community? Things have changed since 1900: the nation counts for more, the community for less. Every year thousands of executives are transferred, thousands of old people move to Florida, thousands of teachers and graduate students move to new universities. Why penalize these people? At least let them vote in national elections.

We started with 155 words, which we cut first to 70 and finally to 64. Nothing worth keeping has been lost in the editing; indeed, as occasionally happens, new material has actually been added. The final version accordingly says more in 64 words than the original said in 155. With the 91 words of static suppressed, the 64 words of message come through more clearly. Our editing has cut away the fat and kept the meat.

Note also the changes in sentence structure. The four sentences of the original were all declarative; in the final version two sentences are interrogative and one is imperative. These changes help make the argument more direct and immediate, and for the first time give something of that sense of the writer's personality (rather a strident one, in this case) which is indispensable to style.

There is nothing absolute about these changes. Brevity is good, but a passage can be too brief for its content: the World War II Navy pilot whose initial radio report read "Sighted sub, sank same" had to submit a longer report when he got back to his base. Interrogative and imperative sentences should be used sparingly; less dramatic devices often serve as well. Above all, you should avoid unnatural changes. *The wind died down* may be unexciting, but *Down died the wind* is no improvement. If you cannot find a natural way to make a sentence shorter or snappier, let it stand and go on to the next one.

Editing at its best will correct obvious errors in spelling, punctuation, and so on, and eliminate the repetitions, awkward wordings, and bits of foolishness that often creep into first drafts. It will correct slips of tone. It will change unnecessarily long phrases like *was due to the fact that* to short ones like *happened because*, and short ones like *the maintenance of* to shorter ones like *maintaining*. It will fashion sentences of different lengths or kinds to lighten the going where it is otherwise heavy.

Too much to ask? Perhaps at first, but it gets easier, and it can even get to be fun if you have a first draft you respect and a good working knowledge of the basic elements and techniques of writing. To these elements—the paragraph, the sentence, the word, punctuation—we turn next.

6

PARAGRAPHS

Paragraphs are not just hunks of prose marked by indentations; they are the basic units of thought out of which an essay is made. They are sometimes classified into three kinds: narrative, descriptive, and expository. The first kind tells a story, or part of one; the second describes something; the third explains something. Our concern here is mainly with the last kind, the paragraph units that make up an expository essay.

BEGINNINGS, MIDDLES, AND ENDS

Every coherent essay has a beginning, a middle, and an end. The beginning may be thought of as a single paragraph; it may grow naturally into two or more paragraphs, but one is usually enough. The end may also be thought of as a single paragraph; usually an essay of ten to fifteen pages requires no more. Finally, the middle may be thought of as a single paragraph that has grown too long to treat as one unit. Accordingly, it must be broken down for the reader's convenience into a series of component paragraphs.

A good way to write a short essay[1] is to begin with a simple three-part plan: beginning, middle, and end. Here is a sample:

Beginning

> Although the novelist E. M. Forster is generally thought of as a liberal, he is in another sense profoundly conservative.

Middle

> To understand this paradox, we must distinguish between the words *liberal* and *conservative* as applied to Forster, see in what ways he is an aristocrat, and trace these issues in his essays and novels.

End

> Although Forster may be a conservative, he is no reactionary, and on this distinction hangs a good part of his importance.

The beginning idea here is worth one paragraph; so is the end idea. The middle idea is worth at least as many paragraphs as there are main points to make—in this case no fewer than four.

The first sentence in this outline happens also to be a "thesis sentence," that is, a one-sentence statement of what the essay is all about. But that need not always be the case. The opening paragraph may simply open a door into the essay by asking the reader a question or by giving him a quick peek at something that is not fully illuminated until, perhaps, the final paragraph. Here is another brief outline:

Beginning

> The so-called silent generation was created by the cultural climate of the 1950's.

Middle

> The Eisenhower administration, the Cold War, and uninterrupted prosperity were the shaping influences on this gen-

---

[1] See Part 3, "The Research Paper," for strategies governing longer pieces of writing.

eration. These forces created a world that felt scared and safe at the same time, a mood reflected in the younger generation in many ways. Thanks to these forces, young people preferred security to innovation, money to self-fulfillment, peace and quiet to social justice.

End

But before we dismiss that generation as dead or decadent compared with the present one, we should ask whether the new activism is a new state of mind or simply a new style.

This is the outline of a fairly long essay. The beginning and the end could be handled as single paragraphs, but the middle might require as many as ten. One thing a simple outline like this helps you do is see how much you are biting off. If you have been assigned a 500-word essay, you have too big a subject here, since paragraphs tend to average about 100 words. This outline also hints at what kind of general organization the essay will have: here the opener is not a thesis sentence, and the end is more of a question than a conclusion.

DEVELOPING THE OUTLINE

Example One: Sentences to Paragraphs

Here are some paragraphs that might be developed from the above abbreviated outlines. The beginning paragraph of the essay outlined first might go as follows:

The novelist E. M. Forster is rightly considered a liberal, but he is at the same time profoundly conservative. This is less of a paradox than it may at first appear. American liberal critics make a mistake when they reproach Forster for his loathing of political action or his affection for the Ivory Tower. What they don't see is the intimate connection between his liberalism and his sense of "aristocracy," a connection far more easily understood in England than in this country. To understand Forster's views on aristocracy is the first step toward understanding his political position.

The first sentence introduces the subject; the next three sentences indicate the general line of the argument; the final sentence is a transition to the heart of the essay. In this instance, the paragraph has a beginning, a middle, and an end just as the whole essay does.

Here is a possible final paragraph for the same essay:

> The "aristocracy of the sensitive, the considerate, and the plucky" is, then, at the very heart of Forster's liberalism. It is an aristocracy without worldly power or property, but it is an aristocracy nevertheless, and on it Forster rests his hope for the survival of mankind. This is a conservative position, but not a reactionary one; indeed, in another sense, it is profoundly revolutionary. But it calls for a revolution in ourselves before we go to work on the social order, a revolution of ideas rather than of actions, of slow change rather than of violence.

The first two sentences serve as a transition from what has gone before and set the theme for the paragraph they begin. The last two sentences make a final point; they pull things together.

An essay should be a package with a string around it, not a gathering of fragments. In your concluding paragraph, do not simply repeat in compressed form what you have already said. We have heard it once and do not want to hear it again—unless, that is, a brief recapitulation (as above) serves in some way for emphasis or clarity. Your last paragraph should in itself be a step in the essay's advance. It should reveal in some fresh light what the essay has been driving at all along, or perhaps open our eyes to something new. It should not clobber our minds with repetition.

Example Two: A Come-on Opener

Now consider this opening paragraph of the second essay outlined. Here the strategy is quite different:

> The "final philosophic statement" of Jack Kerouac's book *The Subterraneans*, published in 1958, was *"I don't know I*

don't care and it doesn't make any difference." Kerouac was the voice of the generation that went to college in the fifties. The college students of that decade didn't want to know much about what America was doing abroad, they didn't care much about the plight of the Negro or injustice at home, and they acted as if nothing beyond their fingertips made much difference. A cozy house in the suburbs with wife, kids, and TV; a cushy job in a safe corporation with built-in retirement benefits—these were the limits of their dream. They deserved their title of the Silent Generation.

Here the beginning sentence is not the thesis of the paragraph, but an idea that will lead into that thesis. It is a come-on, an invitation to find out what this question will lead to. If your come-on is serious and relevant, this is an effective way to begin an essay; if it is there just to jazz things up, like the jokes of some after-dinner speakers, then your reader is likely to feel bored and cheated. It is a good idea to be serious even when you are being amusing, to make every turn of a paragraph serve your purpose.

QUALITIES OF A GOOD PARAGRAPH

Unity and Coherence

Every good paragraph has two qualities: unity and coherence. It has unity in the sense that it is about one subject, and coherence in the sense that its sentences fit together to make a connected whole. Whatever form a paragraph may take, it is always a unit of thought. Just as you should be able to state the thesis of a good essay in one sentence (the thesis sentence), so you should be able to state in one sentence the thesis of each of its paragraphs.

By way of testing for these qualities, there is a game one can play called pinpointing paragraphs. Write the thesis sentence of the whole essay; then write down the thesis sentences of the successive paragraphs. The resulting series of sentences should give you in capsule form the basic argument of the essay. If it does not, the essay probably suffers from logical gaps, irrelevancies, or padding. Further scrutiny of the thesis sentences should tell you where the trouble is and what kind of change would make things better.

Length

Let us examine the following paragraph from John Rosenberg's *The Darkening Glass,* a critical study of John Ruskin:

> The political economists, then, were perhaps naïve but not malevolent. They were naïve to assume that economics is a mathematical science which can be divorced from the human creatures who, unlike Newtonian particles in motion, behave in curiously unpredictable ways. Inheriting the rationalistic, mechanistic assumptions of the eighteenth century, they mistook for universally valid laws certain limited principles which operated to limited advantage in a newly industrialized society. Paradoxically, the more they tried to purge their science of extraneous moral issues, the more they endowed *laissez faire* with a kind of sacred moral sanction. For they appeared to be describing not the local operations of London merchants or Lancashire mill owners, but weighty principles which, with the inevitability of natural law, govern the economic life of man. Tampering with free enterprise was tantamount to meddling with the harmony of nature itself. *Laissez faire* was natural, universal; government imposition of minimum wages or humane working conditions was unnatural and by inference evil. Thus political economy presumed to the objectivity of a science at the same time that it arrogated to itself the subtler authority of a religion.

This paragraph has unity and coherence, and carries its rather heavy freight of ideas with considerable grace and efficiency. Nevertheless, it is a fairly big and forbidding block of prose. A reader unfamiliar with the material might feel daunted at the beginning and somewhat taxed near the middle. Could things be made easier for him? Why not begin a new paragraph at "Paradoxically," where the naïveté of the political economists gives way to the paradox of their pretensions to objectivity? Since the two short paragraphs are each as unified and coherent as the original long one, nothing is lost.

How long should a paragraph be? The only general rule is that it should be long enough to convey one more or less complex thought, and not so long as to alienate or stun its readers. Very short paragraphs are no better than very long ones. A series of one- and two-sentence paragraphs (a favorite strategy in political speeches and witty newspaper columns) suggests that the author is presenting a series of fragments designed to evoke bursts of applause or laughs, rather than a message to be considered and understood as a whole. An occasional one-sentence paragraph may be useful as a transition to a new line of thought, or for dramatic effect; but short paragraphs as a class should be left to the politicians and journalists, who have their own reasons (or alibis) for using them.

Transitions

What ties the sentences of a paragraph together? Sometimes words like *but* and *moreover*, sometimes the repetition of a key word (for example, *naïve* in the first two sentences of the Rosenberg paragraph quoted above), sometimes a wordless promise of details to support a generalization or of a generalization to climax a series of details. Sometimes nothing more than the rhythm of the writer's excitement, or of the reader's interest. Much is made of so-called transitional devices by some teachers, but in our opinion few writers consciously use such devices as a way of constructing paragraphs. In our view, the idea comes first, the writing follows, and the transitions from sentence to sentence are generated strictly as by-products of the writer's effort to make the reader see exactly what he means.

Some transitions are nonetheless more effective than others, if we may judge from the work of skilled writers. The best writers tend, for example, to avoid such routine transitional words and phrases as *and, but, however, moreover,* and *on the other hand.* (Note that only two sentences in Rosenberg's paragraph are so linked, with the unobtrusive and necessary *for* and *thus.*) These words are not bad in themselves, but when used to excess they make a paragraph seem full of hinges, like a trick floor at a carnival; it hangs together but is hard to walk on. If you know what you want to say, as Rosenberg clearly does, you need not rope your sentences together. Your ideas will jump from sentence to sentence like electric sparks, or flow like an underground stream.

Variety in Sentence Structure

Another way of tying a paragraph together is to use different kinds of sentences in composing it. In Chapter 5, p. 72, we demonstrated the use of interrogative and imperative sentences in making what had been a long, dull paragraph brief and lively. Other devices are just as effective. Follow a short sentence with a long one, for example, as Rosenberg does in his sentences 1 and 2. Vary the subject-predicate-object sentence form; begin some sentences with an introductory phrase or a subordinate clause. Don't have all compound or all complex or all simple sentences; have some of each. These rules, like all rules, are made to be broken by masters—the final arbiter is the taste and judgment of the writer—but it is well to be aware that one can bore as much by sameness of one's style as by the dullness of one's thoughts.

We had thought to add, too, that you should avoid that other phenomenon, the paragraph consisting of one monster sentence. But consider this paragraph from Norman Mailer's *Presidential Papers*:

It is not that Los Angeles is altogether hideous, it is even by degrees pleasant, but for an Easterner there is never any salt in the wind; it is like Mexican cooking without chili, or Chinese egg rolls missing their mustard;[1] as one travels through the endless repetitions of that city which is the capital of suburbia with its milky pinks, its washed-out oranges, its tainted lime-yellows of pastel on one pretty little architectural monstrosity after another, the colors not intense enough, the styles never pure, and never sufficiently impure to collide on the eye, one conceives the people who live here—they have come out to express themselves,[2] Los Angeles is the home of self-expression, but the artists are middle-class and middling-minded; no passions will calcify here for years in the gloom to be revealed a decade later as the tessellations of a hard and fertile work,[3] no, it is all open, promiscuous, borrowed, half bought, a city without iron, eschewing wood, a kingdom of stucco, the playground for mass men—[4] one has the feeling it was built by television sets giving orders to men.

Here is variety enough, detail enough, rhythm enough, to keep all readers aboard till the end of the ride. But is this *one* sentence? Only in the most technical sense. If periods were put in at 1, 2, 3, and possibly 4, we probably would not notice much difference—perhaps only a slight slowing down in our reading speed. Which punctuation is better? It is a matter of taste. If you can write paragraphs this good, you can go ahead and punctuate them any way you like.

ORDERING PRINCIPLES

Paragraphs, like essays, tend to follow certain definite ordering principles. Although few paragraphs exhibit these principles in a pure form, the writer can profitably keep three of the main varieties in mind.

Induction and Deduction

When a paragraph (or an essay) begins with a general statement and moves to the particulars supporting it, we call that method of ordering deductive, from the Latin *deducere,* to lead out or away. When, on the contrary, a paragraph or an essay moves from particular facts or details to a general truth, or from a part to the whole, we call its order inductive. Most expository paragraphs, like the ones by Rosenberg and Mailer above, are roughly deductive; that is, they begin with a thesis sentence and lead away from this sentence with further sentences supporting or illustrating its thesis. But inductive paragraphs can be equally effective. Here are two examples:

> The rivers of eastern Virginia slant down toward the sea from the northwest. Some of them are wide and deep and some are quite insignificant except during time of heavy rains, but each one can be a barrier to a moving army. In the spring of 1864 the Army of the Potomac had to cross all of them, and the crossings could be made only where there were no defenders. These facts shaped the route of the army, and all through the month of May it moved in a series of wide zig-zags.

"You could cover the whole world with asphalt," remarked the late Ilya Ehrenburg, "but sooner or later green grass would break through." In this fashion, the process of suppression of modern Russian literature, that began in the late 1920's and persists to this day, has yielded from time to time to these stubborn shoots. A few works, like some of Zamyatin, Pasternak and Tertz, have only made their appearance abroad, while others have broken past the controls that have been greatly eroded in the post-Stalin era.

Comparison and Contrast

Comparison is often a good way of introducing or defining something. If a reader has never seen or heard an English horn but is familiar with the oboe, a comparison of the two instruments is the best way to instruct him about the one he does not know. Even if a reader is acquainted with both elements of a comparison, the comparison may be instructive: in describing a sonata, for example, you may find it useful to say how it differs from another sonata, or from a concerto by the same composer. Contrast, in particular, can be funny. Thus Shaw wrote of a pompous actor that to make a proper Falstaff, he had only to be born again as unlike his present self as nature might permit.

There is often a certain drama in showing how something is like or unlike something else. In James Baldwin's "What It Means to Be an American," for example, the author compares his American habits of mind with those he acquired in Europe. The two are very different, and the reason has to do with differences between the two environments:

> The American writer, in Europe, is released, first of all, from the necessity of apologizing for himself. It is not until he *is* released from the habit of flexing his muscles and proving that he is just a "regular guy" that he realizes how crippling this habit has been. It is not necessary for him, there, to pretend to be something he is not, for the artist does not encounter in Europe the same suspicion he encounters here. Whatever the Europeans may actually think of artists, they have killed enough of them off by now to know

that they are as real—and as persistent—as rain, snow, taxes, or businessmen.

Classification

Classification is the breaking down of a subject into its component parts, listing the categories or units of which it is made up. Here is part of a paragraph from Loren Eiseley's *The Immense Journey*:

> That food came from three sources, all produced by the reproductive system of the flowering plants. There were the tantalizing nectars and pollens intended to draw insects for pollenizing purposes. . . . There were the juicy and enticing fruits to attract larger animals, and in which tough-coated seeds were concealed, as in the tomato, for example. Then, as if this were not enough, there was the food in the actual seed itself, the food intended to nourish the embryo. All over the world, like hot corn in a popper, these incredible elaborations of the flowering plants kept exploding.

This order is by nature deductive: the reader is told that there are three, or four, or five items to be discussed, and the items are thereupon discussed. Most readers are grateful to have this sort of road map. The writer must of course take care, if he has promised three items, to deliver three, and not two or four.

This is by no means an exhaustive list of the way paragraphs can be ordered, but the other principles sometimes invoked—definition, exclusion, cause and effect, and so on—seem to us matters of common sense that need not be illustrated or discussed. To repeat, ordering principles are rarely exhibited in pure form; indeed, paragraphs are almost as various in their contours as the people who write them. Writers do not usually organize their paragraphs by principle, but by what they have to say: form is inseparable from content. The reason that a few ordering principles are nonetheless prominent enough to deserve study is simply that these principles correspond to the most powerful methods of reasoning.

JUDGING A PARAGRAPH

Here is a paragraph from a student paper. Is it a good one?

Young people have always been rebellious, anxious for change. Presented with a group of problems they are not responsible for, they have a great urge to change things, to make a better world. They have not yet met with the discouraging realities of life and the accompanying loss of idealism. In college one is presented with a unique opportunity to voice views without the fear of recrimination that people with a fixed place in the community have. There is relatively little to lose because no roots have been set down. The college student is not tied to his college as the ordinary citizen is to his community. He has a sense of detachment which may give him the feeling that he can bring about great changes and certainly allows him to attempt this without fear.

The first question to ask is this: Is there a single idea that governs the whole paragraph and makes a unit of it? Can one state it as a thesis sentence? How about "Young people, especially college students, are rebellious because they have less to lose than their more established elders"? Since all seven sentences relate in some way to this idea, it is fair to consider the paragraph a unit. But now comes the second question: Is the paragraph coherent? Here one encounters difficulties. The first three sentences are about young people in general, the last four about college students. Is a connection established between these two worlds? None that can be put in words. The reader is supposed to infer a connection, but can only guess what the writer intended.

This brings us to our third question: Is the reasoning in the paragraph, or the way evidence is presented, sound and convincing? It is not, primarily because the generalizations of the first three sentences are too broad to be defended or, really, understood. Not all young people are rebellious; some are timid, some are indifferent, and some like things just the way they are. And not all rebellious young people are out to make a better world; some are simply neurotic, and some are juvenile delinquents. As for the claim that young people "have not yet met with the discouraging realities of life," what about young people in war-torn Vietnam or famine-ridden India? What people are we talking about, anyway? All young people, or only some, and if some, which ones?

As the paragraph stands, then, it has a kind of unity, but little coherence. If the writer had begun by saying "Many young Americans are rebellious today" and otherwise qualified his opening remarks, the paragraph would be better, but since its details are nowhere specific and its point is not clear, it would still be boring and vaguely irritating. With all its defects remedied, the paragraph might read like this:

> In America most young people are brought up to believe in change—to believe that next year's model will be better than this year's, that the new math will supplant the old, that because people are growing taller they must be growing better as well. These illusions are reinforced by the behavior of many American adults, who trade in their cars, their jobs, even their wives and husbands, for new models in the recurrent expectation that the new ones will bring happiness. Small wonder that college students are such active seekers of change. Not only are they encouraged by the training and the example of their elders, but they are uninhibited by responsibility to a profession, a family, or a community, and unsobered by the recollection of their own past errors. In theory, at least, they are the perfect revolutionaries.

The revised paragraph has expressed much the same general idea as the original, but its generalizations are rooted in reality, its details are concrete and alive, and its final sentence makes the writer's message clear. And this is the point we would like to end on: If you have something to say and really want to say it, the chances are that your paragraphs will shape themselves. The person who is full of his subject almost *has* to communicate it clearly and convincingly. That motive in itself tends to be a shaper of good paragraphs.

7

SENTENCES:

BASIC MECHANICS

A generation ago the word *grammar* called to mind a fixed body of rules to be drummed by severe schoolmarms into the thick skulls of successive waves of children. Today we see these things a little differently. In this book, grammar in the classic sense will be considered under three headings: basic mechanics (the present chapter), syntax (Chapter 8), and style (Chapter 9). These terms may be regarded simply as convenient classifications for a discussion of certain recurrent problems that come up in writing sentences.

A problem in *basic mechanics*, as we use the term, is one involving a choice between alternatives differing in number, gender, case, or tense. A *syntax* problem is one involving a choice between alternative ways of relating two or more parts of a sentence to each other. A *style* problem is one involving a choice between equally correct alternatives on the ground of effectiveness. In matters of basic mechanics and syntax, a writer's choice between alternatives is conventionally considered either right or wrong—not absolutely (as is often thought), but by reference to the way educated persons write. Style, by contrast, has no rights or wrongs: here the writer's choice is between better and worse, between what is less likely and what is more likely to get his message across to his readers. Grammar and syntax lend themselves to a certain amount of rote learning. Style is ultimately dependent on taste.

NUMBER AND GENDER PROBLEMS

People (is) (are) my business

Everyone knows that singular subjects take singular verbs and plural subjects plural verbs. The difficulty lies in determining when a subject is singular and when plural, and sometimes in determining which of several words or phrases is in fact the subject. The present section will be confined to common sources of error and confusion, and will not pursue the more bizarre complications to which this deceptively straightforward-sounding rule gives rise.

When the subject is singular but a predicate noun is plural, stick strictly to the rule. All of the following sentences are correct:

My only *source* of support *was* my parents.

My *parents were* my only source of support.

The one *thing* the Allies lacked *was* troopships.

Troopships were the one thing the Allies lacked.

With a subject made up of two or more nouns linked by *and*, use a plural verb: *Wine, women, and song were Bao Dai's downfall.* There are exceptions—for example, *A year and six months was all they needed / Bread and butter is tedious fare*—where the compound subject, being essentially singular in meaning, takes a singular verb; but these exceptions are few. When in doubt, use the plural: *Rain and sleet were forecast for the week of the convention.*

With a subject made up of two or more singular nouns linked by *or* or *nor*, use a singular verb; if the components are all plural, use a plural verb:

Either Egypt or Israel *has* to back down.

The investigation did not reveal whether the pilot, the navigator, or the bombardier *was* responsible.

Neither the ranchers nor the miners *pay* this tax.

If some components are singular and some plural, you may face a nasty choice:

Usually the coaches or the manager (*gives*) (*give*) the signals.

When this happens, either the farmhouse or the crops (*have*) (*has*) to be mortgaged.

Neither the governor nor the local authorities (*were*) (*was*) sympathetic.

Since each of the alternatives in parentheses has its drawbacks, the best thing to do is reword the sentence to avoid the number problem. This is usually not hard: *The signals are usually given by the coaches or the manager / When this happens, either the farmhouse or the crops must be mortgaged / Both the governor and the local authorities were unsympathetic.* If no alternative wording can be found, make the verb agree with the nearest noun or pronoun component of the subject:

Either the Joint Chiefs or one of the field commanders *was* lying.

Has Socrates's question, or Hobbes's and Rousseau's questions, ever been satisfactorily answered?

Who takes (his) (our) (their) turn next?

Number difficulties may involve not only verbs but pronouns and nouns:

Was it Sir Robert or his sister that hanged (*himself*) (*herself*) (*themselves*)?

The teacher wanted me or Ken to read (*my*) (*his*) (*our*) essay.

Either the linebackers or the safety man missed (*his cue*) (*their cue*) (*their cues*).

Here, as so often, the best solution is to avoid the problem by re-wording: for example, *Either the linebackers or the safety man made the wrong move.* If no satisfactory alternative wording can be found, make the pronoun agree in number and gender with the nearest component of the subject, making the nearest component plural if possible and masculine if there is a choice of genders:

Either the safety man or the *linebackers* missed *their* cues.

Was it Lady Nutcombe or *Sir Robert* that hanged *himself*?

We each (have) (has) children of (our) (his) own

Each as a subject takes a singular verb; so do nouns modified by *each* and *every* and the nouns *anyone, anybody, no one, nobody, everyone,* and *everybody.* These words cause few problems with verbs; the trouble comes in determining the number and gender of any following nouns and pronouns. Fowler[1] has a fine pronouncement on this subject:

A perfect language . . . would have words meaning him-or-her, himself-or-herself, his-or-her. But, just as French lacks our power of distinguishing (without additional words) be-tween his, her, and its, so we lack the French power of say-ing in one word his-or-her. There are three makeshifts: first, *as anybody can see for himself or herself;* second, *as any-body can see for themselves;* and third, *as anybody can see for himself.* No one who can help it chooses the first; it

[1] Henry Watson Fowler (1858–1933) was perhaps the greatest of all writers on English usage. His *Dictionary of Modern Usage* (1926), from which this quotation is taken, made his name a household word among writers, editors, and teachers of English. A second edition, with extensive revisions by the late Sir Ernest Gowers, was published in 1965.

is correct, and is sometimes necessary, but it is so clumsy as to be ridiculous except when explicitness is urgent, and it usually sounds like a bit of pedantic humour. The second is the popular solution; it sets the literary man's teeth on edge, and he exerts himself to give the same meaning in some entirely different way if he is not prepared to risk the third, which is here recommended. It involves the convention (statutory in the interpretation of documents) that where the matter of sex is not conspicuous or important the masculine form shall be allowed to represent a person instead of a man, or say a man (*homo*) instead of a man (*vir*). Whether that convention, with *himself or herself* in the background for especial exactitudes, and paraphrase always possible in dubiour cases, is an arrogant demand on the part of male England, everyone must decide for himself (or for himself or herself, or for themselves). Have the patrons of *they* etc. made up their minds yet between *Everyone* WAS *blowing their noses* (or *nose*) and *Everyone* WERE *blowing their noses*?

To the general preference for the singular with words like *each* several exceptions may be noted. First, when *each* modifies a plural noun or pronoun, it takes the plural: thus, whereas the singular is correct in *Each man here has a dollar* and *Each of us has a dollar*, the plural is correct in *We each have a dollar* and *We have a dollar each*. Second, *none*, unlike *no one* and *nobody*, can take either the singular or the plural. If your emphasis is on the individual components of the class of things that *none* refers to, use the singular: *None of these three books is worth reading*. If the components are more sensibly thought of in groups or batches, use the plural: *No letters have been received, and none are expected*. In borderline cases, most good writers use the singular.

Finally, when no combination of *each* or *every* can convey your precise meaning without sounding foolish, use the plural and hope for the best: thus *Some children raised their hands*, which does not tell how many hands each raised, is preferable to *Some children raised one hand each*, which is overexplicit and silly.

The coaches made their own (decision) (decisions)

Whether to use the singular or the plural with the plural possessives *their, our,* and *your* is not always easy to decide. Do we say *The prisoners went to their death bravely* or *went to their deaths bravely? We changed our mind* or *changed our minds?* The English language is in transition on this point, and in borderline cases either form will serve. A rough rule of thumb might be as follows: when the noun is concrete or tangible, use the plural; when it is highly abstract, or when a fixed idiom is involved, use the singular; in between these extremes, take your choice. Thus:

The two girls changed their dresses. (*Concrete.*)

The two girls changed their mind [*or* minds]. (*In between.*)

The two girls changed their religion. (*Abstract.*)

The two girls changed their tune. (*Idiom.*)

Of course, when there is only a single item in question, the singular is used: *We love our country.*

The jury (was) (were) served coffee

With collective nouns—words like *crowd, committee,* and *majority,* which are singular in form but plural in connotation—either singular or plural verbs may be used, depending on context. When in doubt, use the singular: *The crowd was dispersed by the police / The committee is unable to reach an agreement.* If you are not happy with either the singular or the plural, and there are times when you won't be, try a different wording that gets around the problem: *The onlookers were dispersed by the police / The committee members are unable to reach an agreement.*

Where *the majority* simply means *most,* use the plural: *Some agreed, but the majority were undecided.* Use the plural also with such ostensibly singular expressions as *a number of* and *a handful of* when they mean *some* or *many,* as they usually do: *A small number of people were present / A high proportion of Americans go to college.*

A word cannot be simultaneously singular and plural. This difficulty is exhibited in the following sentences, in which conflicting words are italicized:

> The younger generation *has* no patience with legal restrictions; *their* law is action.

> Two days *was* a long time, and what would happen when *they were* over?

> Everyone from the Chinese restaurant *was* there, wearing *tuxedos* and evening *dresses*.

The first two sentences can be made consistently singular by changing *their* to *its* and *they were* to *it was*. In the third sentence, the plural is better: *All the people from the Chinese restaurant were there.*

Mathematics (are) (is) difficult

Some words are plural in form but singular in meaning. For most such words (*scissors, glasses, pants*) the plural is idiomatic. The chief exceptions are *news*, the names of certain diseases (*measles, mumps, shingles*), and words ending in *-ics* when used to designate a more or less formal body of knowledge or course of study: *Politics is the art of the possible / Ethics attracts more modern philosophers than logic.* In less formal uses the plural is more common: *His politics were dirty / Their ethics are questionable.* The Latin plural *data*, being singular in appearance and to some extent in connotation, increasingly takes the singular in modern usage and will someday be as singular as *agenda*, which has traveled the same road; at this writing, however, good usage still favors *data are*.

One of the boys (was) (were) absent

A difficulty to watch out for is the false association of verbs with nearby nouns that are not in fact their subjects. Number errors from this cause, which is sometimes called "attraction," are surprisingly common. The two following examples are wrong:

The pattern of monetary and role allocations in schools *impose* rigid limits on managerial power.

The ways and means of arriving at a workable treaty *remains* to be explored.

The subject of the first sentence is *pattern,* not *allocations;* the subject of the second is *ways and means,* not *treaty.* Errors of this sort come from haste, and should not survive a careful editing.

In this connection, note in particular that *with* and its compounds (*together with, along with*) do not act like *and* to make a subject plural. The following sentences are both correct:

Del Vecchio and ten other rioters *were* fined $50 each.

Del Vecchio, along with ten other rioters, *was* fined $50.

POSSESSIVE PROBLEMS

The rules for forming possessives, including the possessives of singular nouns ending in an *s* or *z* sound, are given in Chapter 11, pp. 156–157, together with a discussion of the main uses and misuses of the apostrophe. We confine ourselves here to two problems that arise in relating possessive forms to their context.

Unwieldy Possessives

When a choice between *s's* and *s'* yields two equally or almost equally unattractive alternatives, try to avoid the choice by rewording. Why make the difficult choice between *the metropolis's growth* and *the metropolis' growth* when you can say *the growth of the metropolis,* or *the growth of metropolitan Toronto?* Most words of over three syllables whether or not they end in *s,* and many three-syllable words ending in *s* or an *s* sound (*wilderness, residence*), take the *of* form much more gracefully than the apostrophe. An especially awkward possessive is *United States':* *the United States' viewpoint* is not wrong, but might better be changed to *the American viewpoint* or *the viewpoint of the United States.*

Possessives of long phrases should also be avoided. *The man in the street's opinion* might just get by, but *the man in the fur coat's car* is too much; the *of* construction is better for both.

Compound Possessives

Short compound possessives of the form *John('s) and Mary's money* are harder to avoid. Whether to use *'s* after the last noun only or after each noun in the series depends on whether the possessors should be thought of as a unit or as separate entities. The following four phrases are correct:

Mother and Dad's wedding anniversary

Mother's and Dad's summer clothing

Ed, Bill, and Charley's bar

Ed's, Bill's, and Charley's responsibilities

OTHER CASE PROBLEMS

Apart from the possessive problems just described, case problems in English are few and are getting fewer. On the one hand, the generations of American farm boys and immigrant children who were exposed at home to the likes of "Me and her get along fine" have given way to the sophisticated television viewers who now fill our kindergartens. Today the basic rules of case in good spoken English are taken in early. On the other hand, teachers have reconsidered the old rules and discovered that some of the expressions they formerly condemned as ungrammatical are not so bad after all. Recent developments in linguistics and lexicography have also encouraged the abandonment of outworn grammatical formulas where they conflict with usage.

The result of all these developments has been a revolution in teaching and grammatical thinking. The fussy-sounding expressions *It is I* and *That is he* are no longer taught, and *Whom are you kidding?* is down to its last dozen defenders. Only Gowers raises a voice against T. S. Eliot's "Let us go then, you and I," on the ground, now generally considered irrelevant, that *I*, being in apposition to the objective *us*, should be the objective *me*. Many teachers no longer even object to *whom* in *They gave him men whom he knew could be trusted,* or to *who* in *Who are they talking about?* The argument against these sentences is sound and logical: it can be grasped, diagramed, explained. The argument for them is simply that this is what most people, including educated people, would actually say. With the triumph of *It's me* and *That's him,* both indefensible in classic terms, both rooted in usage, a new era has dawned.

We cannot yet say with any certainty what the case rules of that era will be, save for the obvious ones that give no one any trouble. Accordingly, in all matters of case (that is, in all choices between *I* and *me, he* and *him, she* and *her, we* and *us, they* and *them, who* and *whom*) our advice is simply to write what you would say—if, that is, you speak something like Standard English.

TENSE PROBLEMS

Foreigners learning English find the tenses difficult to master, but for native-born writers only four kinds of decision may be said to give trouble: between past tense and present in sentences like *She asked herself whether the law (is) (was) just;* between present and perfect in sentences like *He would have been glad to (go) (have gone);* between past and past perfect in sentences like *I had spoken briefly and then (left) (had left);* and between indicative and subjunctive in sentences like *If Nixon (was) (were) president, things would be different.* Although the subjunctive is technically a "mood" rather than a tense, the distinction has no practical effect.

The Past vs. the Present

In a clause following a past-tense verb or a verb in the conditional (*would* + verb), the verb should normally be in the past tense, not the present. The following sentences are correct:

She asked herself whether the law *was* just. (not *is*)

Professor Snyder explained what "atomic weight" *meant.* (not *means*)

One would think he *was* crazy. (not *is*)

The use of the past tense here is natural and idiomatic; the present tense, though not wrong, sounds unnatural. Note especially that the past-tense verb does not connote finality—in the second sentence above, for example, the choice of *meant* rather than *means* carries no suggestion that "atomic weight" means something different today. The present tense is preferable to the past only when the past would be patently awkward or misleading:

> The dispute was over what freedom *means* in the Soviet Union.

> The Senator explained what the Republicans stood for 30 years ago, and what they *stand for* today.

The Perfect

One verb in the perfect tense (*have* + verb) should not be subordinated to another: write *He would have been glad to go,* not *He would have been glad to have gone.* The following sentences are correct:

> She would have given anything *to be chosen.* (*not* to have been chosen)

> Gallman *has enjoyed being* Ambassador to Korea. (*not* enjoyed having been *or* enjoys having been)

> It would have been easy for Myra *to make* her father happy. (*not* to have made)

The Past Perfect

The past perfect (*had* + verb) should not be allowed to obtrude itself unnecessarily. In a passage describing anterior action, a very few *had*'s are usually sufficient to establish the time relationship, and the other verbs in the passage may be in the simple past:

> After she left, he had slept for a while. He had dreamed of her; she was younger in the dream, prettier, more loving. When he awoke, he was hungry, and there was no food in

the house. Now, fifteen years later, he remembered exactly how he had felt.

Since the verbs *left, was* (younger), *awoke, was* (hungry), and *was* (no food) indicate action prior to the time of *remembered,* they should technically be *had left, had been,* and so on. But to stand on this technicality would be to make the passage pointlessly heavy and mannered.

The Subjunctive

The subjunctive offers few difficulties save to those who try to extend its legitimate domain. Its chief accepted uses today are as follows: (1) the use of *were* for *was* in clauses introduced by *if* and *wish* and expressing hypothetical rather than factual conditions (*if I were king / I wish I were dead*); (2) the omission of *should* in clauses introduced by verbs expressing will, command, or desire (*I move that the meeting be adjourned / I insist that my money be refunded*); and (3) the use of infinitive rather than indicative forms in half a dozen old-fashioned expressions, notably *come what may, be that as it may, far be it from me,* and *suffice it to say.*

Much ink has been spilled in defense of the subjunctive in category (1) against the incursions of the indicative; but *if I was king* and *I wish I was dead,* though not yet accepted as proper, are gaining inexorably and seem likely to prevail. Category (2), by contrast, is of recent growth and very vigorous, in large part because the use of *should,* though perfectly correct and natural to many Englishmen, strikes Americans as softening the intended meaning. In English usage, *I insist that my money be refunded* and *I insist that my money should be refunded* mean the same thing. In American usage, the first means "Give it back," the second "By rights I should get it back." The first form, being in this interpretation more manly than the second, has prevailed.

Category (3) offers no problems. In fact, the subjunctive as a whole offers no problems except to writers with a flair for the archaic, that minority in every generation who are prompted by their fondness for an older prose or poetry (*If this be treason / What care I how fair she be?*) to revive a form that is as foreign to modern writing as the casual use of Latin. Here are two sentences from student themes:

Whether his charge *be* true or false, it has the authority of his suffering.

If these conditions *be* made, no man could qualify.

The first *be* should be *is*, the second *were* or *are*. In both cases, *be* was once correct but is no longer. One may regret the change, but one must respect it. As Fowler wrote over 40 years ago, those who traffic in archaic subjunctives run the risk, "first, of making their matter dull, . . . and lastly, of having the proper dignity of style at which they aim mistaken by captious readers for pretentiousness."

8

SENTENCES: SYNTAX

Good syntax is a matter of arranging or grouping words for maximum clarity to the reader. A few typical sentences in which the words are not properly arranged will illustrate the chief problems discussed in this chapter:

> The first stanza is serious, straightforward, and sets the theme of the poem.
>
> Lying in the gutter, she found her watch.
>
> Bill's brother asked the coach if he could go.
>
> In the town, which I grew up in, there was only one drugstore.
>
> Like the AMA plan, private groups were to allocate the subsidies.

The first sentence is unparallel; having established the pattern of a series of adjectives, the writer has veered off before completing it. The writer of the second sentence has improperly attached the phrase *Lying in the gutter* to *she* rather than to *watch*. In the third sentence, there are three possible antecedents for *he*. The fourth sentence may conceivably be correct, but would probably prove in context to require not *the town, which* but *the town that*; the issue here is that of restrictive versus nonrestrictive clauses, a basic distinction in the use of English. The fifth sentence, illustrating one of the three "syntactical battlegrounds" with which we conclude the chapter, misuses *like* as a conjunction. Either it should begin *As in the AMA plan,* or it should end *the new plan called for the subsidies to be allocated by private groups.*

PARALLELISM

According to Blake, there are three main states: innocence, experience, and a higher innocence. Their major symbols are the child, the man, the woman, and Christ. No good writer will subject his readers to conundrums of this sort. A change to *the man and the woman* is essential to make the two series parallel to each other, and hence coherently related to each other; failing this change, the reader will either move on perplexed to the next sentence or have to spend time sorting out the two series. Either way he will be irritated, and with justice.

Although failures of parallelism are rarely so striking, the principle is of the first importance in good writing. Things related to each other in parallel construction are clearly related; where the parallelism is faulty, the relationship may or may not be clear. And where any chance for confusion exists, at least some readers will surely become confused.

The basic requirement for a parallel construction is easily stated: What is true of one element must be true of the others. If one element is a noun, the others must be nouns; if one is a prepositional phrase, the others must be prepositional phrases; if one has a verb, the others must have verbs. There are two main kinds of parallel construction in English: the series of three or more elements (*red, white, and blue*) and the correlative pair (for example, *either/or*).

Series

The most common form of unparallel series is the one illustrated above: *The first stanza is serious, straightforward, and sets the theme of the poem.* Here are two others of the same sort, both, as it happens, inadvertent slips in current handbooks of English:

> Most uses of capital letters are conventional [*adjective*], easily understood [*adjective*], and cause [*verb*] no difficulty.

> She made more sandwiches [*noun*], more hot chocolate [*noun*], and scraped [*verb*] out the last of the pudding.

To correct the faulty parallelism, either make the three terms of the series syntactically identical (*Most uses of capital letters are conventional, easily understood, and easy to apply*), or abandon the series as such (*She made more sandwiches and hot chocolate, and scraped out the last of the pudding*). The latter solution is always available, and is often the better. Some writers shrink from the second *and* ("The first stanza is serious *and* straightforward, *and* sets the theme of the poem"); but in our opinion, far from being a blight, it is a touch of elegance, a welcome sign that the writer knows what he is doing.

The second most common form of unparallel series is one in which an opening word—usually an article, a preposition, or a conjunction—appears before the first element in the series and again before the last element, but is dropped before some or all of the intermediate elements. Here are five examples of unparallel series of this sort, with the key words in italics:

> Among those present were *the* President, Secretary of State, General Abbott, and *the* English Ambassador.

> The rules state that *a* hat, coat, and *a* tie must be worn.

> Cortez was informed *that* the enemy forces numbered 2,000, they were heavily armed, and *that* their stone outworks were impregnable.

> There is no life *on* the sun, the moon, or *on* the stars.

Inexpert writers tend to substitute the dash most commonly *for* the comma, the semicolon, the period, and *for* parentheses.

Parallelism requires that a preposition or a conjunction be used either before every term of a series or before the first term only: that is, either *on the sun, on the moon, or on the stars* or *on the sun, the moon, or the stars.* The choice is a matter of taste. Articles are less flexible. For one thing, it is generally preferable to put the article before each term in the series rather than just the first; in the second sentence above, for example, *a hat, a coat, and a tie* is better than *a hat, coat, and tie,* which tends to make a bogus unit or ensemble out of three clearly separate items. For another, a series may contain some terms capable of taking the article and some not, as in the first and last sentences above (*the General Abbott* and *the parentheses* are impossible). In such cases, the article *must* be placed before each of the other terms—the terms capable of taking an article—to make the series parallel.

There are many other possibilities of unparallelism in series, too many to be illustrated here. The general thing to remember about parallel construction is that it is a principle of order, a way of telling the reader economically what elements go together or have the same weight. A sprawling sentence like *The boy was tall, with long, shaggy hair, and wore sloppy clothes* will slow a reader up unnecessarily; one does not immediately perceive its three parts as describing three roughly equal characteristics of the boy's appearance. Either of two parallel constructions offers a clearer map of the terrain:

The boy was tall, shaggy-haired, and sloppily dressed.

The boy was tall, his hair was long and shaggy, and he wore sloppy clothes.

Correlatives

Parallelism in correlative pairs, like parallelism in series, requires that what is true of one element be true of the other. The four pairs in question are *either/or, neither/nor, both/and,* and *not only/but* (*also*). Errors made under this heading can often be fixed by merely switching the position of one of the correlatives, and can almost always be fixed in more than one way. The following sentences are defective, with alternative corrections indicated in parentheses:

> *Intransigent* dates in England from about 1880; being now established, it should neither be pronounced as French nor spelled *-eant* any longer. (*be neither pronounced*; or *nor be spelled*)

> All-out war on two fronts was impossible: either we concencentrated on defeating Germany or on Japan. (*or we concentrated on defeating Japan*; or *we concentrated either on Germany or on Japan*)

> Water pollution is a problem both in the city and the country. (*and in the country*; or *in both the city*)

> Piero not only collected rare manuscripts, but also paintings and sculpture. (*collected not only*; or *but also collected*)

To take the first sentence as an example, the rule says that if *neither* takes a verb phrase, *nor* should take a verb phrase; and that if *neither* takes a participle, *nor* should take a participle or some equivalent form of adjective. Similarly with the other sentences. In the second, for example, *either* is followed by a complete clause, *or* by a phrase; parallelism requires both to be followed by clauses, or both by phrases.

Correlative constructions in which both parts have the same subject and the same verb may take any of three possible forms:

1. *Not only* did U Thant act quickly, *but* he acted courageously.

2. U Thant *not only* acted quickly, *but* acted courageously.

3. U Thant acted *not only* quickly, *but* courageously.

1. *Either* the sketch was a genuine Picasso, *or* it was a skillful forgery.

2. The sketch *either* was a genuine Picasso *or* was a skillful forgery.

3. The sketch was *either* a genuine Picasso *or* a skillful for-gery.

In sentences 1, the correlatives introduce complete clauses; in sentences 2 they introduce verbs; in sentences 3 they introduce adverbs in one case and nouns in the other. Usually one of the possible choices sounds better than the other two: in the examples above, sentence 3 seems clearly the best choice for both. Once the various truly parallel possibilities are determined, the choice is a matter of taste. The problem is to avoid such unparallel alternatives as *U Thant not only acted quickly, but courageously* or *The sketch was either a genuine Picasso, or it was a skillful forgery.*

A surprisingly frequent error is the false pairing *neither/or,* as in *Neither the Army, the Navy, or the Marines favored American intervention.* Whether in pairs or in series of three or more, *neither* goes with *nor* and *either* with *or.* There are no exceptions.

MISPLACED MODIFIERS

Just as an adjective normally comes immediately before or after the noun it modifies (*a blue car, a tale too sad for words*), so an adjectival clause should be placed as close as possible to its noun. Violations of this principle may produce the absurdities known as misplaced modifiers, of which the largest single class goes by the name of dangling participles.

Dangling Participles

A participle is the adjective form of a verb, ending either in *-ing* (present participle) or in *-ed, -en,* or *-t* (past participle); for all practical purposes, it may be treated exactly like an adjective. When a participle begins a sentence, it must modify the subject of the independent clause that follows. For example, *Ravaged by illness and starvation, Mola's regiment had no choice but to surrender.* Since *ravaged* modifies *regiment,* the subject of the sentence, all is in order.

The classic error is to place the modified noun or pronoun in some subordinate position, or to leave it to inference:

> Following the criminal's trail, the memory of past manhunts came to Inspector Leonard.
>
> Following the criminal's trail, past manhunts occupied his thoughts.

Since Inspector Leonard is doing the following, not his memory or past manhunts, these two sentences are defective.

Sentences of this sort may always be corrected in either of two ways. One is to keep the participle construction but give the independent clause a suitable subject: *Following the criminal's trail, Inspector Leonard thought of past manhunts.* The other is to leave the independent clause as it stands but abandon the participle construction: *As Inspector Leonard followed the criminal's trail, past manhunts occupied his thoughts.* The choice between these alternatives is strictly a matter of taste.

The noun modified by a participle must be a full noun, not a possessive form, and must be complete in itself, not part of a compound subject or buried in a verb. The following sentences are wrong:

> Surprised at the compliment, her eyes sparkled with pleasure.
>
> Being the oldest, his word was law.
>
> Having borne him two boys, Mrs. Lincoln and her husband were hoping for a girl.

Her eyes were not surprised by the compliment; *she* was. *His word* was not the oldest; *he* was. As for Lincoln, his part in the bearing of his sons was no doubt as large as a loving husband could make it, but the equal of Mrs. Lincoln's it was not.

Other Danglers

Not only participles may be misplaced, but other adjectives and adjective phrases as well:

> Twice the size of her brother, they called her Big Bertha.
>
> While out for a stroll one morning, a thief broke into my apartment.
>
> Sad and bitter at first, Chopin's good spirits soon returned.

The remedy here is the same as for misplaced participles. Either convert the opening phrase to a subordinate clause, or see that the independent clause begins with a suitable noun:

Twice the size of her brother, she was known as Big Bertha.

While I was out for a stroll one morning, a thief broke into my apartment.

Sad and bitter though Chopin was at first, his good spirits soon returned.

Participle Prepositions

A number of participles have acquired the status of prepositions in some uses. In these uses they are no longer subject to the rules of attachment and can be placed without concern for how they relate to the nearest noun. For example:

Given his view of the chances of success, how can we blame him for seeking help?

Barring acts of God, no more money was to be spent on welfare measures.

Six more votes remained to be cast, not *counting* those of the New York delegation.

Some two dozen participles have entered this category, in the wake of such earlier participle prepositions as *according* and *concerning*; and many more will no doubt follow. Most participles, however, are untouched by this trend, and seem likely to remain so. When in doubt, attach participles carefully to suitable nouns, or avoid the participle construction altogether.

One adjective phrase for which preposition status is hotly disputed is *due to*. It is correct to say *His success was due to hard work,* but can we say *Due to hard work he succeeded?* That is, can the adjective form be used adverbially? *Due to* in this sense is gaining ground, but is not yet generally accepted. Our advice is to use *owing to, thanks to,* or *because of* where an adverb is needed and restrict *due to* to its undisputed adjectival use.

ANTECEDENTS

Ambiguous Antecedents

The noun to which a pronoun refers should be unmistakable. Such a farrago of pronouns as *He told him that his father had lost his shoes* is impervious to rational analysis, but a sentence with only one pronoun may be just as baffling. *During the war between China and Japan, their industrial output rose twenty percent.* Whose industrial output? Both countries'? And if so, both equally, or is the twenty percent some kind of average? And does it make sense to quote a joint statistic like this for two countries that are fighting each other? It is to spare the reader puzzlements of this sort that clear antecedents are desirable.

The main thing to avoid is pronouns that can refer to any of two or more possible antecedents. In the following sentences, the ambiguous pronoun is italicized and the ambiguity is elaborated in parentheses:

Cliff asked Jack if *he* could go. (*who?*)

The congressmen who heard the strikers' complaints described *their* experience as harrowing. (*whose experience, the congressmen's or the strikers'?*)

Oakland is losing population to San Francisco and *its* suburbs. (*Oakland's suburbs or San Francisco's?*)

They spend a lot of time drinking, and *that* is something I don't approve of. (*drinking in general, or spending so much time drinking?*)

Omitted Antecedents

Another error is to bury the antecedent in an adjective, or to leave it to inference:

French cooking is *their* chief claim to fame.

The Dean's Office welcomes *student* inquiries about *their* draft status.

The children were *singing,* but I couldn't hear *it.*

Often the best way to correct sentences of this sort is to get rid of the pronoun altogether: "French cooking is *France's* chief claim to fame." Alternatively, the pronoun should have a legitimate and unmistakable antecedent: "I welcome *students'* concern about *their* education"; "The *children* were singing, but I couldn't hear *them*," or "The children were singing *something*, but I couldn't hear what *it* was."

Ideas and Phrases as Antecedents

It was once considered incorrect, but is now perfectly correct, to use *which, this,* or *that* to refer to a general idea or statement rather than to a specific noun antecedent, provided there is no ambiguity in the reference. It is essential, however, that this condition of no ambiguity be fulfilled. The following sentences are good English:

Few Negroes voted, *which* is understandable in the circumstances.

Thirty-five people were killed and two hundred wounded; *that* is all we know.

An empty icebox, dirty dishes, mud on the floor—*this* is what we get for giving Uncle Mort a key.

The following sentences, by contrast, contain ambiguities (indicated in the parenthetical questions), and are accordingly unacceptable:

The audience booed and threw fruit, *which* caused the manager to lower the curtain. (*the audience reaction in general, or the fruit in particular?*)

The commission vetoed the mayor's plan to ban weekday traffic on midtown streets; for my part, I think *this* was the right thing to do. (*what? ban traffic or veto the plan?*)

RESTRICTIVE AND NONRESTRICTIVE CLAUSES

Definition

In the first of the following examples *John* is nonrestrictive; in the second *John* is restrictive:

> I have one brother and one sister. My brother, *John,* lives in New York.

> I have two brothers, John and Elmer. My brother *John* lives in New York.

In the first example, *my brother* is enough to tell the reader precisely who is meant, since he knows that I have only one brother. My addition of *John* does not restrict or alter the meaning of *my brother,* but simply adds a piece of information to a sentence that makes perfect sense without it. In the second example, *my brother* does not tell the reader who is meant; he knows I have two brothers, and cannot know which one I refer to until I add a name. My addition of *John* accordingly restricts the meaning of *my brother* to the particular brother I have in mind: my brother John, not my brother Elmer. Without the addition the sentence is unintelligible.

As the example indicates, the distinction between restrictive and nonrestrictive nouns in apposition is made with commas: the restrictive takes no commas, the nonrestrictive two commas (one if the noun comes at the end of the sentence). The distinction between restrictive and nonrestrictive relative clauses, our main concern here, is made the same way. A further refinement favored by most good writers, and one that we heartily recommend, is to make writing conform to idiomatic speech by using *which* for the nonrestrictive clause and *that* for the restrictive.

The first of the following examples has a nonrestrictive clause, the second a restrictive clause:

> I borrowed a lawn mower and a rake. The lawn mower, *which needed sharpening,* was hard to use.

> My neighbor has two lawn mowers. To be considerate, I borrowed the lawn mower *that* needed sharpening.

In the first example, the lawn mower has already been identified by the time we get to the relative clause; *which needed sharpening* does not distinguish it from other lawn mowers but simply adds to our information about it. In the second example, *that needed sharpening* tells us for the first time which lawn mower was borrowed; *the lawn mower* alone, or *the lawn mower, which,* would be nonsense.

That and Which

It is not always easy to determine whether a sentence should be restrictive or nonrestrictive. How does one choose between *I have a lawn mower that needs sharpening* and *I have a lawn mower, which needs sharpening?* Between *There was a drought in 1964 that dried up the lake* and *There was a drought in 1964, which dried up the lake?* None of these alternatives is wrong, and our advice in borderline cases of this sort is simply to take your pick. When in doubt, use *that.* In ordinary speech the restrictive (*that*) construction is six times as common as the nonrestrictive (*which*); the ratio in writing is much lower, but is probably at least two to one.

We have recommended using *that* for the restrictive and *which* for the nonrestrictive, following the almost universal pattern of spoken English. Another characteristic of spoken English is to omit *that* altogether when it serves as the object (as opposed to the subject) of a restrictive clause. Here again we recommend making writing conform to speech:

Awkward

the first books *which* Dickens wrote

Acceptable

the first books *that* Dickens wrote

Better

the first books Dickens wrote

We think that if you would omit *that* in speaking, you should omit it in writing. Similarly in the following:

the security which it gives

the security that it gives

the security it gives

the kind of person which he was

the kind of person that he was

the kind of person he was

Even writers who reject the highly formal *which* in such phrases sometimes retain an unnecessary and faintly irritating *that* in deference to the supposed requirements of formality. Formality has its requirements, to be sure, but this is not one of them.

Other Relative Clauses

The distinction between restrictive and nonrestrictive extends to other relative clauses, notably those in *who, whom,* and *whose* and in *of which, in which,* and the like. The distinction, as always, is made by using a comma for the nonrestrictive (two commas if the clause is in the middle of the sentence rather than at the end), and no comma for the restrictive. The following sentences are correct:

Restrictive

Senator Fulbright is a man *who* knows his own mind.

Nonrestrictive

Senator Fulbright, *who* cast the one dissenting vote, is a Democrat.

Restrictive

Clean government is a goal *to which* most officials give only lip service.

Nonrestrictive

Kavanaugh's goal was clean government, *to which* most officials give only lip service.

SOME SYNTACTICAL BATTLEGROUNDS

A number of simple principles of syntax have been developed over the years by teachers of English in an effort to come to some sort of workable terms with the complexities of a living language. Some of these principles are sensible and to the point: the main ones have been dealt with earlier in this chapter. Others have been ill served by oversimplifiers or eroded by contrary usage; if they are still worth heeding, their claims must be convincingly restated. Still others were nonsense from the start, having nothing but their simplemindedness to recommend them.

With these last we need not concern ourselves. It was never incorrect to begin a sentence with *But* or *And*; it was never incorrect to write sentences without verbs; and if it was ever incorrect to end a sentence with a preposition, that stuffy day is long past. Our concern here is rather with practices over which tradition and usage are to some extent at war, and in particular with three members of this class: the split infinitive, the fused participle, and the use of *like* as a conjunction.

The Split Infinitive

The split infinitive can be traced back to the fourteenth century. Its chief modern forms appeared in the early seventeenth, and in the past hundred years there has been scarcely a major writer in the United States or England whose works are free of it. Is the form then completely acceptable? No, say the traditionalists; yes, say the impatient; not quite, is the advice here.

There are three possible positions for the adverb modifying an infinitive: before it (*completely to understand him*), splitting it (*to completely understand him*), and after it (*to understand him completely*). The last is recommended as natural:

> In the end she decided to live *openly* with Paul.

> They were too busy to look after the children *properly*.

> Captain Larsen requested permission to explore the matter *further*.

The first position, before the infinitive, is less often natural, but should be preferred to splitting when it is not objectionable: "I do not want you *ever* to take such chances," "*Even* to wish for mercy would be cowardice." Only if neither outside position will do justice to the meaning should the infinitive be split:

The glare caused the men to *half* close their eyes.

He appeared to *suddenly* lose all control of the boat.

Mother had to *simply* take over the accounts.

The chief difficulty with split infinitives today is not that conservatives oppose them absolutely, but that radicals split them too freely. The battle for permission to split has long been won; the issue today is where to draw the line. Rightly or wrongly, split infinitives jar many readers and make them uneasy. Since the last thing you want to do is jar your readers, it follows that you should split infinitives only when any alternative arrangement would be even more jarring.

The Fused Participle

"Fused participle" is the name given by Fowler to a very common construction midway between the pure participle or adjective form in *-ing* and the pure gerund or noun form. The three constructions may be illustrated as follows:

Participle

I saw them dancing.

Gerund

I enjoyed their dancing.

Fused participle

I like them dancing together.

In the first example, *dancing* is an adjective modifying *them.* In the second, it is a noun, the direct object of *enjoyed.* In the third example, *dancing* has the noun quality of the second (it is the direct object of the verb), but the adjective form of the first; it is neither a pure gerund or noun, which would necessarily take the possessive *their,* nor a pure participle or adjective, which could not serve as a direct object. It is a fusion of the two forms.

Fowler considered the fused participle a plain error, to be corrected by converting to the pure gerund form with the possessive (*I like their dancing together*), or to the pure participle form (e.g. *I like to see them dancing together*); or by switching to a different construction altogether (e.g. *I like watching them dance together*). We disagree. The following sentences, all of which contain fused participles, seem to us perfectly acceptable:

> It was impossible to imagine so small a *ship being* torpedoed.
>
> They could talk in the garden without the *servants hearing* what they said.
>
> There was a skit about two *men* from Mars *walking* down Broadway.

The question, then, is whether all fused participles are acceptable or only some. Is it all right to say *They insisted on us paying for the tickets*? How about *John being appointed surprised everyone*? It is all right, we suppose, but most writers and all editors would say *our paying* and *John's being appointed,* and that is what we advise. In general, follow your ear. When in doubt, it is better to fuse a participle than to avoid fusing it at the cost of an awkward possessive or an unnatural wording.

Like and As

The distinction between *like* and *as* is easily made. *Like,* a preposition, compares nouns, pronouns, and noun phrases: *I am like my father / Like the women who had brought him up, Neil hated braggarts.* *As,* a conjunction, compares adverbs, adverbial phrases, and clauses: *For Johnson, as for Kennedy, there were no easy answers / Mme. de Sévigné was afraid of mice, as many women are.* *As* has other uses as well, some of which are discussed on pp. 223–224. We confine ourselves in this section to uses of *as* that bring it into conflict with *like.*

The classic error is to use *like* to introduce a clause. The following sentences illustrate this error:

> Harry drives like Jack does.
>
> These recurrent symbols clarify the poem's meaning, much like the action of a Greek drama is clarified by the chorus.

The patient sits before a screen that looks like it came from a television set.

The more vocal champions of *like* apparently consider the correct use of *as* in these sentences (*as if* in the third) affected or snobbish. However this may be, *like* is now routinely used to introduce clauses by perhaps half the English-speaking world, and bids fair in the end to drive *as* from the field.

The advice here, nonetheless, is to hold the line. The distinction between *like* and *as* is easily learned, and its proper application is regarded by discriminating people as basic to good English. If you shrink from using *as* to mean *in the way that,* for example in *Harry drives as Jack does,* use *the way* instead: *Harry drives the way Jack does.*

The following sentences illustrate the correct use of *like, as,* and *the way*:

Marvin walks *like* an ape.

Marvin walks *the way* an ape *walks.*

I have been lonely, *as* you *have been.*

Like you, I have been lonely.

Shakespeare, *like* Marlowe before him, wrote with actors and an audience in mind.

Shakespeare wrote *as* Marlowe before him *had written,* with actors and an audience in mind.

The principle followed in constructing these sentences is easily summarized. When there is a verb in the phrase governed by *like/as,* use *as* (or *the way*): "the way an ape *walks,*" "as you *have been,*" "*as* Marlowe before him *had written.*" When there is a noun only, use *like.*

What goes for *like* goes also for *unlike,* a word often misused out of desperation because there is no word *un-as* and no good equivalent. *Unlike* can only compare nouns, pronouns, or noun phrases: *Unlike Harry, I was tired* / *My old Chevrolet, unlike Bill's Buick, could go 200 miles on a tank of gas.* The following sentences are wrong (suggested revisions in parentheses):

Unlike in the previous election, few charges of fraud were made. *(Unlike the previous election, this one evoked few charges of fraud.)*

To Sue, unlike her sister, the afternoon seemed pleasant. *(Sue, unlike her sister, found the afternoon pleasant.)*

Unlike what both sides had expected, the battle was soon over. *(Contrary to what both sides had expected, the battle was soon over.)*

Finally, there is a growing tendency, especially among college students, to write *as* erroneously for *like;* for example, *Byron, as Keats and Shelley before him, died young.* This curious construction apparently comes from an excessive fear of falling into the opposite error, that of using *like* for *as,* which, as we have seen, is by far the more common and the more loudly deplored. The new error, with its prissy, toe-in-the-water effect, seems if anything more deplorable than the old.

As this chapter has suggested, good syntax is not just a matter of rules, though rules are its necessary point of departure. It is also a matter of judging when and to what extent the rules apply, when and to what extent time and usage have passed them by, when convenience may properly be indulged at the expense of fastidiousness, and when the line should be held. The best arbiters of such matters, we think, are professional writers and editors, whose sense of the language is constantly elaborated and modified by their work. Their current practice has been the basis for our pronouncements in this chapter.

Several dozen other errors and pitfalls of syntax are discussed briefly in the Index to Current Usage, pp. 220–261.

9

SENTENCES: STYLE

In Chapter 5, "About Technique," we discussed the general problem of writing effectively. In this chapter, we are concerned specifically with writing at the sentence level, and in particular with choosing the most effective wording from among two or more equally correct alternatives. The aggregate of such choices amounts to a writer's style. Grammar and syntax are matters of precision; style is a matter of grace. Poor grammar or syntax may puzzle a reader or mislead him; poor style will irritate him or put him to sleep. Under the impact of awkward or leaden writing the reader's brain becomes first overtaxed, then inefficient, and finally stupefied. Good writers try to spare their readers this distress by the practices set forth in this chapter.

BASIC PREFERENCES

Most good writers agree on five basic preferences:
1. Prefer verbs to nouns.
2. Prefer the active to the passive.
3. Prefer the concrete to the abstract.
4. Prefer the personal to the impersonal.
5. Prefer the shorter version to the longer.

Prefer Verbs to Nouns

New nouns and noun compounds pour into the language daily like so many boulders into a river, until one wonders if they will someday dam the flow forever. From electronics and space technology alone we have thousands of new names for things, ranging from simple compounds like *thermostress* and *countdown,* through contrived acronyms like *sonar* and *laser,* to sodden six- and seven-noun strings like *nozzle gas ejection ship attitude control system.* The effect of these nouns is to displace verbs. We do not begin *to count down* (verb); we begin the *countdown* (noun). We do not have a system by which gas *is ejected* through nozzles *to control* a ship's attitude (two verbs); instead, we have the monstrosity cited above (seven nouns), from which our only hope of delivery is the grotesque acronym NGESACS.

Indeed, the mere proliferation of new nouns is less alarming than the increasing tendency to overuse all nouns, new and old alike, at the expense of verbs, which give language most of its life and movement. Fifty years ago it would have been natural to write *McCormick also invented a machine for picking corn;* today we incline to write *Another of McCormick's inventions was a mechanical cornpicker.* Fifty years ago, *This book tells you how to promote local sports without spending much money;* today, *The subject of this book is low-budget sports promotion techniques.* The modern versions are heavy and lifeless. Not only have the verbs given way to nouns, but the nouns themselves have lost their color: *corn* is buried in *cornpicker, sports* hangs grayly on a clothesline between abstractions, *money* has disappeared.

One finds writing of this sort everywhere. Scientists and technologists are perhaps the worst offenders, government officials the second worst, but no large class of writers is free of the disease. Remember our muffin-mouthed school principal in Chapter 1? Here is a history professor (nouns and pronouns italicized):

> The Allen-Hamilton-Shippen *connection* represented for the Proprietary *party* a *leadership* comparable to *that* of the Pemberton-Logan-Norris *combination* of the *Quakers,* though the *former* exhibited less *unity* and *effectiveness* in *politics.*

There are ten italicized nouns and pronouns in addition to the six proper names, or five nouns for each of the sentence's two verbs.

The proportion is too high, and the sentence is heavy-footed. The nouns can easily be cut to three, and the verbs increased to the same number:

> Allen, Hamilton, and Shippen served the Proprietary *party* much as Pemberton, Logan, and Norris served the *Quakers*, though the Proprietary *leaders* were less unified and less effective politically.

Here is a sentence from an academic report with its nouns italicized: "There has necessarily been a *tendency* on the *part* of *researchers* to continue *studies* with *equipment* now approaching *obsolescence*." As rewritten to cut down the nouns: "*Researchers* have necessarily gone on using obsolescent *equipment*." Here is an Army dispatch: "The *enemy* has had no *opportunity* to assemble *forces* in sufficient *quantity* to mount an *offensive* against *Danang*." As rewritten: "The *enemy* has failed to assemble a big enough *force* to attack *Danang*."

Nouns are of course indispensable; the problem is to avoid using them at the expense of livelier words. A sentence with too many nouns—and "too many" may usually be defined as one more than is strictly necessary—takes slightly more effort to read than it is worth. Multiply this extra effort by six or eight paragraphs and you have a fatigued reader, which is to say no reader at all.

Prefer the Active to the Passive

Verbs in the passive voice tend to yield unnecessarily dull sentences, as the following examples show:

> She was not told by anyone.
> No one told her.

> Words are seen as bricks in an edifice of beauty.
> Shelley sees words as bricks in an edifice of beauty.

> A fair decision was rendered difficult by the judge's evident bias.
> The judge's evident bias made it hard for him to decide fairly.

All three active versions are more forceful and direct. Moreover, there are secondary advantages. In the first example, the active saves two words; in the second, it makes the subject, Shelley, explicit; in the third, it makes for lighter and less formal language. Such advantages are common in switching from passive to active.

Another difficulty of the passive is that it avoids placing responsibility. It presents no subject, no actor, only the action and its object. Typical is the following murky recommendation from a government report: *It is urged that special study be given to the question of how the positive values in migrant life can be exploited in improving the teaching of the migrant child.* Urged, given, exploited by whom? We can only guess. Here are two sentences from student themes:

> Frost's work contains much symbolism, symbolism that is strongly felt.

> Pathos is aroused at Andrea del Sarto's meek submission to his wife.

By whom, the reader wonders, is Frost's symbolism strongly felt? By Frost? By his readers? By the writer? Whose pathos is aroused in the second example, and by whom or what? The answers to these questions make a difference, but there is no knowing what they are from the agentless passive construction.

To be sure, the passive has its legitimate domain. Sometimes the subject of a verb is irrelevant or too complex to identify: *He will be released from prison tomorrow / Two majors were promoted to lieutenant colonel / For we were nursed upon the self-same hill.* The point is not to avoid the passive altogether, but to use it sparingly. Use the active, with its superior vigor and directness, when you can; use the passive only when the active is clearly inconvenient or unidiomatic.

This rule has a corollary: Prefer the action verb to the linking verb, and the more forceful action verb to the less forceful. Linking verbs are the handful of verbs that take noun or adjective complements (predicate nouns or adjectives, as opposed to direct objects); the main ones are *be, become, seem, appear, grow,* and *feel.* These pallid verbs, especially *be,* are flourishing as never before in this golden age of nouns. Where once people said *George drives well / George drives a bus,* we now say *George is a good driver / George is a bus driver;* an action verb, *drive,* has dwindled into a noun, leaving the field to the linking verb *is.* *Is* supplies no motion to a sentence, no grace; it is inert, a kind of equals sign between nouns. No writer, of course, can avoid *is* and *are, was* and *were,* but good writers are always on the lookout to replace them with verbs of greater impact. The following alternative versions of a single sentence are listed in order of increasing effectiveness:

Passive

> It has been decided that a ten percent tax increase is necessary.

Active, linking verb

> Our conclusion is that taxes must be increased ten percent.

Active, action verb

> We have decided on a ten percent tax increase.

Active, more forceful action verb

> We propose to increase taxes ten percent.

Verbs are the wheels of writing; as they move, so moves the message they carry. If all the verbs in a paragraph are forms of *be* and *have,* the wheels will move slowly.

Prefer the Concrete to the Abstract

Concrete nouns stand for things. They are words like *hog, heart, helicopter, Harry:* specific designations for specific entities. Abstract nouns stand for ideas. They range along a spectrum from near-concrete words like *housing* through relatively simple concepts like *sympathy* and *difficulty* to more general terms like *situation* and *socialism,* and on to the formidable abstractions of modern scholarly discourse. At the extreme, we find such sentences as this one, the work of a doctoral candidate in philosophy:

From the standpoint of the historical development of empirical observation in scientific inference, it is worth noting De Morgan's acceptance of a subjective viewpoint in probability.

Writing that runs heavily to abstract nouns is hard to read, partly because such nouns tend to be long and lifeless, partly because they take the tamer sort of verb (abstractions never *kick* or *ogle* or *revere* each other; they *cause* or *refer to* or *consist of* each other), but above all because they require the reader to invest time and effort in translating the writer's generalities into particulars. To be sure, some writing is slow going for the reader because it deals with genuinely difficult or complex matters; but much more is slow going solely because the writer did not know how to make his meaning immediately clear.

Abstractions are general, intangible, elusive. The human mind works best on particulars: on tangible, finite units. *The poor need better housing* is a simple enough sentence, but no two people can truly agree on its meaning until *better housing* is defined in terms of number of units, size of rooms, rental rates, and so on; and until *the poor* are defined as a particular class of people— for example, families of four or more persons living in New York City with an annual family income of under $3,000. Similarly, *Tom is brave,* or *The situation is desperate,* makes no sense without particulars. For example, we may know that Tom is brave because he stood up against a bully or saved a child from a fire; the situation may be desperate because enemy tanks are only a mile away, or because Dad cannot find a job.

In short, to make sense of abstractions we must see them in concrete terms. The beginning explanation of Einstein's theory of relativity is commonly made in terms of two trains: to a person on Train A, the apparent speed and direction of movement of Train B will depend on which directions the two trains are in fact moving in, and at what speeds. Complexities like De Morgan's "subjective viewpoint in probability" must be explained in similar concrete terms if we are to understand what they mean.

Some writers mistakenly feel that abstractions lend tone to writing, that they are more dignified than everyday words like *cat* and *dog.* Others use abstractions to avoid committing themselves to particulars—which means, in effect, to avoid the kind of careful thinking and articulation of thought that goes into all

good writing. In both cases, the results tend to be vague and irritating. The following sentences from student themes are illus-
trative:

> Other lessons were absorbed through his experiences.

> Attitudes and opinions resulted from these environmental
> occurrences.

> There is no way to overcome the situation of racial
> relationships.

The first writer seems to mean simply *He learned other lessons as
well*; the second seems to mean *He got his ideas from what he
saw and heard*; the third seems to mean *There is no way to end
racial tensions*. Note that we say "seems to mean"; in none of
the three cases can we be sure. It is as if the writer had tried
deliberately to keep us guessing. Not only must a reader strain
his mind to interpret such unexplained abstractions in concrete
terms, but he must move on to the next sentence uncertain
whether his interpretation of the previous one is correct.

In general, specific concrete details make for clearer communication; and the more specific, the clearer. Here are our three defective sentences made clear by the addition of details:

> He learned even more from talking with the lumberjacks.

> All he knew about Portland was what he could see from
> his window and what his nurses told him.

> Tensions between whites and Negroes are inevitable in a
> mixed neighborhood.

Whatever the original writers meant, they would have done better to explain their meaning in concrete terms like these. Tell your
readers what you mean in words they can understand. If you do
not, you may lose the attention of most of your readers, and confuse and irritate the few who stay with you.

Prefer the Personal to the Impersonal

Sentences with people in them make more interesting reading
than sentences without people. Most sentences have people in

them in the nature of things. Others have no people and no room for any: *The water was six feet deep/Transistors have replaced vacuum tubes.* Our concern here is with a third class of sentences, those that can go either way: that is, those whose meaning, though it involves people to some extent, can be expressed clearly and idiomatically either with or without a personal noun or pronoun. Our advice is to put the people in.

The point is illustrated in the following pairs of sentences. In each pair the first is perfectly acceptable, but the second is slightly better:

It was necessary to get some sleep.
The boys had to get some sleep.

The drug would be lethal if it were swallowed.
The drug would kill anyone who swallowed it.

What was the casualty count?
How many people were hurt?

It is also a good idea to replace abstractions like *membership,* when used of people, with concrete nouns like *members,* which sounds more human than anything ending in *-ship.* In each of the following pairs, the second sentence is the more effective:

The leadership was completely replaced last summer.
The leaders were all replaced last summer.

The medical profession considers the practice unsafe.
Doctors consider the practice unsafe.

The police department soon had the crime wave under control.
The police soon had the crime wave under control.

The principle extends to more formal writing as well. Here is a passage from a preface to a book of readings:

Literary criticism as such did not seem useful for the purposes of this book. This is not to denigrate the art of criticism, but only to suggest that literary criticism, to be properly appreciated, must be accompanied by the texts it examines.

Here is the same passage livened up by the addition of people:

I decided against including literary criticism in this book, not because I have anything against it, but because readers cannot properly appreciate a critic's ideas without first reading the works he is discussing.

Prefer the Shorter Version to the Longer

Other things being equal, the shorter of two versions is the better. To be sure, other things *must* be equal—that is, the shorter version must convey the same information as the longer, and convey it just as clearly. The idea is not to reduce all writing to three-word sentences, but to eliminate the redundancies and dead words that so often clog the pipes. Why write *It was Harry that did it* when you can write *Harry did it*? Why write *There is a lot for us to talk about* when you can write *We have a lot to talk about*? What do the extra words add besides deadweight?

This principle was illustrated in Chapter 5, pp. 71–72, by the paring down, in two stages, of an unnecessarily wordy paragraph. A few further illustrations may be helpful:

It was clear to me on what basis the request for my resignation had been made.

I knew why they wanted me to resign.

The fact that Susan had made up her mind to leave college was distressing to her parents.

Susan's decision to leave college distressed her parents.

As a result of the labor policies established by Bismarck, the working class in Germany was convinced that revolution was unnecessary for the attainment of its ends.

Bismarck's labor policies convinced the German working class that revolution was unnecessary.

In each of these pairs, the shorter version is only about half the length of the longer. Savings of this order are fairly common in editing first drafts written at full tilt. But smaller savings are also worth making:

> There was nothing for Alice to do.
> Alice had nothing to do.

> Banks in England are more helpful than banks in this country.
> English banks are more helpful than ours.

> It is not uncommon to see shooting stars.
> We often see shooting stars.

Notice that the shorter sentences often represent improvements not only in brevity, but also in the other particulars discussed in this chapter. In the *resignation* example, three abstract nouns disappear, a linking verb becomes an action verb, a passive construction becomes active, and some people (*they*) are added; all of this, plus a halving of the word count, makes a conspicuously better sentence. In the Susan example, and in two of the three shorter examples that follow it, linking verbs are replaced by action verbs. In the Bismarck example, a passive construction becomes active and the nine nouns of the original are reduced to five. Conversely, nearly all the changes recommended under our four earlier headings—that is, changes to make sentences less noun-ridden, more active, less abstract, and more personal—had the additional effect of making the sentence shorter. Clearly the five rules are interrelated, and each reinforces the others.

We conclude this section with a horrendous example of academese from a recent book on juvenile delinquency:

> Contemporary economic perquisites and differential standards have an important conscious and unconscious effect upon the individual's expectation of what he considers to be his right. If the degree of social permissiveness generally sanctioned for attaining pleasures and status is not adequately available to the less economically or culturally favored, the deprivation begets resentment.

The passage violates every one of our five rules. It is sodden with nouns, twelve of them, all but one abstract. Though none of its four verbs is passive, only one, *begets,* has any motion. Its only human component, if human is the word, is a faceless social unit called *the individual.* It is at least a dozen words too long. One can only guess at what it means. Not only does such writing offend the ear and stun the mind; it separates the writer from the specifics that were his original point of departure, in this case the pressure of poverty and powerlessness on flesh-and-blood people.

Our first advice to a beginning stylist is to be honest and unpretentious; our second advice is to learn the five preferences listed on p. 118 and learn to apply them in practice. They are the very foundation stones of style.

EMPHASIS

Word Order

In writing, as in speech, most sentences mirror the natural sequence of ideas in the mind whenever no particular emphasis is sought: subject—object—circumstances—afterthoughts. Emphatic sentences, by contrast, are a matter of deliberate artifice. Typically, the chief element to be emphasized is placed at the end; the lesser elements precede it, setting the stage for the main act.

Compare the following versions of the same incident, the first in natural word order, the second with the word order changed to emphasize *sister*:

> I started at the noise and looked up guiltily. My sister stood there in the doorway.

> I started at the noise and looked up guiltily. There in the doorway stood my sister.

Although, as this example suggests, the word or statement to be emphasized should come at the end of the sentence if possible, you can get the same effect, with somewhat diminished intensity, before a semicolon, a colon, a dash, or even a comma. The emphasis comes from a sort of echo in the moment of silence signaled by the punctuation mark. The stronger the punctuation, the longer the moment; the longer the moment, the more impressive the emphasis. In the emphatic versions of the sentences that follow, the emphasized elements (in italics) come before a period, a semicolon, and a comma, respectively:

Unemphatic

> Ellen had her first sight of the sea at 24, after living in Kansas all her life.

Emphatic

> At 24, after living in Kansas all her life, *Ellen had her first sight of the sea.*

Unemphatic

> He was skinny and weak when I first knew him; today he must weigh 200 pounds.

Emphatic

> When I first knew him, *he was skinny and weak*; today he must weigh 200 pounds.

Unemphatic

> Lincoln was such a man, it is said.

Emphatic

> *Lincoln,* it is said, was such a man.

Although the emphatic versions here seem better than the unemphatic in getting the emphasis where it belongs, the emphatic treatment is by no means always to be preferred. Most unemphatic sentences are inoffensive, and many are eloquent. The best writing mixes the two kinds.

Coordination and Subordination

There is, however, one kind of unemphatic sentence to guard against. That is the compound sentence: the sentence of two or more clauses joined by coordinating conjunctions, usually *and* or *but.* Sentences of this form have neither the potential elegance and strength of the simple sentence, nor the possibilities of emphasis afforded by the complex sentence. They have an inherently boring symmetry: *John played baseball, and Mary went to the movies.* An occasional sentence of this sort is fine. A sprinkling of them makes for writing that is blander than necessary. A preponderance of them is fatal to good prose.

Lazy writers like the compound sentence because it covers all possibilities without committing itself to any. Does *He was rude and she was angry* mean that his rudeness made her angry, or were their reactions simultaneous, or what? The writer who uses *and* this way saves himself the trouble of deciding and specifying which of these relationships he means, if indeed there is any relationship at all. Here are two typical compound ramblers:

> I don't think I ever actually talked to him, *but* he was the ultimate symbol of authority, *and* the mere sight of him used to fill me with physical terror.

> The play is very funny *but* it is also sad, *and* one is never allowed to forget the theme.

In the first, there is no *but* or *and* relationship worth the name. Properly reorganized, the sentence becomes two sentences with no conjunctions at all: *He was the ultimate symbol of authority; the mere sight of him used to fill me with physical terror. I don't think I ever actually talked to him.* The second sentence needs subordination of the less important ideas to the more important one: *Funny as the play is, one is never allowed to forget the underlying sadness.* Both writers, by reaching mechanically for their old friends *and* and *but,* have obscured the true relationships between the elements they are relating.

Before you connect two clauses with *and,* stop and think. Is there really any *and* connection at all? Do we need *and* in a sentence like *Steve was a hero-worshiper, and his hero was John F. Kennedy,* or would a semicolon or a period be enough? Even if there is a legitimate *and* connection, is the *and* construction the best possible, or is one idea in fact subordinate in meaning or importance to the other? Which is better, *Mary went away, and John was unhappy,* or *After Mary went away, John was un-*

happy? Most good writers would vote against *and* in both these examples. Write *and* in your first draft if you must. But in editing, get rid of as many *and*'s as you can.

In Chapters 5 and 6 we discussed how to write effective paragraphs by varying sentence types—simple, compound, and complex; declarative, interrogative, and imperative—and by varying sentence lengths. Readers interested in the present discussion of emphasis at the sentence level may want to review these discussions, which appear on pp. 71–72 and p. 81.

SOME JARRING CONSTRUCTIONS

So far we have been concerned with ways of making writing more lively; in this section we shall consider ways of making it less irritating. Writing can be irritating in many ways: it can be perverse, superficial, dishonest, cryptic, boring, cute. Bad grammar is irritating, so is bad syntax, and so are the various forms of dull writing discussed earlier in this chapter. Our concern here, however, is exclusively with the minor irritations produced by clumsy sentence structure in sentences otherwise perfectly acceptable.

We shall consider three irritating constructions here: the subordination of one *that, who,* or *which* to another; the following of one *but* or *however* with another; and false telegraphy, that is, allowing the reader to suppose a sentence has one construction when in fact it has another.

Double That

The irritation caused by the double-*that* construction should be plain from the following examples:

> The *Times* editorial said *that* Alston was afraid *that* he would be fired.

> It was the National Council *that* made the prediction *that* no Republican would be elected.

> Professor Aaron is the one *who* introduced the poet *who* won second prize.

Sometimes you can repair this construction by simply dropping one of the two relative pronouns: *The* Times *editorial said that Alston was afraid he would be fired.* Where *said* is the main verb, another option is *according to*: *According to the* Times *editorial, Alston was afraid that he would be fired.* Sometimes the construction can be fixed only by rewriting: *The prediction that no Republican would be elected came from the National Council.*

Note that the objectionable construction is always subordinate: one *who, which,* or *that* clause is subordinated to, or contained in, another. In coordinate constructions, by contrast, repetition of *who, which,* or *that* after the conjunction is not only acceptable but usually preferable. The following sentences are correct:

> The report confirmed *that* her father was too ill to work, *and that* her mother was crippled.

> It was a small, irregularly shaped vase, *which* no one at that time could place, *but which* Paddock later identified as of Mixtec origin.

Deleting the second *that* would make the first sentence ambiguous: did Helen know her mother's condition, or does only the writer know? Deleting the second *which* makes the construction of the second sentence less immediately clear.

Double But

The double-*but* construction jerks the reader's mind back and forth from *but* to *but* like the eyes of someone watching a tennis game. *However, yet, nevertheless,* and other action-reversing words are as irritating with *but* as another *but* would be. Some examples:

> She wanted to go, *but* her father would not let her, *but* then he changed his mind.

> Earl, *however,* hung back, *but* no one even noticed.

> I was good at translation, *though* my pronunciation was only fair; *however,* I did well on the test.

To repair such a construction, get rid of at least one *but* or *however*. As with the double-*that* construction, this is sometimes simply a matter of dropping one word of the pair: *Earl hung back, but no one even noticed.* More often, rewriting is necessary:

At first her father refused to let her go, *but* later he changed his mind.

Even *though* my pronunciation was only fair, I was good at translation and did well on the test.

The objection to the double-*but* construction applies only when each *but* introduces or governs a complete clause, as in the examples above. In particular, it is a bad idea to begin two successive sentences with *But.*

False Telegraphy

Some sentences confuse the reader by telegraphing one construction and delivering another. Here are a few examples:

To Germany, France, England, and Russia are natural enemies.

Police told the astounded dean of students who had thrown firecrackers and fruit at the Governor's limousine.

Mr. Hastings, the Secretary of Defense, and General Benton were absent.

I said that Tuesday was impossible, not every Tuesday.

In the first sentence, the reader infers a series of four; this does not work, and he has to read the sentence carefully to discover that it breaks after *Germany.* In the second, the reader mistakenly makes a unit of *dean of students.* In the third, is Mr. Hastings the Secretary of Defense or are they two different men? In the final sentence, the writer means "I said [that] that [particular] Tuesday was impossible, not [that] every Tuesday [was impossible]." The most adroit reader would have trouble extracting this meaning from the sentence as it was written.

False telegraphy is easy enough to fix; the problem is to spot it. Here is one place where it helps to allow sufficient time between first draft and final typing. After a day or so, you can approach your own writing as another reader might, critically and with a fresh eye. If you find a sentence baffling at first—however momentarily—so will other readers, and revision is accordingly in order.

HOBSON'S CHOICES

Thomas Hobson was an irascible Englishman of Elizabethan times who rented horses to travelers on the condition that they take the horse he chose for them or none at all. His horses were a sad lot, and "Hobson's choice" has accordingly come to mean a choice between alternatives all of which have serious drawbacks.

Confronted by a Hobson's choice between a technically correct sentence that sounds awkward and a good-sounding sentence that is technically deficient, many students resignedly opt for one or the other without reflecting whether there may be some third alternative that is neither awkward nor unsound. Consider the following sentences:

> Either you or I (*are*) (*am*) wrong.

> There was a furor about the Undersecretary of (*State*) (*State's*) not being invited.

> Mays is as good an (*outfielder*) (*outfielder as*) or better than Joe DiMaggio in his prime.

> It is one of the best, if not the best (*sonnet*) (*sonnets*) ever written.

> Bohr thought of Einstein as much as a friend (*as*) (*as as*) a teacher.

In each of these sentences, the first alternative listed is the more natural or unobtrusive, but is technically defective; the second is better technically, but is rhetorically ugly. A Hobson's choice, then, but with one important difference: Hobson's customer had to choose between the alternatives offered him, and we do not. Why confine ourselves to the possibilities in parentheses? Why not rewrite the sentence to get around the difficulty?

> Either you are wrong or I am.

> There was a furor when people learned that the Undersecretary of State had not been invited.

> Mays is at least as good an outfielder as Joe DiMaggio was in his prime.

> It is one of the best sonnets ever written, maybe even the best.

> Bohr thought of Einstein not only as a teacher, but as a friend.

Never just give up and allow an awkward sentence to stand. Except, perhaps, in the higher reaches of science and technology, ideas can always be expressed in sentences that are simultaneously grammatical and graceful. If a sentence is intractable on its own terms, choose other terms. If you find yourself wound up in a construction you cannot see all the way around, choose another construction, one you are more at home with. The language is flexible; it has many ways of saying what you want to say. Why run into a wall that you can as easily walk around?

10
WORDS: DICTION

Thirty years ago American textbooks spent many pages correcting some five dozen classical diction errors: *lay* for *lie*, *he don't* for *he doesn't*, *principle* for *principal*, and the like. Some of these errors and confusions are rarely encountered today. Others persist, not only among the educationally underprivileged but among college students with a good background in high school English. Brief discussions of the most troublesome of these questions will be found in the Index to Current Usage, pp. 220–261. Here we shall confine ourselves to questions of a more general nature.

USING THE DICTIONARY

Diction begins with the *dictionary*, a word that for some reason makes many students wince. As the following discussion shows, there is nothing impenetrable about the way information is arranged in a dictionary. Most of the conventions not illustrated in the sample entry we discuss below are no harder to decipher than the ones discussed, and the rest are easily mastered with the help of the brief explanations at the front of every dictionary.

The entries for the word *delay* shown below on the page appear in *Webster's Seventh New Collegiate Dictionary*. The first entry, ¹de·lay, is for the noun (*n*); the second, ²delay, is for the verb (*vb*). The dot between *de* and *lay* in the first entry indicates that *delay* may be divided at this point if it comes at the end of a line. The notation \di-'lā\ is the standard pronunciation; the exact weight of *i* and *ā* and the meaning of ' are explained on the dictionary's endpapers. The information in brackets is the standard derivation of the word: through the Middle English verb *delayen* from the Old French *delaier,* a compound of *de-* and *laier,* "to leave," which in turn derived, through its alternative form *laissier,* from the Latin verb *laxare,* "to slacken." By convention, when there are separate entries for the noun and verb forms (or whatever) of a single word, the word-break, pronunciation, and derivation indications are given only once.

The entry ²delay has two major divisions, *vt* and *vi. Vt* stands for "verb, transitive," the kind of verb that takes a direct object: *He delayed his decision / The soldiers delayed the train. Vi* stands for "verb, intransitive," the kind of verb that does not take an object: *Even when urged to hurry, they delayed.* Two derivative forms, the noun *delayer* and the adjective *delaying,* are listed without definitions, since their meaning can be unmistakably in-

---

¹de·lay \di-'lā\ *n* **1** : the act of delaying : the state of being delayed **2** : the time during which something is delayed
²delay *vb* [ME *delayen,* fr. OF *delaier,* fr. *de-* + *laier* to leave, alter. of *laissier,* fr. L *laxare* to slacken — more at RELAX] *vt* **1** : to put off : POSTPONE **2** : to stop, detain, or hinder for a time ∼ *vi* : to move or act slowly — de·lay·er *n* — de·lay·ing *adj*
    syn DELAY, RETARD, SLOW, SLACKEN, DETAIN, mean to cause to be late or behind in movement or progress. DELAY implies a holding back, usu. by interference, from completion or arrival; RETARD applies chiefly to motion and suggests reduction of speed without actual stopping; SLOW and SLACKEN both imply also a reduction of speed, SLOW often suggesting deliberate intention, SLACKEN an easing up or relaxing of power or effort; DETAIN implies a holding back beyond a reasonable or appointed time
    syn DELAY, PROCRASTINATE, LAG, LOITER, DAWDLE, DALLY mean to move or act slowly so as to fall behind. DELAY usu. implies a putting off (as a beginning or departure); PROCRASTINATE implies blameworthy delay esp. through laziness or apathy; LAG implies failure to maintain a speed set by others; LOITER and DAWDLE imply delay while in progress, esp. in walking, but DAWDLE more clearly suggests an aimless wasting of time; DALLY suggests delay through trifling or vacillation when promptness is necessary

---

ferred from what precedes. Finally, two separate synonymies are given, one for the transitive *delay* in its second sense, the other for the intransitive. Synonymies are one of the most useful features of the modern dictionary, discriminating as they do between near-synonyms like *illusion* and *delusion, postpone* and *defer, show* and *demonstrate,* alternatives that most of us find it hard to choose between without expert guidance.

The boldface numbers indicate the various definitions of a word. In *Webster's Seventh* and most other dictionaries, the sequence of definitions is strictly historical: that is, sense 1 of a word is neither necessarily better (in any way) nor necessarily more frequently encountered than sense 2, but simply entered the language earlier than sense 2. The historical examples on which most such decisions are based are presented in the greatest of all dictionaries, the *New English Dictionary on Historical Principles* (1884–1928), reissued in thirteen volumes in 1933 as the *Oxford English Dictionary* and known familiarly as the OED. Approximately one-fifth of the OED entry for *delay* and its derivatives is shown on the facing page.

College students rarely have occasion to consult the OED, and many can go for months at a time without consulting its nearest equivalent, the 2,662-page, 13-pound, 4-inch-thick *Webster's Third New International Dictionary,* with its 450,000 entries and its controversial hands-off approach to status labels. Your own abridged dictionary, whether *Webster's Seventh* or another, should be sufficient for all but the most recondite uses.

A good dictionary will answer a thousand questions if you will only ask them: on spelling (*indispensible* or *indispensable*?), on pronunciation (*boo-kay* or *bo-kay*?), on word breaks (*plea-sure* or *pleas-ure*?), on definitions (what does *strophe* mean?), on the choice of words (*compulsory* or *obligatory*?), on the choice between different forms of a word (*dwelled* or *dwelt*?), on levels of usage (can I call someone a *hophead* in a term paper?), on any subject having to do with the form, meaning, and status of words. And not only ordinary lowercase words either, since most dictionaries include geographical names, personal proper names, common abbreviations, and other material, either in the main alphabetical sequence or in separate sections at the end. The dictionary may not be the liveliest book around, but to a writer—

1. *trans.* To put off to a later time ; to defer, postpone.   † *To delay time* : to put off time.

c **1290** *S. Eng. Leg.* I. 87/30 And bide þat he it delaiȝe Ane þreo ȝer.   **1297** R. GLOUC. (1724) 513 Ne nolde nouȝt, that is crouninge leng delaied were.   **1393** GOWER *Conf.* III. 290 For to make him afered, The kinge his time hath so delaied.   **1489** CAXTON *Faytes of A.* I. xxii. 68 To delaye the bataylle vnto another day.   **1586** B. YOUNG *Guazzo's Civ. Conv.* IV. 181 b, Delaie the sentence no longer.   **1594** WEST *2nd Pt. Symbol.* Chancerie § 140 Who .. with faire promises delaied time, and kept the said C. D. in hope from yeare to yeare.   **1611** BIBLE *Matt.* xxiv. 48 My Lord delayeth his comming.   **1737** POPE *Hor. Epist.* I. i. 41 Th' unprofitable moments .. That .. still delay Life's instant business to a future day.   **1821** SHELLEY *Prometh. Unb.* III. iii. 6 Freedom long desired And long delayed.   **1847** GROTE *Greece* I. xl. (1862) III. 433 He delayed the attack for four days.

b. with *infin.* To defer, put off.

a **1340** HAMPOLE *Psalter* vi. 3 How lange dylayes þou to gif grace.   **1611** BIBLE *Ex.* xxxii. 1 When the people saw that Moses delayed to come downe.   **1799** COWPER *Castaway* v, Some succour.. [they] Delayed not to bestow.   **1847** TENNYSON *Princ.* iv. 88 Delaying as the tender ash delays To clothe herself, when all the woods are green.

† **c.** With personal object : To put (any one) off, to keep him waiting. *Obs.*

1388 WYCLIF *Acts* xxiv. 22 Felix delayede hem.   **1512** *Act 4 Hen. VIII*, c. 6 § 2 If.. the same Collectours .. unreasonably delay or tary the said Marchauntes.   **1530** PALSGR. 510/1, I delaye one, or deferre hym, or put hym backe of his purpose.   **1639** DU VERGER tr. *Camus' Admir. Events* 88 It was not fit shee should delay him with faire wordes.   **1768** BLACKSTONE *Comm.* III. 109 Where judges of any court do delay the parties.

2. To impede the progress of, cause to linger or stand still ; to retard, hinder.

1393 GOWER *Conf.* III. 261. Her wo to telle thanne assaieth, But tendre shame her word delaieth.   **1634** MILTON *Comus* 494 Thyrsis ! whose artful strains have oft delayed The huddling brook to hear his madrigal.   **1709** STEELE *Tatler* No. 39 ⁋ 4 Joy and Grief can hasten and delay Time.   **1813** SHELLEY *Q. Mab* II. 197 The unwilling sojourner, whose steps Chance in that desert has delayed.   **1856** KANE *Arct. Expl.* II. xv. 161 To delay the animal until the hunters come up.

3. *intr.* To put off action ; to linger, loiter, tarry.

1509 HAWES *Past. Pleas.* XVI. lxix, A womans guyse is evermore to delaye.   **1596** SHAKS. *1 Hen. IV*, III. ii. 180 Aduantage feedes him fat, while men delay.   **1667** MILTON *P. L.* V. 247 So spake th' Eternal Father .. nor delaid the winged Saint After his charge receivd.   **1850** TENNYSON *In Mem.* lxxxiii, O sweet new-year delaying long.. Delaying long, delay no more.

b. To tarry in a place.   (Now only *poetic*.)

1654 H. L'ESTRANGE *Chas. I* (1655) 3 Paris being .. in his way to Spain, he delaid there one day.   *a* **1878** BRYANT *Poems, October,* Wind of the sunny south ! oh still delay, In the gay woods and in the golden air.

c. To be tardy in one's progress, to loiter.

1690 LOCKE *Hum. Und.* II. xiv. § 9 There seem to be certain bounds to the quickness and slowness of the succession of those ideas .. beyond which they can neither delay nor hasten.

any writer—it is by far the most useful. Keep one on your desk, and use it.

CONNOTATION

Connotation and Denotation

The meaning of a word has two aspects, denotative and connotative. A word's denotation is what it literally means, as defined by the dictionary; its connotation is the associations it evokes. These associations may be of several types. Some are simply echoes of one of the word's other established meanings: it is for this reason that the Tenth Commandment's injunction not to covet our neighbor's ass evokes snickers today. Others are historical associations: *appeasement,* for example, formerly a neutral word, acquired heavy connotations of betrayal and dishonor after 1938, when it was widely used to describe Neville Chamberlain's concessions to Hitler at Munich. Still others are social: *square,* for example, in the sense of a person seen as offensively conventional, is used by some kinds of people and not by others.

The meeting of connotation may be illustrated by contrasting two sentences from the same paragraph of *Education at Berkeley,* the report of a faculty committee issued following the student disturbances at the University of California, Berkeley, in 1964:

> The search for genuine experience leads also to experimenting with non-addictive hallucinatory drugs.

> This desire for instant poetry, instant psychoanalysis, and instant mysticism is a further form of escape from hard work.

The first sentence is standard expository prose; its words mean what the dictionary says they mean. In the second something quite different is going on. Not only is *instant* a surprising modifier of activities that we normally think of as contemplative and introspective, but it calls to mind instant coffee, instant cake frosting, instant TV dinners—all the mass-produced gimmickry of the modern supermarket. By modifying *poetry, psychoanalysis,* and *mysticism* with a word that not only denotes an unsuitable speed but connotes an unsuitable level of quality and individuality, the authors are denigrating the students' views. They are saying that these spoiled kids want to know life's greatest experiences with no more work or waiting than it takes to warm up a TV dinner. The connotations of *instant* in this sentence carry almost the whole burden of the authors' critical intent.

Thus, by astute manipulation, a new combination of words creates a new idea, a new impression, a new meaning. Human experience and history and literature are always doing this to words. *Collaborator,* from *co-* (with) and *labor* (work), once meant simply one who worked together with someone else; later the word came to be restricted largely to literary work, and still later it acquired the connotation of working willingly with one's country's enemies. Thanks in part, perhaps, to the Women's Christian Temperance Union, *temperance,* which once meant nothing more than moderation in speech and conduct, has come to connote not only abstinence from liquor but an offensively high-minded moral strictness.

Euphemism is another powerful force for change. *Undertaker,* which originally meant nothing more than one who undertakes an assignment, came by euphemism to mean one who prepares the dead for burial; after acquiring negative connotations from this association, it was discarded by sensitive American undertakers in favor of the tonier *mortician,* which in turn acquired the same connotations as *undertaker* (not to mention the scorn normally accorded transparent euphemisms by outsiders) and has subsequently been replaced by *funeral director.* An airline company now insists that one experiences *motion discomfort* instead of *airsickness.* Before about 1935, *liquidation* in American usage referred mainly to bankruptcy proceedings; it acquired a new meaning when Hitler and Stalin used it as a euphemism for murder.

Connotation and the Dictionary

Time and accident corrode words, change them, encrust them with connotations. The dictionary sometimes spells these connotations out, either by adding them as new denotations ("**square**. . . . 8:** a person rejected for conventionality or respectability"), or by adding qualifying phrases to existing denotations ("**collaborate 1:** to work jointly with others esp. in an intellectual endeavor"), or by labeling a word slang, substandard, archaic, or what have you. More often, however, the dictionary is no help. *Webster's Seventh,* for example, gives no hint that the second meaning of *suggestive* ("tending to suggest something improper or indecent") has all but routed the first and neutral meaning ("giving a suggestion," "full of suggestions"); and it does not even mention the heavy sexual connotations acquired in recent decades by *provocative.* Its definition of *gamesmanship,* "the art of winning games by doubtful expedients without actually violating the rules," gives no idea of the sardonic, post-Christian, under-the-Bomb connotations of this word and such allied compounds as *brinkmanship* and *oneupmanship.*

Though the dictionary can sometimes help, then, the main burden of getting connotations straight falls squarely on the writer's experience and observation. No advice is possible or necessary here except to keep your eyes and ears open. If you do not know exactly what a word means but think it may be dirty, you presumably refrain from using it in a conversation with your girl friend's mother. Do the same in your writing. Try to use only words whose connotations you feel confident you understand. If you are moved to use other words as well—and of course you will be and should be—see who else is using them and how they are being used, in conversation, in lectures, in what you read. There is no need to use them in writing until you have made them your own.

STANDARD AND NON-STANDARD ENGLISH

One of the most important aspects of connotation is status. A word's status has no necessary connection with its meaning: there are "respectable" words for nonrespectable things, and nonrespectable words for respectable things. For example, in the sentence *I was snowed,* the word *snowed* has the perfectly respectable meaning "overwhelmed," perhaps with work, perhaps by someone's good looks or suave approach. And yet the connotations of *snowed* make it less than perfectly respectable; it is a teen-age word, suitable for casual teen-age conversation or a letter to a friend but too colloquial for formal writing. *Overwhelmed* has the opposite connotation; one rarely hears the word spoken, but it is acceptable in formal use as *snowed* is not. One word is acceptable spoken English, at least for teen-agers; the other is acceptable written English.

How do such distinctions come about, and what are we to make of them? They come about naturally rather than artificially. New words are introduced into the language to denote new things, new ideas, new shades of meaning; and immediately people face a choice between the new word and whatever word or phrase was used to express roughly the same idea before. Some new words are accepted immediately: *television* is an example. Others are accepted after a brief struggle with an existing equivalent (*radio* versus *wireless*) or with an alternative new word or form (*automation* versus *automatization*). Still others spend years in colloquial status before they win formal acceptance: the word *swamped*, a precursor of *snowed* in the sense "overwhelmed with work," ran this course many decades ago. Finally, some words—for example, the names of such ephemeral dances as the *frug* and the *watusi*—never rise beyond colloquial status and ultimately drop from the language altogether.

At any given time, then, the language consists broadly of two kinds of words, those acceptable for formal use and those acceptable for informal use only, plus a borderland of words on probation. By formal use we mean primarily serious expository writing, though the term extends to public speaking, business letters, conversations with eminent men, and so on. Whether a word is acceptable or unacceptable for formal use is determined by a consensus of educated persons, as evidenced in what they write and read. Until recently, dictionaries signaled this consensus by status labels: Standard English was unmarked; non-Standard was marked *colloq.*, *slang*, or the like, or left out of the dictionary as trivial or ephemeral. Since the advent of *Webster's Third* in 1961, however, lexicographers have largely abandoned these labels, in part because they are too crude to do justice to the complexities of usage, in part because no such body of pronouncements can keep pace with the rapid changes in our language and our ideas about its use. The burden of distinguishing between Standard and non-Standard has accordingly fallen directly on the writer.

The category non-Standard embraces not only colloquialisms (words like *snowed* and *cops*, abbreviations like *prof* and *D.A.*, expressions like *no sweat*), but also words peculiar to a single region, ethnic group, profession, or gang. These words, variously classifiable as dialect, jargon, and slang, need not be discussed here. Many of the more irresistible, like the Yiddish *schlemiel* and the astronauts' *splashdown*, are now, or are becoming, Standard. Others will run their course and drop from sight.

In expository writing, a departure from Standard English is at least as serious a flaw as an error in spelling or grammar. You may believe that a non-Standard word *ought* to be Standard, that the language needs it, that only stuffy people are against it. You may even be dead right, and ultimately your opinion may help to form the subtle consensus that changes a word's status. But until that time proceed with caution. A distinction between words is like a statutory distinction: it may be unjust or obsolete, its repeal may be imminent, but while it is on the books the prudent man observes it.

Important as the distinction between Standard and non-Standard is, however, too much should not be made of it. The life and vigor of the language are in the spoken word. Vigorous writing has the accents and rhythms of speech; it should have, so far as possible, the words natural to speech. We have drawn the line at non-Standard English, but this implies no superiority in the other extreme. If the student who writes *I blew my cool* offends the dignity of the reader, the student who writes *My reaction was intense to the point of excess* achieves an empty dignity at the expense of vigor. Good English can be said to lie between these extremes.

But how are you to know whether a word is Standard or non-Standard? Given the constant flux of the language, you can never know for certain about every single word, but you can get a good idea of the canon from serious books, magazines, and newspapers, and from the formal and informal speech of educated people. As indicated above, the dictionary is no longer much help. No teacher in America, for example, would accept *The GI's goofed when they hooked the Commies' booze,* and yet one finds no hint in *Webster's Seventh* that this sentence is other than impeccable English. When in doubt, be cautious, but not so cautious that you sound wooden. Standard means standard, not stuffy.

THE CHOICE OF WORDS

The five basic rules of good diction, in the formulation given by Fowler and his brother in *The King's English*, are as follows:

> Perfer the familiar word to the far-fetched.
> Prefer the concrete word to the abstract.
> Prefer the single word to the circumlocution.
> Prefer the short word to the long.
> Prefer the Saxon word to the Romance.

"These rules," they add, "are given in order of merit; the last is also the least." Later writers objected to the last two rules as requiring heavy qualification before they could be accepted, and the most influential formulation of recent times, that of Sir Ernest Gowers in *Plain Words* (1954), omits them entirely. The Gowers rules are worth quoting in full:

> Use no more words than are necessary to express your meaning, for if you use more you are likely to obscure it and to tire your reader. In particular do not use superfluous adjectives and adverbs and do not use roundabout phrases where single words would serve.
>
> Use familiar words rather than the far-fetched, if they express your meaning equally well; for the familiar are more likely to be readily understood.
>
> Use words with a precise meaning rather than those that are vague, for they will obviously serve better to make your meaning clear; and in particular prefer concrete words to abstract, for they are more likely to have a precise meaning.

Brevity

The first of these rules, which has to do more with style in general than with the choice of words as such, we have discussed at length in Chapters 5 and 9, pp. 71–72 and 126–28. We confine ourselves here to observing that one can be too brief. *The tables were arranged in quincunx fashion* is briefer than *Four tables formed the corners of a square, and the fifth was in the middle,* but the longer version will be clearer to most readers. Again, *according to Marcel* is briefer, but may be much less helpful, than *according to the Catholic existentialist philosopher Gabriel Marcel*. Readers for whom *Marcel* would have been enough will not be troubled by the extra words, and other readers will be glad to have them. It is basic good sense (not to mention courtesy) to explain matters that may be unfamiliar to your reader. To put this another way, it is only after the reader's potential discomforts have been attended to that brevity becomes paramount.

Familiarity

Gowers's second rule is to "use familiar words rather than the far-fetched." He had in mind a once-numerous class of British writers, many of them journalists, who used ornate words like *septentrional* and foreign expressions like *tête-à-tête* in preference to their plain English equivalents. Today's college student tends to be ornate in a somewhat different way. His departures from the familiar are not so much to the farfetched as to the imperfectly understood, terms like *organic unity, identity crisis,* and *ontological despair,* which he uses before he has altogether mastered them. Although the issue here is concepts, not just words, Gowers's advice still applies. Use familiar words and your meaning will be clear—not only to your reader, but to yourself.

Precision

Gowers's third and last rule is to "use words with a precise meaning rather than those that are vague." Consider the following pairs of sentences:

> The authorities took favorable action on the proposal.
>
> The board of trustees voted to accept the proposal.
>
> Our whole football program will be affected if any further difficulties develop.
>
> Our new stadium will not be ready in September unless the cement workers' strike is settled soon.

The situation soon required them to seek financial help.

To buy the second printing press, they had to borrow $15,000 from a bank.

In each case the second sentence is the better. Vague, abstract words like *authorities, affected, develop,* and *situation* do not clarify meaning but obscure it. To some writers—notably those who are trying to deceive their readers, to sell them something, or to allay their anger—obscurity may have its uses. But to the honest writer there is no substitute for the precise word and the necessary detail. If *the situation* can be described, describe it. If *difficulties* means a cement workers' strike, or the likelihood of a riot, or somebody's inexperience, say so. A certain decorum is conventionally observed in sex and bathroom matters; but these aside, your duty as a writer of expository prose is to say as well as you can exactly what you mean.

A second and equally self-defeating kind of imprecision is found in such a sentence as *Communism is finished.* What does this mean? Does it mean that Marx's ideas have been definitively discredited? That the present Communist world is reverting to capitalism? That the threat of Soviet or Chinese Communist territorial expansion has receded? There is no knowing. Such large abstractions as *communism, democracy, the people, nature, freedom,* and *education* mean different things to different people. If you do not make clear the exact sense in which you are using such a word, your readers are likely to mistake your meaning.

A final kind of imprecise expression is the cliché. Precision is a function of thought; one chooses the right word by weighing it against alternatives. The cliché is the enemy of thought; writers choose it not because it is right, but because it is there. In going over your first draft, be on the lookout for clichés—not only for such stale metaphors as *leave no stone unturned* (see pp. 53–54), but also, and perhaps especially, for the colorless but insidious three- or four-word phrase that has elbowed out a perfectly good single word or shorter phrase of the same meaning. Of these phrases Gowers writes:

> They slip past the barrier without scrutiny. Thus (to take a
> few examples of the many that might be given) a writer

may say *climate of opinion* without asking himself whether he means anything more than *opinion,* or *within the framework of* instead of a bare preposition, or that something is *grinding to a halt* which is doing no more than slowly stopping; or he may find that *in this day and age* has thrust aside the plain word *today,* which was all that he needed, or that *in the ultimate analysis* has done the same thing to *in the end.*

George Orwell, in his splendid essay "Politics and the English Language," is more succinct: "Prose consists less and less of *words* chosen for the sake of their meaning, and more and more of *phrases* tacked together like the sections of a prefabricated henhouse." He goes on to make an important point that we have touched on earlier:

> A scrupulous writer, in every sentence that he writes, will ask himself . . . Could I put it more shortly? Have I said anything that is avoidably ugly? But you are not obliged to go to all this trouble. You can shirk it by simply throwing your mind open and letting the ready-made phrases come crowding in. They will construct your sentences for you— even think your thoughts for you, to a certain extent—and at need they will perform the important service of concealing your meaning even from yourself.

In the end, we are back to brevity. To write effectively you must make every word count, and not use three words where one or two will serve as well. The French philosopher Pascal once apologized to a correspondent for writing him so long a letter. "This letter is so long," he wrote, "because I have not had time to make it shorter." What he meant is plain: that to make one's meaning clear, time spent in pruning—for example, in changing *in this day and age* to *today*—is time well spent.

IDIOM

Idiom is a complex and irrational business. For example, although *l'ardeur du combat* is idiomatic French for *the heat of the battle,* and although English has literal equivalents for *ardeur* and *combat, the ardor of the combat* is not idiomatic English. Idiomatic English is English as reasonably well-educated native speakers speak it. Unidiomatic English, by contrast, not only rings oddly in the ear, but also, by virtue of its departure from the familiar, unnecessarily taxes the understanding. Small departures from idiom may go unnoticed, especially if they are few. Large departures, or small ones in large numbers, make for the hardest kind of reading. Unidiomatic language is sometimes colorful—the authors cherish a Korean student's sentence, *He just like a monkey, he up and down the tree*—but in expository prose any pleasure it may give is soon lost in the effort to understand what is being said.

Native speakers of English have far less trouble writing idiomatically than foreigners who learn English as a second language. We do not have to learn, for example, when to say *the* and when to omit it: we learn as children that people go *to the* movies but go *to* church, that people watch television but listen to *the* radio. There is no rational basis for these distinctions, just as there is no reason why *the heat of the battle* should have vanquished *the ardor of the combat* or *the passion of the struggle*. The language has simply come in the course of time to favor one form over another. The efficiency of this process is its own excuse. By learning the idiomatic forms of the more common expressions as children, we clear our minds of the many thousands of rejected alternatives with which the uncertain foreigner must grapple.

The difficulty comes with the less common expressions. Everyone knows that we say *bad weather* rather than *ill weather*, but should we say *bad omen* or *ill omen, bad tidings* or *ill tidings, bad health* or *ill health*? Should we describe Grandma as *kind, kindhearted,* or *kindly*? Does one *make, take,* or *reach* a decision? Does one differ *with* or *from* someone, and is one's view then different *from* or *than* his? More than one of these alternatives may be acceptable. What is important is not so much that "correct" answers be found to questions of this sort, as that the questions themselves be asked—that is, that the writer have some sense of the alternatives and not settle for a lazy first stab.

The following sentences illustrate only a few of the many possible kinds of errors in idiom (corrections in parentheses):

Rousseau's argument was the opposite to Hobbes's. (*of*)

The need of action should have been apparent. (*need for*; or *necessity of*)

When we finished sweeping the sidewalk, we considered the job as done. (*considered the job done*; or *regarded the job as done*)

Most importantly of all, the Giants' shortstop was ill. (*important*)

She confessed to have seen neither accident. (*to having seen*)

The Tonkin Gulf Resolution made a mountain of a molehill. (*out of*)

Trivial as these errors are, they are irritating, and they are also hard to avoid. The only defense against them is attention. Read a sentence over. If it sounds wrong, even though you cannot say exactly how, switch to a more manageable construction. For example, if you are uneasy with both *opposite to* and *opposite of* in the first sentence, try *He and I presented opposite arguments*; if you are not sure what is wrong with *confessed to have seen,* try *confessed that she had seen.* No one alive has a complete mastery of English idiom at the *opposite to/of/from* level.[1] It is plain common sense to stick as much as possible to constructions that you know are idiomatic.

For more subtle questions of word choice—for example, between *kind* and *kindly,* between *informer* and *informant,* between *evoke, extract,* and *elicit*—the dictionary is often helpful, especially in its explicit comparisons of near-synonyms, as given, for example, in the entry for *delay* discussed earlier in this chapter. Another useful book is a thesaurus, which gives synonyms and near-synonyms for all the most common nouns, verbs, adjectives, and adverbs. If you cannot think of precisely the right word but can think of a word meaning roughly the same thing, the thesaurus will probably lead you to the word you want.

[1] If you want to be the first, the place to start is with Frederick T. Wood's *English Prepositional Idioms* (New York, 1967), which runs to 562 tightly packed pages.

It is perhaps fitting to conclude with some indication of how the various precepts of the last part of this chapter relate to each other and to the problems confronting writers—in short, with what the advertising industry calls a "take-home message." If all our pronouncements about the choice of words had to be reduced to a single rule, it would be this: Choose the shortest and most familiar word or phrase, consistent with idiom, that will express your meaning without loss or distortion.

11

WORDS: ORTHOGRAPHY

Words must be not only correctly chosen but correctly written, which is to say correctly spelled, divided, capitalized, and italicized as general usage or a specific context may require. Questions of orthography are generally less interesting than questions of diction, but they can be just as important to the writer's message. Small, even niggling, as most of them are, you cannot ignore them or answer them carelessly except at the expense of your reader's understanding.

SPELLING

For spelling, there is only one rule: if you are not absolutely sure how a word is spelled, look it up in the dictionary. If you are not allowed to use a dictionary—for example, during a test— you are on your own. English spelling is so irregular that no one should be required to memorize the spelling of more than a thousand or so of the most familiar words. A teacher who does not allow you to use a dictionary on a test will probably allow you a spelling error or two without penalty. Unless, of course, it is a spelling test.

HYPHENATION

The hyphen has three uses: to divide words at the end of a line *(Mac-/beth, syca-/more)*, to divide prefixes from certain root words (*un-American, anti-imperialist*), and to pull together compounds of two or more words into visual units (*brown-and-serve muffins, a get-together*).

Word Division

The word-division use poses no problems: simply follow your dictionary, which indicates all possible word divisions for a given word. Thus the dots in **syc·a·more** show that the word may be divided either *syc-/amore* or *syca-/more*. Proper names and words not in a dictionary should be divided between syllables; if you cannot tell for certain where a syllable ends, your best guess will probably serve. Never divide a one-syllable name, and never divide after the first letter or before the last.

Prefixes

The use of a hyphen with prefixes is easily learned. (1) If the root word begins with a capital letter, use a hyphen (*pre-Christian*). (2) If the prefix ends with a vowel and the root word begins with the same vowel, check your dictionary. Some such words are unhyphenated (*cooperate, preeminent*); others are hyphenated (*co-opt*); others do not appear in the dictionary, in which case use a hyphen (*co-owner, pre-educate*). (3) In all other cases do not hyphenate, save in the rare instance in which a hyphen may be used to distinguish one reading of a word from another: thus *re-cover*, "to cover again," is distinguished from *recover*.

Compounds

The third use of the hyphen—to pull together compounds of two or more words into visual units—is the most important of the three and the most complex. Two main classes of such compounds may be distinguished: noun compounds and adjective compounds. They may be illustrated as follows:

Noun compounds

> My brother is a *sergeant first class.*
>
> We bought an *air-conditioner.*
>
> I want to build a better *mousetrap.*

Adjective compounds

> Mother is a *clearheaded* woman.
>
> That store has *hard-to-get* parts.
>
> Mr. Adams is a *life insurance* salesman.

For noun compounds alone, *Webster's Third New International* prescribes the following bewildering variety of forms:

pocket-handkerchief	half-wit	off-season
pocket battleship	half brother	off year
pocketknife	halfback	offshoot
birthrate	makeup	vice-president
death rate	shake-up	vice admiral

How in the world, then, is one to know whether a compound should be hyphenated, run as two separate words, or made into a single word? For noun compounds the answer is easy: look up the compound in the dictionary. If you find it, use its dictionary form; if you don't find it, write it as separate words unless a hyphen seems necessary to eliminate a possible misreading.

Adjective compounds are harder to handle. Most are not listed in the dictionary at all, or are listed in their noun form only. We know, for example, that we should write *high school* thus as a noun, but should we hyphenate it or not as an adjective compound in the phrase *high school teacher?* The dictionary does not say. In effect, usage on this point is in transition, but the following broad guidelines may help.

If an adjective compound appears in your dictionary as a consolidated or hyphenated word, use the dictionary form: thus *Webster's Seventh* shows *fainthearted, hardworking, clear-sighted, hard-boiled.* If an adjective compound is not listed as such in your dictionary, either hyphenate it or write it as two (or more) words. Hyphenate number compounds (*a twenty-year period*), participle compounds (*a card-carrying Communist*) except with adverbs ending in *-ly* (*a recently built factory*), preposition compounds (*a made-up story, an after-dinner speech*), compounds of coequal nouns (*the second Clay-Liston fight*), compounds expressing degree (*a large-scale enterprise*), and compounds of three or more words (*a door-to-door salesman, a high-silicon-content alloy*).[1] Write other adjective compounds as two words: *high school teacher, senior class party, civil rights agitation.* A hyphen would not be wrong in such expressions; but it may be a bit stilted or overformal.

Is usage in general moving slowly away from the hyphen? There are signs that it is. We know that British literate usage runs to more hyphens than American literate usage, which in turn hyphenates more freely than American illiterate and scientific usage. At the same time, we find influential English writers like the late Winston Churchill spurning the hyphen as "a blemish to be avoided wherever possible," and Gowers echoing this judgment to the point of recommending consolidated forms like *aftereffects* and *panicstricken* without turning a hair. The Merriam-Webster editors go even further, endorsing such extreme specimens as *radiobroadcasting* and *fluidounce.* When English grammarians and stylists agree with American illiterates, scientists, and lexicographers, who can stand against them? It is a good guess that the hyphen is on its way out.

THE APOSTROPHE

The apostrophe is used to form possessives; to form plurals of numbers, letters, and abbreviations; and to form contractions.

---

[1] This last construction is not attractive. At its worst, it provides horrors like this sentence, cited by Gowers: *A large-vehicle-fleet-operator mileage restriction has now been made imperative.* As Gowers remarks, such a sentence should be rewritten with prepositions: *It has now become imperative to impose a mileage restriction on the operators of fleets of large vehicles.* It still does not sing, but at least it has stopped croaking.

Forming the Possessive

To form the possessive, use *'s* for the singular (*John's hat, the dog's dish*) and an apostrophe only for the plural (*the ladies' bridge club, the Smiths' car*). For words that do not form the plural in *s*, notably *men, women,* and *children,* add *'s* for the plural possessive (*the children's toys, the alumni's wishes, the people's choice*).

Some singular common nouns and many proper names end in an *s* or *z* sound. Most of these, along with all names ending in silent *s* or *x* (*Descartes, Malraux, Illinois, Arkansas*), form the possessive in *'s* just like any other singular noun:

Henry James's novels	for appearance's sake
Essex's plot	Degas's paintings
our hostess's husband	Columbus's crew
in Jesus's name	Alcatraz's first warden

A few such words, however, notably ancient Greek and biblical names of three or more syllables ending in a *z* sound, become too awkward to pronounce with the extra syllable added by *'s* and conventionally form the possessive with the apostrophe only: *Aristophanes' comedies, Socrates' wisdom*.

No apostrophe is used in the possessive pronouns *his, hers, its, ours, yours, theirs,* and *whose*. Errors on this point, particularly *it's* for *its,* are common in student writing. *It's* means *it is* or *it has* and nothing else (*It's a rainy day / It's been fun*); *who's* means *who is* or *who has* (*Who's there? / Who's seen Mary?*). The forms *her's, our's, your's,* and *their's* do not exist. Note, by the way, that *whose* may be used freely in place of the awkward *of which* irrespective of whether it refers to a person or a thing: *the house whose garden we admired* is Standard English.

Misplaced Apostrophe

In some idiomatic phrases involving possessives, it is not immediately obvious where the apostrophe goes. Is it *state's rights,* for example, or *states' rights?* Is it *bull's-eyes* or *bulls'-eyes* or *bullseyes?* Is is *hornet's nest* or *hornets' nest, doctor's orders* or *doctors' orders?* Try your dictionary on questions like this, or better yet an unabridged dictionary. If you can find no pronouncement one way or the other, your best bet is usually the singular. In proper names, the plural is the more common: *Reserve Officers' Training Corps, Professional Golfers' Association.*

The practice of eliminating the apostrophe from what is properly a possessive form has become° established in some proper names (*the Veterans Administration, the Artists Workshop*), and is now being extended to some common compounds as well (*teachers college, citizens group*). There is no warrant, however, for the wholesale elimination of the apostrophe in terms of this form. In particular, keep the apostrophe where dropping it would yield a nonexistent word like *mens* or *childrens*. For the same reason, take care to put the apostrophe where it belongs, not one letter away. It is *women's club*, not *womens' club*; *sheep's wool*, not *sheeps' wool*; *womens* and *sheeps* are not English words. The opposite error (*John Adam's presidency, the United State's viewpoint*) evokes nonexistent singulars: a president named *John Adam*, a country named *the United State*.

Beware of adding an apostrophe to a nonpossessive plural noun being used as an adjective: it is *physics test*, not *physics' test* or *physic's test*. And never use an apostrophe to form the plural of a word that has a perfectly good plural of the normal form. Errors of this sort are common on signs: *Strawberry's for Sale, We Charge Battery's*. On doorplates we may find *The Jones's*, implying that some sinister figure known as The Jones lurks within, rather than an innocent family of Joneses. This last error in particular smacks of illiteracy: if it creeps into a first draft, it should creep no further.

Miscellaneous Plurals

An apostrophe is ordinarily used to form plurals of numbers (*the 1960's, two size 9's*), letters (*two A's and three B's*), and abbreviations (*sixteen Ph.D.'s, some MP's*), and to form plurals of words used as words, book titles, and the like (*do's and don't's, and's instead of but's, a dozen* Life with Father's). Apostrophes should not be used to form other plurals. As we have seen, Mr. Jones's family is *the Joneses*, not *the Jones's*. Similarly, the plural of *New York*, for example, is not *New York's* but *New Yorks*: *Two New Yorks would be one too many.*

Contractions

Contractions are formed by substituting an apostrophe for some part of a word that is not pronounced in informal discourse. The words most commonly contracted are *not* (*isn't, don't*) and the various forms of *have* (*he's been, you've gone*), *will* (*I'll stay, they'd complain*), and *be* (*I'm, you're*). Although the standard contractions of *have, will,* and *be* involve pronouns, other contractions of all three are possible in dialogue: *I wouldn't've dared / The sun'll be up soon / The sky's the limit.* Contractions are basically a way of rendering informal speech; they should be used sparingly in formal writing except in quoting spoken dialogue. In writing them, take care to get the apostrophe in the right place (*hadn't,* not *had'nt*) and not to leave a space before or after it (*you'll,* not *you' ll* or *you 'll*).

Such poetic contractions as *'twas* for *it was* and *o'er* for *over* are obsolete or jocular save for a few words like *Hallowe'en* and *ne'er-do-well.* Cute contractions—*'cause* for *because,* *'n* for *and*—should be rigorously restricted to the personal correspondence of girls under seventeen. Only one contraction of this form has come down to us from the past: *o'clock,* a contraction of *of the clock.* No more are needed.

Contractions like *'teens* (as in *girls in their 'teens*) and *'sixties* (meaning the 1960's), where the apostrophe indicates that part of a word is being used for the whole, are increasingly, and we think properly, written without the apostrophe. Some earlier travelers along this path were *'bus* for *omnibus* and *'coon* for *raccoon.*

CAPITALIZATION

Capitalization is the bane of many a writer. The basic rules—to capitalize the first word in a sentence and such proper names as Henry Smith, Thursday, *War and Peace,* and the Chicago Bears—are easily learned, but once beyond the basics even the most experienced writer encounters difficulties. In this section we shall discuss some of the more persistent trouble areas.

Direct Quotations

When a direct quotation makes a complete sentence within a sentence, you may either capitalize or lowercase the first word, depending on how the quotation relates to the rest of the sentence and without regard to whether or not the word is capitalized in the original. Thus, the same quotation may properly be begun with a capital letter in one context and a lowercase letter in another:

> The Bible says: "Look not upon the wine when it is red."
> The Bible asks that we "look not upon the wine when it is red."

> In the words of Harold Wilson, "The worst is over."
> Harold Wilson argues that "the worst is over."

By contrast, when a sentence within a sentence is not in quotes, do not capitalize the first word:

> According to Harold Wilson, the worst was over.

> The truth was plain: we had been deceived.

> Art's job (he was test-flying helicopters) had been classified as hazardous.

A capital letter may follow a colon when the colon introduces a formal or weighty pronouncement, even if no quotation marks are used. For example, *He had his own version of the Golden Rule: Do unto others all you can get away with.* When in doubt, however, use lowercase after a colon.

Personal Titles

Good writers capitalize personal titles when they are attached to names (*General Bat Guano, Professor Rainier*), but lowercase them when they are used alone (*Bat Guano was promoted to general / Mr. Rainier is a professor of French*). The problem comes when a title is used in place of a specific name. In a specific reference to General Guano, for example, should we write *The General called for volunteers* or *The general called for volunteers*? Both forms are common; neither is wrong. If current usage has any pattern at all, it is that the most eminent titles are the most frequently capitalized: few if any writers lowercase *the Pope, the President of the United States, the Queen of England.*

For slightly less eminent titles, though lowercase is increasingly common, capitalization remains usual: *the Secretary of State, the Governor of Alaska, the Prime Minister, the Archbishop, the General.* At lower levels of eminence lowercase prevails: *the president of General Motors, the major, the professor, the judge, the coach.*

Parts Standing for the Whole

Eminent titles apart, the lowercasing of key words substituted for formal proper nouns now generally prevails. Thus, after an initial reference to the Mississippi River, we refer to it as *the river,* not *the River;* we refer to World War II as *the war,* to the French Communist Party as *the party,* to the Chicago Public Library as *the library,* to the University of Wisconsin as *the university,* and so on. Naturally, this practice applies only when the lowercased word faithfully conveys the meaning of the full expression: a restaurant named the Old Barn cannot be referred to as *the barn,* or the Chicago Bears as *the bears.*

Points of the Compass

North, east, south, west, and their derivations cause all sorts of trouble. Should it be *Western Europe* or *western Europe, in the north* or *in the North*? Probably the most workable rule is to capitalize these words when they stand for a formal or semiformal political or geographic unit, and to lowercase them when they are used in a general geographical sense or merely to indicate direction. Thus *Southeast Asia* designates the area south of China and east of India and politically independent of both, whereas the geographical region *southeastern Asia* would include much of China and part of India. Similarly, *the East* refers to New England and the Central Atlantic states, *the east* to where the sun rises. A few more examples may make the distinction clearer:

Semiformal	General
West Germany	a west wind
South Korea	the south of France
North Africa	drive north to Seattle
the Far East	the east bank of the Rhine
the Southwest	southwestern Arkansas

By a semiformal name, we mean one that is sanctioned by usage (*West Germany*) or convenience (*North Africa*) rather than by formal political decree. *West Germany* is the common name for the Federal Republic of Germany, as *South Korea* is for the Republic of Korea; *North Africa, the Far East,* and *the Southwest* are convenient names for areas having no formal unity. Although not formal in the sense that *West Virginia* and *North Carolina* are formal, these names are in practice treated formally. The distinction between semiformal and general is more important, and is not always easy to make; when in doubt, lowercase. Adjectives derived from capitalized nouns in this class should themselves be capitalized: *Far Eastern policy, Middle Western roads, Southern hospitality.*

Book and Article Titles

In titles of books, magazine articles, songs, and other formal compositions, and in the titles and subheadings of papers that you write, capitalize the first and last words and all other words except (1) articles and (2) prepositions and conjunctions of five or fewer letters:

What Is an American?	"When the Saints Come Marching In"
"A Choice Between Two Evils"	
Of Mice and Men	*Love in a Cold Climate*
	"What It Means to Be Ill"

ITALICS

Titles of Publications and Compositions

Italics are indicated in manuscript or typescript by underlining. Underline the names of newspapers and magazines; the titles of books, plays, and other longish pieces of writing, especially if published separately; and the names of movies, paintings, and long musical compositions:

the *Washington Post*	*Paradise Lost*
Life magazine	movies like *La Strada*
The Caine Mutiny	Cézanne's *View of Auvers*
The Merchant of Venice	Mozart's opera *Don Giovanni*

Do not underline the titles of newspaper or magazine articles, short stories, poems, songs, and other shortish pieces of writing, or of unpublished works. Use quotation marks:

> "The Situation in Asia," editorial in the *San Francisco Chronicle,* May 27, 1967, p. 28.
>
> a senior thesis entitled "The Renascence of the English Stage"
>
> Milton's "Lycidas"
>
> the "Dear Abby" column
>
> the short story "Epstein"
>
> Cole Porter's "Begin the Beguine"

When in doubt, use quotation marks rather than italics.

Foreign Terms

Underline only the most unfamiliar foreign words, not relatively common terms like ruble, fiancé, and prima donna. If a foreign expression is in quotation marks, underlining is unnecessary unless foreign and English words are mixed:

> "Le coeur a ses raisons que la raison ne connaît pas."
>
> "Oji wa doko desuka?" was the only Japanese he knew.
>
> BUT: "Time to go now, *nicht wahr?*" said Charlie.

Do not underline foreign proper names:

> The Comuneros and the Alumbrados joined forces in 1534.
>
> I met her at the Piazza San Marco.
>
> The Jeunesses Agricoles is a sort of French 4-H club.

The whole idea of underlining a foreign expression is to set it off clearly from the surrounding English. If quotation marks or capital letters accomplish this purpose, underlining is superfluous.

Emphasis

Underlining for emphasis is almost always a mistake; if you have this tendency, do your best to suppress it. Writers who underline for emphasis usually do so for one of two reasons. One is the desire to clarify a badly constructed sentence for the reader without going to the trouble of reconstructing it:

Clumsy

It was not so much the things she *had* done that made people annoyed with her as the things she had *not* done.

Rewritten

What she had done annoyed people much less than what she had not done.

The other is the desire to give writing some of the body English that intonation and gesture give to speech. Novelists sometimes use italics effectively in dialogue to convey kittenishness and other unprepossessing (or at best amusing) characteristics: "In *Holly*wood! How *mar*velous! What's he *do*ing?" exclaims a girl in *The Catcher in the Rye,* and we know immediately what sort of girl she is.

In nonfiction, it is usually the writer who ends up sounding foolish. Here are three examples of excessive underlining from student themes:

Dogged

I feel that punishment *can* be detrimental to a child's character or that it *could* cause damage to his psyche, but I do not think it usually *does.*

Strident

Some people *really* have *no idea* that their parents were ever young.

Girlish

His giggle nearly drove me *crazy,* and I thought to myself, "How am I *ever* going to survive this ghastly picnic?"

The temptation to underline can be very strong, particularly when you are exasperated at not being able to get the kind of emphasis in writing that comes so easily in speaking. But there is almost always a better way to get the reader's attention than by shouting at him. A change in wording, often a very slight one, will usually do the trick.

12
PUNCTUATION

Punctuation is partly a matter of rules and partly a matter of taste. Those who would make it altogether a matter of rules paint themselves into a corner: no rules can anticipate the millions of possible combinations of words that a writer may be moved to use, or his need to relate words in various ways for various effects, or his desire to slow down or quicken the reader's pace. Those who would make it altogether a matter of taste make an even more serious mistake. There are, after all, certain well-established rules or conventions for relating words, phrases, and clauses to each other, and most readers expect to see them followed, at least for the routine connections and separations.

THE PERIOD

A sentence or sentence fragment should end with a period unless it ends with a question mark or an exclamation point. A sentence occurring within another sentence must be punctuated according to the needs of the larger sentence: *She said "I am tired," but she didn't mean it / Bill spoke crossly (he was tired).* Periods are misused chiefly in making an illegitimate sentence fragment out of what is in fact properly a subordinate clause in the preceding sentence:

Wrong
> He always goes fishing on August 1. Which is his birthday.

Right
> He always goes fishing on August 1, which is his birthday.

Right
> He always goes fishing on August 1. That is his birthday.

Another difficulty is the converse of this last, namely, making what is properly two sentences into one:

Wrong
> He always goes fishing on August 1, that is his birthday.

Poor
> I was hungry, I wanted some lunch.

Right
> I was hungry. I wanted some lunch.

You may use a semicolon if a period seems too abrupt: *He always goes fishing on August 1; that is his birthday / I was hungry; I wanted some lunch.*

Notice that the sentence *I was hungry, I wanted some lunch* is labeled *poor*, not *wrong*. For many years this punctuation—known as the comma splice or comma fault—was anathema to teachers and editors, a sign of gross illiteracy; in some colleges it was grounds for an automatic F on a paper. But good writers persisted in using the construction, especially for certain effects of nervousness, tentativeness, and haste that no other punctuation could quite capture; and gradually it became acceptable in principle, however greatly abused in practice. The sentence fragment has come the same road, from outright rejection to qualified acceptance. Both constructions, the comma splice and the sentence fragment, have their unique uses. The problem is not how to avoid them altogether, but how to use them well.

A particular source of difficulty with the comma splice is the handling of direct quotations:

Wrong

"I am hungry," Marie said, "I want some lunch."

Right

"I am hungry," Marie said. "I want some lunch."

Right

"I am hungry," Marie said, "and I want some lunch."

The writer of the first sentence has punctuated it as if it were the third; that is, he has mistaken two sentences for one. In the second sentence, a semicolon rather than a period may be used; but a period is usual, perhaps because semicolons seem too formal for informal dialogue.

THE COMMA

The comma is the most important unit of punctuation; as befits this status, its usage is both complex and hotly disputed. The disputants come largely from two schools of thought. One is the old-fashioned or rhetorical school, which concerns itself with marking the natural pauses in a sentence as it might be spoken by an able speaker, and which accordingly caters to the ear. The other is the modern or logical school, which concerns itself with clarifying the sense units of a sentence and bringing out their proper relationship to one another; this school caters primarily to the eye. Current usage draws on the insights of both schools, with the modern school favored by most authorities in cases of out-and-out conflict.

The following discussion begins with some basics (use of the comma in appendages, series, compound sentences), moves on to more difficult matters (introductory phrases, parenthetical phrases, confluences), and ends with some general remarks on over- and underpunctuation. The basics are both the most important and the easiest to learn, but the later material is indispensable to a mastery of the comma.

Appendages

Most appendages preceded by a comma are also followed by a comma in running text:

Washington, D.C., is	June 14, 1967, was
Athens, Ohio, is	Sunday, June 14, was
The University of California, Berkeley, is	Trinity College, Oxford, is

The chief exceptions to this practice are *Jr., Inc.,* and academic degrees:

Alexander H. Jones, Jr. is	Textron, Inc. is
Robert Abrams, M.D. is	Unilever, Ltd. is

There are also, of course, appendages that take no commas at all:

John D. Rockefeller III is	8:30 A.M. is
The fifth century B.C. is	Queen Elizabeth II is

Still others take parentheses: 12:15 P.M. (EST) is.

All these last cause no problems. The thing to remember is the comma *following* appendages of the sort illustrated in the first examples above.

Series

In a list or series of three or more members, put a comma after every member but the last:

De Gaulle, Adenauer, and Churchill are mentioned most frequently.

Detectives were stationed in the drawing room, on the patio,
and in the garden.

Landis was a big, fat, slovenly, but extremely agile man.

One kind of confusion caused by omitting the comma before *and*
is illustrated by this sentence from the *New York Times*: "Bravo,
who is justly famous for his five wives, fourteen serious gorings
and love affairs with Hollywood actresses, was easily the favorite
of the first-nighters."

When two adjectives precede a noun, use a comma if they modify the noun independently, that is, if their relationship is an *and*
relationship. *A little, funny-looking dog* is a dog that is both
little and funny-looking. If the first adjective modifies the unit
composed of the second adjective and the noun, omit the comma.
A wild young man is a young man who is wild; we read *young
man* as a single unit. Most people find this distinction hard to
apply, and it is accordingly breaking down, with the no-comma
form increasingly favored.

Compound Sentences

In general, put a comma before the conjunction (*and, but,
or, for, nor*) in a compound sentence:

I went with Jack, and my sister went with Roy.

The reason was not altogther clear, but clarity was not altogether desirable.

Official invitations were sent to McNamara and Udall, and
several other Cabinet members were invited informally.

In such sentences, the comma enables the reader to divide the
sentence instantly into its two components. Sometimes it may eliminate false trails: for example, *Jack and my sister* in the first
sentence. But even where such ambiguities are no problem, as in

our second sentence, the comma offers the most economical possible clue to the sentence structure. The reader confronted with
an unpunctuated sentence like *The reason was not altogether
clear but clarity was not altogether desirable* must in effect hunt
down the turning point for himself and put in his own mental
comma, a labor the writer should have spared him.

Three exceptions may be noted. First, a compound imperative
sentence does not usually take the comma:

> Shoot and be damned.

> Go down to the drugstore and get some aspirin.

Second, a short compound sentence with an introductory adverbial phrase governing both verbs is sometimes more clearly
punctuated with a single comma after the opening phrase:

> In Montaigne's view, the Spanish Armada was good and
> Sir Francis Drake was bad.

> As my grandfather used to say, most people are fools and
> the rest are swine.

Third, the comma can be omitted in a very short sentence (except before *for*):

> I forgot and so did Mary.

> He went but she stayed home.

Opening Phrases

Many writers put a comma after an opening phrase or clause
only if it is seven words long or longer:

> In the Sudan there are very few large cities.

> Among the Wolagusi warriors of the northern Sudan, prop-
> erty squabbles are frequent.

> When Aunt Laura arrived the fun began.

> When Aunt Laura and Uncle Harry arrived, the fun began.

Other writers put a comma after all introductory phrases, regardless of length:

> In 1917, the Bolshevik Revolution occurred.
>
> When Lincoln died, the nation mourned.

These practices are equally acceptable; our advice is to choose one or the other and stick with it. In borderline cases let your ear be your guide. Single words like *however* and *incidentally*, short phrases like *for example* and *in other words*, are commonly followed by a pause in speech, and hence by a comma in writing. Other single words like *thus* and *therefore*, other short phrases like *in some ways* and *at one time*, are commonly followed by little or no pause in speech, and normally by no comma in writing. If you simply cannot decide, add the comma.

When an opening phrase or clause ends with a preposition, always add a comma to keep the preposition from being read as part of what follows it:

> To begin with, the overture is weak.
>
> From late June on, the beach is crowded.
>
> Whatever condition he is in, the office is no place for him.

Parenthetical Phrases

Place commas before and after a phrase or clause in a sentence that would be complete and coherent without that phrase or clause:

> Mother was amused, oddly enough, and so was Dad.
>
> "You are a fool," she said quietly, "and a coward."
>
> Only San Salvi, the home of Andrea del Sarto's *Last Supper*, was spared.

If such a phrase ends the sentence, a comma should precede it: *Oveta Culp Hobby was the first WAC colonel, if I am not mistaken.*

This convention applies only to truly parenthetical or nonre-strictive phrases, phrases that might as readily have been put be-tween parentheses as between commas: *Mother was amused (oddly enough), and so was Dad / The total amount was under ten dollars (I think).* The convention does not apply to defining or restrictive phrases, phrases that could not be placed in paren-theses without distorting the intended meaning. In the following sentences, a comma at any of the points indicated by brackets would be wrong:

> He was a friend of the poet [ ] Matthew Prior.
>
> Stores [ ] with high reputations [ ] often overcharge.
>
> A man [ ] who would do that [ ] would do anything.

Here the phrases following the opening brackets do not merely comment parenthetically on the preceding words but complete them. *Stores (with high reputations) often overcharge,* for ex-ample, would be nonsense; not all stores are in question, only *stores with high reputations.*

In some sentences, notably those in which a conjunction is fol-lowed by a longish introductory phrase or clause, the distinction between parenthetical and nonparenthetical expressions is hard to apply, largely because the ear and eye approaches to punctua-tion clash. The following sentences, with brackets where commas are possible, illustrate the problem:

> The repairman said that [ ] for all practical purposes [ ] the heating system could be regarded as adequate.
>
> Cromwell had made his preparations, and [ ] if the worst hap-pened [ ] he was ready.

The logical school would plump for two commas in each case, to telegraph the construction of the sentence clearly. The rhetorical school would omit the opening commas, on the ground that since there would be no pause in speech after *that* and after *and,* a comma after either would be irritating.

We incline to the rhetorical school. If the phrase is too long to leave without commas, put a comma at the end but do not slav-ishly add one at the beginning. Follow your ear. In the following sentences one comma seems adequate:

He said that *whatever the judge's decision might be,* he would accept it.

Mr. Abbott was at first inclined to sue, but *when he remembered the promise he had made,* he changed his mind.

Confluences

"Confluence" is Fowler's term for constructions in which two syntactically parallel elements, one following the other, flow simultaneously into the sentence somewhere short of its end:

Some, if not all [,] of the teachers were on strike.

His approach was more delicate, more ingenious [,] than mine.

Ney's courage was his foremost, perhaps his only [,] virtue.

Many people are opposed to, or at least annoyed about [,] the new zoning regulations.

The question is whether the comma shown in brackets should be added or not. We think it should be in all these cases, and in general, so as to connect the first element of the sequence more securely with the words that follow the second. Without the comma, the construction is not immediately clear.

Clarity

Consider the following sentence:

The headmaster of the academy would on ceremonial occasions refer to the school as a patriotic institution [,] and to the boys and the recent alumni as their nation's best hope for a glorious future.

Although this is not a compound sentence, to add the comma shown in brackets is a service to the reader. It converts an unwieldy mass of 34 words into two more manageable units of 17 words each; and it adds weight to the *and* immediately following it, which might otherwise appear to be coequal with the lesser *and* 4 words farther on. In the following sentences, the commas help to separate units of thought that might otherwise be muddled by the proliferation of *and*'s:

> There are two kinds of great men: men of wit and wisdom [,] and men of power.

> He distrusted the Americans [,] and the Canadians and the English as well.

Commas must not, of course, he added indiscriminately simply to break up a long sentence for the eye, or to distinguish one weight of *and* from another. In the following sentences it would be wrong to add commas at the bracketed points:

> Whether it is right or wrong to imprison for life a man [ ] who has committed four or more relatively trivial offenses [ ] has been for years a subject of debate in the law schools.

> Given the situation in Eastern Europe and Germany [ ] and Hitler's megalomania, war was inevitable.

Although the first sentence is long and some division of it for the eye would be welcome, none is possible; commas at the indicated places, by making the *who* clause parenthetical rather than defining, would make the sentence unintelligible. In the second sentence, the later *and* marks a bigger division than the earlier, but a comma would make the sentence lame. Neither sentence can be improved by adding commas; both must be left as they are or rewritten.

Over- and Underpunctuation

In the end, there remains a great region of discretion, in which writers may use commas or not as strikes their fancy. Within this region of discretion, some like their punctuation heavy, some medium, some light. We like ours medium.

A distinguished exponent of heavy punctuation is the *New Yorker*, from which the following extract is taken:

> During the morning, more or less as Toperih-peri had predicted, the Turkana, avoiding the pass, which, as Tope-

rihperi could have told them, was sure to be guarded, had entered the district between Morukore and Kalapata and, turning north instead of south, raided a neighborhood on the plain.

Here we agree with Fowler: "Any one who finds himself putting down several commas close to one another should reflect that he is making himself disagreeable, and question his conscience, as severely as we ought to do about disagreeable conduct in real life, whether it is necessary."

As an example of light punctuation, here is James Joyce's *Portrait of the Artist as a Young Man*:

> His heart trembled; his breath came faster and a wild spirit passed over his limbs as though he was soaring sunward. His heart trembled in an ecstasy of fear and his soul was in flight. His soul was soaring in an air beyond the world and the body he knew was purified in a breath and delivered of incertitude and made radiant and commingled with the element of the spirit.

Underpunctuation of this sort causes the very trouble, especially with *and*, that we have mentioned earlier as a reason for adding commas; many of Joyce's sentences have to be read a second time to be read properly. Where a Joyce leads we gladly follow, but few would be as quick to indulge a lesser writer of nonfiction.

In short, the extremes of heavy and light punctuation seem to us excessively hard on the reader: the first belabors him to no purpose; the second ignores his needs. We accordingly recommend medium punctuation. We close this section with a brief passage from the *New Yorker*, first as that magazine printed it, next as Joyce might have punctuated it, and finally as we would punctuate it:

Heavy punctuation

> But the people had delayed, and, seemingly by accident, had speared the ox just as the Turkana were coming in. Moreover, the ox, of its own volition, had run in a circle for almost a mile.

Light punctuation

> But the people had delayed and seemingly by accident had speared the ox just as the Turkana were coming in. Moreover the ox of its own volition had run in a circle for almost a mile.

Medium punctuation

> But the people had delayed, and seemingly by accident had speared the ox just as the Turkana were coming in. Moreover, the ox of its own volition had run in a circle for almost a mile.

THE SEMICOLON

The semicolon weighs about twice as much as a comma and half as much as a period. From its weight we may infer its two main uses: as a strong comma, and as a weak period. As a strong comma, it is used chiefly between phrases with internal commas:

> Those missing were R. A. Abramovits, the director of the bank; Elma Snyder, the chief cashier; and two tellers, Joseph J. Petrullo and Louise Kreps.

> Despite the news from the Far Eastern front, the invasion was not canceled; but weekend passes were given out, at least to some of us.

As a weak period, it connects independent clauses that are too closely linked to be separated by a period, or too short and undramatic to stand by themselves:

> Such sentiments are not rare; on the contrary, they are very common, especially among policemen.

> *Probe* is a good word for headlines; it takes less space than *investigate*.

An excess of semicolons gives writing a stuffy and pompous air. They are particularly inappropriate in dialogue, and should be used sparingly in any writing that aspires to be lively. In standard expository writing, however, the semicolon is indispensable. Its chief glories are two. As a strong comma, it makes possible the clear and orderly grouping of complex units, especially in series. As a weak period, it helps make possible the pleasing variation of pace and rhythm that is essential to good writing.

THE COLON

The colon was initially, many centuries ago, nothing more than a strong semicolon, halfway in weight between a semicolon and a period. Today, its use is very different. In Fowler's phrase, the colon "has acquired a special function: that of delivering the goods that have been invoiced in the preceding words." The colon in its modern use is the equivalent of *namely* or *that is*:

> I have seen every National League team but three: the Giants, the Braves, and the Mets.

> The message was clear: our views were not welcome.

> I remember her words: "May God forgive these men!"

As remarked in Chapter 11, a normally lowercase word following a colon should not be capitalized even when it begins a complete sentence, unless the sentence is either in quotation marks or especially formal or weighty.

There are three restrictions on the use of the colon. First, do not subordinate a colon to a lesser piece of punctuation. A colon yields only to a period: the goods it delivers must accordingly consist of all the words from the colon to the end of the sentence. Not some; all. The following sentences improperly subordinate colons to a comma and a semicolon, respectively:

> If he said: "I am innocent," he was lying.

> There were three men: Taylor, Adams, and Szyszniewski; and two women.

The first sentence can be fixed by simply deleting the colon, the second by changing the colon and the semicolon to parentheses or dashes. Alternatively, *There were two women and three men: Taylor, Adams, and Szyszniewski.*

Second, do not subordinate a colon to another colon; in other words, never use more than one colon in a sentence. The following sentences violate this restriction:

> The American delegation was distinguished: Johnson, Humphrey, and two Cabinet members: Rusk and McNamara.

> The vote was as follows: California: aye, 85; nay, 15; Oregon: aye, 60; nay, 7.

The colons in sentences like this are visually equal but syntactically of different weight; the writer knows how they dovetail, but the reader is left the work of sorting things out for himself.

Third, a period should not be subordinated to a colon. Consider the following examples:

> We hesitated to rent the house for several reasons: the garage had no roof. The bathroom had no fixtures. And the yard was piled high with junk.

> Remember two things: first, the dependent countries will be hard hit; their coal supply may be cut in half. Second, the rich industrial countries will benefit most.

In each example, the first period, which the reader expects will mark the end of what the colon has promised to deliver, marks instead a mere halfway point. The first example above can be fixed simply by changing the periods to commas. In the second, since there is no apparent way of delivering the invoiced goods without an internal period, we recommend making "Remember two things" a separate sentence.

THE DASH

The overuse of dashes gives writing a breathlessness that is rarely appropriate, and at worst a bogus dramatic quality. Dashes may legitimately be used for emphasis (for example, to bring out a paradox), or in pairs for long or complicated parenthetical insertions. They should not be used where commas would serve as well.

There are two dash constructions: the double dash (*Johnny ran away again—he does every Sunday—and was brought home by Uncle Bob*) and the single dash (*We were broke—not a penny left*). In a given sentence neither of these constructions may be used more than once, nor may the two be used together. The following sentences are all unacceptable:

Two double dashes

For Austria—Hitler's fatherland—not a penny; for Hungary—the cradle of freedom—all possible aid.

Double dash plus single dash

He loved his work—he lived for nothing else—but he was fired—no one ever knew why.

Two single dashes

Napoleon was his idol—the greatest man of the age; but Guizot was his master—the man of the moment.

The single dash, like a colon, governs everything from itself to the end of the sentence; the first of two dashes governs everything up to the second. It follows, among other things, that a dash and a colon should not be used in the same sentence. If dashes are used with a semicolon, the semicolon should be subordinate, as in this sentence from the *New Yorker*: "I found myself getting annoyed with Gould, not because of his gloating over the settling of old scores—that was all right with me; I believe in revenge—but because of his general air of self-satisfaction." Compare this sentence with the incorrect Napoleon sentence above, in which the sequence of punctuation is identical.

PARENTHESES

In the nineteenth century and earlier, commas and semicolons were used in immediate conjunction with dashes, but in modern usage no punctuation may immediately precede or follow a dash. Parentheses, which do not suffer from this restriction, can sometimes clear away ambiguities that pairs of dashes or commas cannot handle. In the following ambiguous sentences parentheses are the obvious remedy:

> The card featured Peterson, Gilroy—known as the "Terre Haute Tiger"—Morse, and Martin.

> Three vegetables—carrots, beans, and brussels sprouts—and two fruits—avocados and raspberries—were particularly vulnerable to "smog fallout."

> The men who went to England were Mr. Ward, the sales manager, and Mr. Tyler.

In the first sentence, parentheses rule out the possibility that we are talking about somebody named Gilroy Morse: *The card featured Peterson, Gilroy (known as the "Terre Haute Tiger"), Morse, and Martin.* In the second, parentheses bring order to an impossibly fragmented sentence: *Three vegetables (carrots, beans, and brussels sprouts) and two fruits (avocados and raspberries) were particularly vulnerable.* In the third, parentheses show us that two men went to England, not three: *Mr. Ward (the sales manager) and Mr. Tyler.*

Beginning writers make two errors in using parentheses. One is overusing them: their residual connotation of a whispered aside, or a trivial qualification, makes them irritating in large quantities. The other is making them enclose too long a parenthetical passage, especially one so long that the reader loses his bearings before he gets to the end of it. Make your passages in parentheses few, and make them short.

A sentence with parentheses in it is punctuated exactly as it would have been if the passage in parentheses had been omitted. The punctuation follows the closing parenthesis except when the passage consists of a whole sentence or several sentences, in which case the final period is placed inside the closing parenthesis. Thus:

> There were only two of us (me and my sister).

> (There were only two of us, me and my sister.)

QUOTATION MARKS

Quotation marks have two main uses: to set off passages attributable to speakers or writers other than the present writer at the time of writing, and to alert the reader to words or phrases that are being used in some unfamiliar or unusual sense.

Punctuation and Capitalization with Quotation Marks

Always put a comma or a period inside the closing quotation marks, a semicolon or a colon outside. This is one of the very few rules of writing that have no exceptions, and at the same time one of the rules most frequently violated in student writing.[1] For other punctuation, use your common sense: a question mark or an exclamation point, for example, goes inside the quotation marks if it is part of the quotation, otherwise outside. If a quotation runs to more than one paragraph, all paragraphs should begin with quotation marks, but only the last should end with them. With this exception, all quotation marks come in pairs.

Quotation marks following *said* and equivalent words may be preceded either by no punctuation, or by a comma, or by a colon, depending on the context and the writer's taste. The following sentences are all acceptably punctuated:

She said "I dare you!"

He replied, "I'll do my best, but I can't promise anything."

The ad read: "Experienced waitress wanted; age 21–45; short hours; no Sundays."

Single quotation marks are used exclusively for quotations within quotations: *"That's unfair," said his wife. "All I said was 'You're wrong.'"* Note that the closing quotation marks both go outside the period.

---

[1] Perhaps students are led astray by older books and books printed in England, many of which follow a different system for commas and periods. The system recommended here is all but universal in current American publishing.

If words in quotation marks make a full sentence, or a sentence fragment or exclamation used as a sentence, the first word quoted should be capitalized. Otherwise a normally lowercase word should be left lowercase:

> According to Schlesinger, Kennedy replied "Never again."
>
> When he said "Where's the food?" everyone laughed.
>
> Red Smith calls the 1927 Yankees "the greatest baseball team of all time."

Superfluous Quotation Marks

Quotation marks should be used sparingly to set off words and short phrases from their context. If you use a word in an unusual sense, or if you coin a new word for some special use, explain matters clearly the first time you use the word and thereafter write it without quotation marks. If you use slang, use it boldly; quotation marks make slang look defensive and self-conscious. In general, if quotation marks do not make any distinction worth making, drop them. In the following sentences, all the quotation marks should be eliminated:

> When I was little, my family called me "Bobo."
>
> "Communism" has a different definition in every country.
>
> I was feeling "blue."
>
> In the summer Mario offers "fresh vegetables" for sale.

As the last example suggests, quotation marks may be worse than superfluous; carrying as they do the connotation of something-fishy-here, they may actually suggest the opposite of what the writer intends. Thanks to the quotation marks, we get the feeling that whatever Mario is up to, it is something decidedly more sinister than selling fresh vegetables.

PART 3
THE RESEARCH PAPER

13

RESEARCH
AND NOTE-TAKING

Every educated person should be able, on assignment, to investigate a subject, evaluate the facts and opinions he encounters, and present his findings in a readable and orderly way, taking pains to acknowledge in approved form his sources of information. Training in how to do this is what the research paper is all about. It is a practical as well as an academic exercise. As our society grows more complex and organized, it places increasing demands on its educated citizens to sift out from the glut of available information the knowledge relevant to a particular need, and to report that knowledge reliably. The day when an engineer or a business executive could make it through life without ever reading or writing a word is fast disappearing. Professional men and women in particular are called on frequently to write papers and present them at professional meetings. Scoutmasters, PTA activists, even mere writers of letters to the editor, need training of the sort the research paper provides.

Some English courses now require a so-called critical paper rather than the traditional research paper. The critical paper is based on a relatively circumscribed body of information, usually literary or historical. This information is increasingly supplied in the form of "source books" like David Levin's *What Happened in Salem?*, a gathering of the testimony from five Salem witchcraft trials in 1692. There are now hundreds of source books—on novels and poems, on subjects like war, comedy, and tragedy, and on literary and historical figures. With their help, both the teacher and the student can conveniently become familiar with a body of knowledge, and emphasis can be given to discussion, thinking, and writing rather than to legwork, often futile, in the understocked college library.

For all its conveniences, however, this approach has its dangers. The library is your prime educational resource; you should know its treasures and pleasures early and not get detoured around them. Even if library work is not assigned, you would do well to supplement the source book with a look at some of the library's books and articles on your subject. It is better that you learn your way around the library as a freshman than as a junior —or as a middle-aged graduate lost in a labyrinth that should long ago have become familiar.

CHOOSING A SUBJECT

Even if you are using a source book, you will be asked to choose a subject. Your teacher's first advice will undoubtedly be to limit your subject to something you can handle in the relatively small space available (usually around five thousand words). With a book like *What Happened in Salem?* you might choose to compare one of the witchcraft trials with Arthur Miller's play *The Crucible*, or the Salem trials with the political "witch-hunting" of the early 1950's. Above all, the subject should be one you can respond to, that you can relate to and take a personal interest in. This does not mean that you should stick to what you know, or what you know you like; exploring new areas of intellectual interest, after all, is one of the rewards of the research paper. But there should be a point of contact with where *you* live, with your own experience. The trouble with the pre-source-book kind of research paper was precisely here: it tended to encourage topics like "The History of Badminton" or "The Introduction of the Camel into America"—topics of little interest to the student himself and chosen out of desperation or the *Reader's Digest*.

How do you know what you are interested in before you have investigated it? In a sense, of course, you do not; you must play some hunches. Let us assume that your teacher has assigned a conventional research paper and suggested the following general topics, which he would expect you to limit and refine:

Civil rights: law and reality
Freud as a social critic
Who wants fraternities?
Toward a safer automobile
The ethics of LSD

Let us say that you decide on the last topic. Perhaps you have read some magazine articles on LSD, or perhaps you even know someone who has taken it. At any rate, you are interested in LSD and would like to know more about it. The possibility of getting some of your information from interviews increases your interest.

RESEARCH: BOOKS

Your first step is to consult the card catalog in your college or university library. You look up "LSD" there and find a cross-reference card to "Lysergic acid diethylamide," the proper name of the drug. Under that head you find nine books entered, all published after 1961 and most since 1964—an indication of how recent public interest in the subject is. But since you have only five weeks for this research, you know that you will be lucky to read even one book thoroughly, so right at the outset you begin to limit your selection. You have the good luck to find seven of the nine books in the stacks. They are as follows:

Blum, Richard H., et al. *Utopiates: The Use and Users of LSD-25.* New York: Atherton Press, 1964.

Dunlap, Jane. *Exploring Inner Space: Personal Experiences under LSD-25.* New York: Harcourt, Brace & World, 1961.

Leary, Timothy; Metzner, Ralph; and Alpert, Richard. *The Psychedelic Experience: A Manual Based on the Tibetan Book of the Dead.* New York: University Books, 1964.

Masters, R.E.L., and Houston, Jean. *The Varieties of Psychedelic Experience.* New York: Holt, Rinehart and Winston, 1966.

Newland, Constance A. *My Self and I.* New York: Coward-McCann, 1962.

Solomon, David, ed. *LSD: The Consciousness-Expanding Drug.* New York: G. P. Putnam's Sons, 1964.

DeBold, Richard C. and Leaf, Russell C., eds. *LSD, Man and Society.* Middletown, Conn.: Wesleyan University Press, 1967.

Of this collection, you tentatively decide to concentrate on the Blum and Solomon books, since they are collections of articles by many authors and would probably give you a representative sampling of opinions and attitudes; and on the book by Masters and Houston, since it is one of the most recent and from a cursory inspection seems to be well written and researched. You reject *The Psychedelic Experience,* since it is primarily a handbook for those who intend to use the drug; you also reject *My Self and I,* after reading three chapters and taking a few notes on some of its illuminating appendixes, since it is primarily the account of a personal experience with LSD by a believer in it rather than by a disinterested observer. You reject *Exploring Inner Space* and *The Human Nature of Science* as seemingly too personal, too one-sided, or too far from your specific concern with the *ethics* of LSD.

Figure 1 shows the Library of Congress catalog card for the Blum book, as it appears in a library card catalog. Some of the items at the bottom of the card are of interest mainly to librarians, but you should be interested in most of the others. For whatever books you intend to use, you should immediately make out your own bibliography card (see p. 195).

Besides the card catalog, you may have occasion to use one of several useful guides to lists of books on certain subjects. One of

Figure 1

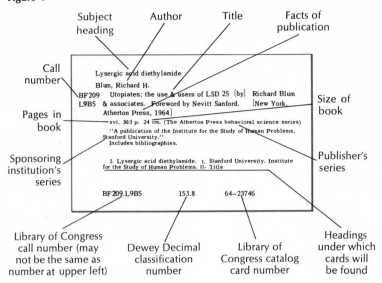

the best is the *Bulletin of Bibliography,* a periodical listing bibliographies on certain selected subjects and reviewing books containing bibliographies—often very amusingly. It so happens that the *Bulletin* has nothing on LSD; but it was worth taking a look. Another book to check is the annual *Bibliographic Index,* which lists recent bibliographies by subject for a great many subjects.

Still another book that can save you time is the *Book Review Digest.* Here, for example, are some entries for the book edited by David Solomon as listed in the BRD for 1965:

> The Solomon volume, though interesting, does not appear to be so significant a work [as *Ethics and Science,* by Henry Margenau, or *Heredity and the Nature of Man,* by Theodosius Dobzhansky, both BRD 1965]. Without doubt, however, the assault against the conventional consciousness by such agents as hallucinogenic drugs is a part of the radical

reorientation that science thrusts at us, a reorientation within which the church must minister if it is to minister at all.

Philip Hefner

Christian Century   82:368   Mr 24 '65   200w

The treatment of the subject is on the whole thorough and direct, each writer stating his position clearly. The questions that are left unanswered must necessarily exceed those answered, for the subject of "consciousness" itself must be scrutinized in the process of evaluating the effect of these substances on the person. Sophisticated lay readers will find this book especially informative. For special collections in psychology, psychiatry and the related disciplines.

Library J   90:258   Ja 15 '65   180w

One of the high points in the volume is the chapter contributed by Charles Savage, James Terrill, and Donald D. Jackson. These scientists are well versed in the use of LSD and similar compounds—and their knowledge of the behavioral and mental changes produced is worth study. Sanford N. Unger's description of LSD, mescaline, psilocybin, and personality change is thoughtful, authentic, and provocative.

H. A. Abramson

N Y Times Bk R   p 10   Ja 3 '65   750w

Clearly these reviewers see the book from their different points of view, the one as a churchman, the next as a librarian, and the last as a spokesman for the lay reader. The first reviewer in particular seems to offer something useful for your subject, so you make out a tentative bibliography card for the *Christian Century*, Volume 82, page 368, for March 24, 1965; "200w" means 200 words. The references that the third reviewer, H. A. Abramson, makes to specific authors in the volume seem to you valuable, so you make out a card also for the *New York Times Book Review*, page 10, for January 3, 1965.

Suppose now that you are trying to decide whether the Solomon book or Blum's *Utopiates* is better for your purposes. You find these two reviews of the Blum book in the BRD *Supplement* for May 1966:

Trick-titled, this is a mixed bag of articles by persons mostly competent to speak for their diverse points of view —sociological, psychological, pharmacological, legal, or whatnot. It is the whatnot which must bear the brunt of criticism here, though the sociologists and psychologists herein are wordy and trivial enough and sometimes stupefyingly dull, the psychiatrists correct, uncritical, and superficial, and only the law administrator level-headed, plausible, and pleasantly articulate. . . . The designation "consciousness expanding" for psychedelic drugs is itself question-begging. . . . Institutionalized modes of self-deception—advertising and mass "entertainment"— . . . are already Establishment enough for us not to need further pharmacological escape for the young. . . . The book is therefore inadequate even in propaganda terms.

Weston La Barre

Am Anthropol   67:595   Ap '65   1000w

[This] is a brave study in that the relevant data are hard to come by. No one knows the extent of the use of this drug nor the distribution of the users. This makes the location and justification of a sample, for what is largely an epidemiological study, a problem. It is an honest book in that problems such as these are faced directly and the solutions chosen are explicitly stated. . . . Although the data analysis is no more sophisticated than a comparison of percentages, some trends are clear and illuminating. . . . The repeated users . . . seek and appear to find a sense of "loving" or caring for others and a sense of meaning or of putting their lives into a context. . . . Tighter legal control of the drug will not dispel these needs. The book helps to highlight their importance and persistence and our failure to provide for them adequately in our driving, achievement-oriented world.

R. D. Cartwright

Am J Soc   71:576   Mr '65   650w

You have an interesting difference of opinion here. To the anthropologist the book is "inadequate"; to the sociologist it is a "brave study." Which can you believe? Since the first reviewer concentrated on the content of the articles, and the second on the techniques of data-gathering, you have no common ground on which to base a choice between them. But you make out a bibliography card for Blum anyway; a book that stirs such heat is worth looking into.

RESEARCH: PERIODICALS

You learn from an appendix in Constance Newland's book that LSD's psychedelic properties have been known only since 1943, when they were discovered by a Swiss chemist, A. Hofmann. Because the controversy about the drug's use has raged only since about 1963, you decide to concentrate mainly on newspaper and magazine articles published since 1961. If time permits—or if your quarry leads you on—you will go further into the past. You should know the main periodical indexes, even if some of them are not usable in your present research:[1]

Poole's Index to Periodical Literature (indexing many nineteenth-century periodicals)

Reader's Guide to Periodical Literature (covering popular magazines from 1900 to the present)

Social Science and Humanities Index, known until April 1965 as *International Index to Periodical Literature* (listing articles in a wide range of scholarly journals)

Remember that the *Reader's Guide* covers only popular magazines. You must consult the *Social Science and Humanities Index* or other guides for more scholarly articles.

Consulting the *Reader's Guide*, you find 24 articles listed under "Lysergic Acid Diethylamide" in the eight years from March 1955 through February 1963. In the next three years, from March 1963 to April 1966, you find 50 articles listed, 17 of them appearing in one month alone, June 1965. In the *International Index* you find

[1] There are vast numbers of other indexes and reference books as well. A good list of such books appears in Constance M. Winchell, *Guide to Reference Books*, 7th ed. (1951). And nearly every medium-sized and large college library has a reference librarian who specializes in helping people find information.

nothing listed under "LSD" or "Lysergic Acid Diethylamide," but you do find the heading "Hallucinogenic Drugs." Only one article is listed under that head between April 1960 and March 1965; but that one, which is not listed in the *Reader's Guide,* strikes you as possibly of great interest and importance.[2] The entry reads:

Do drugs have religious import?　H. Smith　J. Philos
61:517–30　O 1 '64

You then ask the reference librarian what other indexes might be useful. She suggests *Psychological Abstracts,* an annual collection of résumés of new books and articles in various psychological categories. You decide, since the abstracts are short, to start checking from the first mention of the subject, which turns out to be in 1948. One article is listed for that year: W. A. Stoll, "Lysergsäure–diathylamid, ein Phantistikum aus der Mutterkorngruppe," *Schweitzer Archiv für Neurologie und Psychiatrie,* LX (1947), 279–323. Since you have problems enough without tackling articles in German, you decide to skip this one; but you are interested to note that European interest in LSD apparently preceded American interest. You later discover that a Swiss firm is the only legal manufacturer of the drug.

As you continue your inspection, you find no articles in 1949–1950, 1 in 1951, 2 in 1952, 4 in 1953, 2 in 1954, 14 in 1955 (a significant jump), 20 in 1956, 11 in 1957, 15 in 1958, 54 in 1959 (clearly something happened that year), 23 in 1960, 5 in 1961 (things quieting down?), 14 in 1962, 13 in 1963, 26 in 1964, and 37 in 1965 (interest was apparently on the upswing). These figures may or may not give you important clues; at the very least they indicate when interest in the drug was most intense. Despite the highly technical nature of most of these articles, some may help to clarify the ethics of the problem. For example, whereas the early reports seem to emphasize the good effects of the drug,

[2] It is well to check both guides. The *Reader's Guide* has more on some subjects, the *Social Science and Humanities Index* more on others. For example, on "Imagery," listed in both indexes, the *Reader's Guide* for 1966–67 refers you to "Figures of Speech," where only one entry is listed; the *Social Science and Humanities Index* for the same period has 24 entries under "Imagery," plus cross-references under "Figures of Speech" to "Metaphor," "Synecdoche," "Clichés," and "Shakespeare."

in 1964 one finds an index entry listing "adverse reactions" to LSD, and in 1965 another listing "controversy about" LSD. Clearly, articles dealing with the medical pros and cons of LSD might be of use to you, and you make a note of them.

What are you going to do with all this material? You have already decided, so far as possible, to get your objective data on LSD from books, and to get arguments and expressions of opinion from periodicals. To be sure, you have also decided not to be rigid in these procedures: this is only a general working strategy, and you are ready to pick up diamonds where you find them. Here are a few of the articles listed in the *Reader's Guide* that seem to offer what you might want:

> Can this drug enlarge man's mind?   G. Heard   Horizon 5:28–31   My '63
>
> Danger in happy drugs   E. Mirel   Sci N L   84:138 Ag 31 '63
>
> Don't fool around with LSD   Sci Digest   54:42   S '63
>
> Dangerous LSD   Sci Am   214:54   F '66

In these abbreviations the first item is the title, the second the author (omitted for anonymous articles), the third the periodical title, the fourth the volume number followed by the page or pages, the fifth the date.

BIBLIOGRAPHY CARDS

As you gather lists of the books and articles you intend to read or consult (or better still, while you are consulting them), you should make out cards to be used ultimately in preparing the bibliography for your paper. A card for the Newland book will read as shown in Figure 2. The entry for this book that ultimately appears in the bibliography at the end of your paper will include everything on this card except information about collaborating authors, which is optional:

> Newland, Constance A. *My Self and I*. New York: Coward-McCann, 1962.

Figure 2

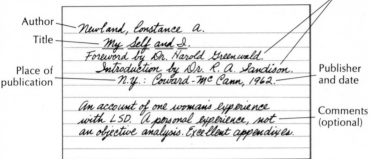

Collaborating
authors

Author — Newland, Constance A.

Title — My Self and I.
Foreword by Dr. Harold Greenwald.
Introduction by Dr. R. A. Sandison.

Place of
publication — N.Y.: Coward-Mc Cann, 1962. — Publisher
and date

An account of one woman's experience
with LSD. A personal experience, not — Comments
an objective analysis. Excellent appendixes. (optional)

Figure 3

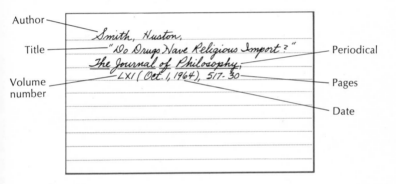

Author — Smith, Huston.

Title — "Do Drugs Have Religious Import?"

The Journal of Philosophy, — Periodical

Volume
number — LXI (Oct. 1, 1964), 517-30 — Pages

Date

Figure 3 shows a sample bibliography card for a periodical. Volume numbers may be given in arabic numbers rather than roman numerals, but be consistent one way or the other. A particularly handy style is "28:13 (May 1960)," meaning that the article begins on page 13 of the May 1960 issue of the periodical, which issue will be found in Volume 28 of the bound series in the library. The same style can be used for footnotes, in which case the second number is not (necessarily) the first page of the article, but the page being cited. Note that whenever the volume number of a periodical is given, "p." or "pp." is omitted before the page citation that follows.

The bibliography for this paper, in final typed form, appears on p. 207. Footnote citations, which differ in form from bibliography entries, are illustrated on pp. 209–212.

NOTE-TAKING

Although there are many ways of taking notes, the beginning researcher does well to keep his notes on 3 × 5 or, preferably, 5 × 8 cards.[3] There are, roughly, four kinds of notes he will take: quotations from his reading, paraphrases of his reading, statements of fact, and original ideas inspired by his reading. A word on these four.

In quoting material, make sure that you are quoting exactly, and that you indicate by ellipsis (. . .) any material omitted. Let us say you want to quote a statement from the Smith essay mentioned above. You are not sure you will use it, but it seems promising enough to save for future reference. Your card is shown in Figure 4.

Figure 5 shows a card paraphrasing a comment that did not

Figure 4

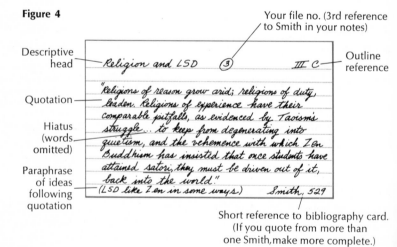

Your file no. (3rd reference to Smith in your notes)

Descriptive head

Religion and LSD ③ III C

Outline reference

Quotation

"Religions of reason grow arid; religions of duty, leaden. Religions of experience have their comparable pitfalls, as evidenced by Taoism's struggle . . . to keep from degenerating into

Hiatus (words omitted)

quietism, and the vehemence with which Zen Buddhism has insisted that once students have

Paraphrase of ideas following quotation

attained satori, they must be driven out of it, back into the world."
(LSD like Zen in some ways.) Smith, 529

Short reference to bibliography card. (If you quote from more than one Smith, make more complete.)

[3] Many teachers recommend using 3 × 5 cards for bibliography entries and larger cards for notes. This system has the virtue of keeping the two kinds of information clearly distinguishable.

Figure 5

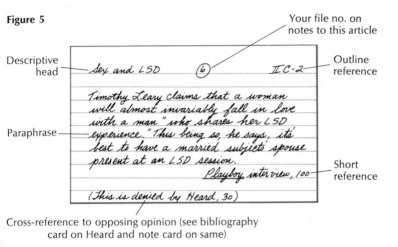

Your file no. on
notes to this article

Descriptive head — Sex and LSD ⑥ · II C-2 — Outline reference

Paraphrase —
Timothy Leary claims that a woman
will almost invariably fall in love
with a man "who shares her LSD
experience." This being so, he says, it's
best to have a married subject's spouse
present at an LSD session.
          Playboy interview, 100 — Short reference

(This is denied by Heard, 30)

Cross-reference to opposing opinion (see bibliography
card on Heard and note card on same)

seem worth quoting in full. The words "who shares her LSD experience" are in the original, and hence are put in quotation marks
on the note card to keep the author's words distinct from your
paraphrase. This is important; you must never appropriate words
or phrases that are in any way the unique creation or invention
of the author you are paraphrasing. For example, Leary elsewhere in this same article refers to "the psychedelic dropouts"
and to American society as "an air-conditioned anthill"; to use
such language in your notes without putting it in quotation marks
is to risk plagiarism (see pp. 214–219).

On your final paper it may strike you as awkward to put "who
shares her LSD experience" in quotation marks, since the phrase
is not particularly eloquent; at the same time, you may find it
hard to come up with a paraphrase that does not alter the
meaning. But you should deal with this possible difficulty when
you get to it, not anticipate it in your note-taking. Since you will
ultimately have to give credit in your text or footnotes not only
for material quoted verbatim, but for paraphrased material as
well—and since the credit you give will depend heavily for ac-
curacy and completeness on what you have written on your cards
—it only makes sense to bend over backward to keep things
straight in the note-taking stage.

Figure 6 shows a card containing a statement of fact. Since

information about the discovery of LSD can be found in encyclopedias and in nearly all books on the subject, it requires no special acknowledgment in your paper. You see no immediate use, perhaps, for this information in your outline, but it is so fundamental that you decide to record it anyway for probable use early in your paper.

The fourth kind of card records ideas that come to you as your reading progresses. These notes will contain some of your best insights; often you can transcribe them to your paper with little alteration. Make sure, however, that when you jot down reactions you record what you are reacting *to*. These notes will often be in the form of value judgments or conclusions; in your paper you will need evidence to back them up, and this evidence will usually be found in the printed passage to which your idea is a response. Figure 7 shows this sort of card.

Getting your information on these cards straight and complete from the outset will save you at the very least one thankless trip to the library to fill in what you left out and clear up what you got wrong. And very frequently it will spare you more: the confusion of writing weeks later from notes too sketchy to make sense of, or even the agony of hunting in vain for something you remember having seen but did not think to record. Don't count on your memory. When you see something you think you may use, write it down and write down where to find it.

Figure 6

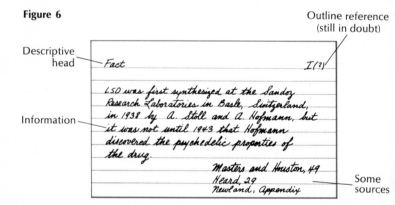

Figure 7

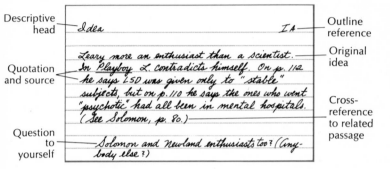

Descriptive head — *Idea*   *I A* — Outline reference

Quotation and source — *Leary more an enthusiast than a scientist. In Playboy L. contradicts himself. On p. 112 he says LSD was given only to "stable" subjects, but on p. 110 he says the ones who went "psychotic" had all been in mental hospitals. (See Solomon, p. 80.)* — Original idea / Cross-reference to related passage

Question to yourself — *Solomon and Newland enthusiasts too? (Anybody else?)*

THE OUTLINE

All the note cards shown in Figures 1 to 7 carry outline references: numbers tentatively keyed to your emerging idea of the possible structure of your paper. Early in your reading you sense the main issues with which you will deal and start to chart your course. You conclude that LSD has more or less profound effects in three areas—physical, psychological, and social—and you decide that these are the main areas of ethical controversy. Since these three categories cover a lot of ground, your paper may have to be far less ambitious than your outline. That is quite normal; outlines are made to be trimmed. The chief use of your outline is as a frame of reference for your notes, a way of keeping them in order; and as a way of limiting and focusing your project from the start. So, early on, playing on hunches and sparse knowledge, you jot down the following tentative outline plan:

Is LSD a Force for Good or for Evil?

Thesis: People who object to the use of LSD argue (1) that it can cause physical and psychological damage, (2) that it can lead to criminal and immoral (i.e. sexual) acts, and (3) that it can cause otherwise responsible people to escape into fantasy. Those who take the opposite view argue (1) that physical and psychological damage is caused not by the use of LSD but by its misuse, (2) that criminal acts have never been directly traced to LSD and that its sexual effects are by no means necessarily immoral, and (3) that the responsibility question revolves about what "reality" is, and whether the LSD experience does in fact lead toward reality rather than away from it.

From this plan, you work out a possible outline for your paper, entering items and ideas from your reading at the appropriate places.

Is LSD a Force for Good or for Evil: Outline

I. Are there medical-psychological reasons for or against the use of LSD?
- A. Claims are common that psychoses have resulted.
- B. Claims are equally common that remarkable therapeutic cures have been effected.

II. Does LSD lead to immoral acts, criminal or sexual?
- A. Cases of murder and suicide have been associated with the use of LSD.
  1. The Kessler case.
  2. Other case histories cited by Masters and Houston.
- B. Proponents claim that, rightly used, the drug actually saves lives.
  1. The therapeutic cure of Constance Newland.
  2. The deepening of religious, aesthetic, and personal experience as cited in Masters and Houston, Smith, Solomon, and Leary.
  3. The sloughing off of "robot existence" (Leary and Solomon).
- C. The argument over the sexual morality of LSD hangs largely on what generation the critics belong to, and their attitude toward sex in the first place.
  1. The tendency of certain conservative journals and critics to see LSD users as a "meta-

beatnik" fringe using LSD for kicks, indulging in orgies and "acid parties," etc.

2. The tendency of its proponents to see the aphrodisiac aspects of LSD as part of its goodness, and to see hostility to it as hostility to love and sex.

3. Differences of opinion, on both sides, over whether LSD really has aphrodisiac qualities.

III. Perhaps the most serious argument against the drug is that it encourages a philosophy of escapism.

A. The arguments made by Harvard authorities against Leary and Alpert hinged on this point.

B. The "aesthetic" appeal of LSD, so valuable to its proponents, tends to arouse suspicion in its critics—since those critics tend to connect aestheticism with escapism.

C. The "mystical" effects of LSD, like the aesthetic, are also controversial.

1. Can chemistry lead to religious experience?

2. Controversy over "The Miracle of Marsh Chapel" at Harvard in 1962.

IV. Conclusion.

This is a working outline, not a final one. It is neither a pure topic outline nor a pure sentence outline, but a mixture of the two; the sentences tend to become topics at the lowest level because you do not want to make firm commitments yet. (If you are asked to submit an outline of your finished paper, you should choose one or the other pure form: either all sentences or all topics, not a mixture.) Note that all subdivided topics have at least two subtopics. Why? Because if you divide something, you get at least two parts; a topic divided into one subtopic is an absurdity.

Now, with your research done and your tentative outline complete, you are ready at last to begin writing.

14

WRITING
THE RESEARCH PAPER

The outline with which the previous chapter ends is not the sort of thing a person can strike off after an hour's thought, or even after a weekend's reading. It has taken shape slowly in the course of two weeks or more of reading and thought on your part, and perhaps after one or more false starts. It is the product of your total information at the end of your research: that is, it represents what you know at the time you have stopped reading and are ready to start writing.

This does not mean that your working outline is necessarily the best possible one for your topic. Indeed, if you have done a thorough job of research, your outline will often be too broad in scope for the short or medium-length paper that you have been assigned. That is exactly what has happened here. But you have been more and more drawn to one aspect of the LSD question anyway: why people react so strongly, pro and con, to the drug. You decide to make this your topic, and you make a second working outline to reflect this new and narrower focus.

In the next five pages we give the beginning, middle, and end of the paper that may have emerged from the process just described, and the paper's bibliography.

LSD: DANGER OR BLESSING?

In the spring of 1963 two young Harvard psychologists, Timothy Leary and Richard Alpert, were dismissed from their academic posts-- "the first firings in Harvard's history."[1] Owing to their open and well-publicized experiments with psychedelic drugs (mainly LSD-25 and psilocybin), they had become an embarrassment to that liberal institution.[2] Mr. Leary, in violation of an agreement not to involve undergraduates in the drug research, was dismissed on May 27, and Mr. Alpert had been dropped earlier, allegedly for failing to show up for an honors program committee meeting.[3]

The heart of the trouble lay less in the use of the drugs themselves than in the unconventional nature of the methods Leary and Alpert used. One critic said: "Their program has an anti-intellectual atmosphere. Its emphasis is on pure experience, not on verbalized findings. It is an attempt to reject most of what the psychologist tries to do."[4] Another critic, Dr. Herbert G. Kelman, declared: "I question whether this project is carried out primarily as an intellectual endeavor or whether it is being pursued as a new kind of experience to offer an answer to man's ills."

These criticisms were typical. Leary and Alpert were challenging orthodox methods of scientific investigation. They became participants in

---

[1] Huston Smith, "Do Drugs have Religious Import?" The Journal of Philosophy, 61:517 (Oct. 1964).
[2] "Playboy Interview: Timothy Leary, a Candid Conversation . . . ," Playboy, 13:95 (Sept. 1966).
[3] Dan Wakefield, "The Hallucinogens: A Reporter's Objective View," in David Solomon, ed., LSD: The Consciousness-Expanding Drug (New York, 1964), p. 50.
[4] Alan Harrington, "A Visit to Inner Space," ibid., p. 75.
[5] Quoted by Wakefield, ibid., p. 49.

experiments and not, as scientists normally are, rigorously objective observers.[6]
For this reason, among others, many members of the scientific-academic
community found the experiments alarming, and they passed their misgivings
along to the public, which reacted to the drugs as it might to a new outbreak
of plague or Communism.

Leary and Alpert did little to calm the opposition. Rather, they deliberately cast themselves in the role of prophets and revolutionaries, as in this
statement:

The free expansive vision is molded into the institutional. Hardly has the institutional mortar set before there is a new cortical upheaval, and explosive,
often ecstatic or prophetic revelation. The prophet is promptly jailed. A
hundred years later his followers are jailing the next visionary. . . . The
university is the Establishment's apparatus for training consciousness-
contractors. The intellectual ministry of defense.[7]

This sort of messianic talk understandably annoyed their more conservative colleagues, and it has continued to do so, for Leary and Alpert by
no means went out of business after they were dismissed from Harvard.

But the most dramatic (and dangerous) part of this controversy is not
the academic debate, but the public outcry. Here the discussion is far less
informed and objective, and is daily being inflamed by newspaper writers,
politicians, and others. "There can be little doubt," writes Donald B. Louria,
"that the communications media bear a heavy responsibility for the spread of
LSD abuse."[8]

---

[6] Timothy Leary writes: "We are engaged in what is called a trans-
actional research design. The researcher sees himself as part of the transaction, and is an active learner in the experiment. Most American psychology today is only a description of what the researcher sees . . . . The
subject-object method of research is inadequate for studies of human consciousness." Quoted by Wakefield, p. 53.

[7] Harvard Review (Summer 1963), quoted by Wakefield, p. 50.

[8] "The Abuse of LSD," in Richard C. DeBold and Russell C. Leaf, eds.,
LSD, Man, and Society (Middletown, Conn., 1967), p. 41.

It seems fairly clear from the record that LSD, used therapeutically under medical supervision and not just for kicks, may be a powerful instrument for curing rather than creating psychoses.[19] The experiments of Dr. G. W. Arendsen-Hein of the Netherlands with "psychopathic criminals" seem to bear this out,[20] and LSD has been used, according to Masters and Houston, "to produce marked improvement in mentally retarded and schizophrenic children and also in psychotic adults."[21] The findings of Sidney Cohen[22] have also influenced the conclusions of Masters and Houston:

It seems safe to conclude that for certain kinds of patients, and also for certain kinds of therapists, these drugs have present value and an enormously greater potential value. However, . . . the psychedlics are of little use with highly dependent individuals (or) persons of low intelligence, or in the treatment of compulsion neuroses . . . . Thus the psychedelic drugs are no more a panacea for all mental ills than an agent that "makes people crazy." [23]

This sort of balanced statement should reassure the anxious. But it doesn't seem to, partly because, inflamed by prophets like Leary, they are more worried about the drug's sexual aspects than its physiological dangers. Leary called LSD "the most powerful aphrodisiac ever discovered by man"[24] --a misleading remark that he later qualified.[25] But such conclusions, far more calmly stated, are supported by Constance Newland (who was cured of frigidity by LSD) and, interestingly enough, by Cary Grant, who claimed, as a result of taking LSD, "Now I can truly give a woman love for the first time in my life, because I can understand her."

---

[19] See Humphrey Osmond, "A Review of the Clinical Effects of Psychomimetic Agents," in Solomon, ed., pp. 128-51, and the remarkable case study cited by Donald D. Jackson, "LSD, Transcendence, and the New Beginning," ibid., pp. 196-97. Newland makes the same point throughout My Self and I.
[20] Masters and Houston, p. 52.
[21] Ibid., p. 54.
[22] Sidney Cohen, "Lysergic Acid Diethylamide: Side Effects and Complications, "Journal of Nervous and Mental Disorders, 130:30-40 (1960).
[23] Masters and Houston, pp. 55-56.
[24] "Playboy Interview," p. 100.
[25] Louria, "The Abuse of LSD," p. 42.

Still, granted all these dangers, there would seem to be one greater: the danger of an uninformed or half-informed public setting out on a new witchhunt. It seems strange, given the sad state of our modern world, that any large body of public opinion should oppose cautious experimentation, under proper auspices, with drugs that offer such remarkable possibilities for human insight and happiness. But that is just what is happening. Politicians, responding to the public outcry, have already begun to pass laws that class LSD with addictive narcotics like heroin and opium. Leary was fined $30,000 and sentenced to 30 years' imprisonment for possession of marijuana (another non-addictive drug) in Laredo, Texas, as he was about to cross the border from Mexico. From any point of view, this is a vindictive sentence; and it is probably a sign of sterner attitudes to come. Macaulay once said that there was nothing quite so depressing as the British public in one of their periodic fits of morality. I wonder if they were any worse than the American public in a comparable state of mind.

BIBLIOGRAPHY

Blum, Richard H., et al. Utopiates: The Use and Users of LSD-25. New York: Atherton Press, 1964.

Cohen, Sidney, "Lysergic Acid Diethylamide: Side Effects and Complications," Journal of Nervous and Mental Disorders, 130:30 (1960).

DeBold, Richard C., and Leaf, Russell C., eds. LSD, Man, and Society. Middletown, Conn.: Wesleyan University Press, 1967.

"Epidemic of Acid-Heads: Post-LSD Symptoms after Non-Medical Use," Time, 87:44 (Mar. 11, 1966).

Heard, Gerald, "Can This Drug Enlarge Man's Mind?," Horizon, 5:28 (May 1963).

Leary, Timothy, "Playboy Interview: Timothy Leary, a Candid Conversation . . .," Playboy, 13:95 (Sept. 1966).

_____; Metzner, Ralph; and Alpert, Richard. The Psychedelic Experience: A Manual Based on the Tibetan Book of the Dead. New York: University Books, 1964.

Masters, R. E. L., and Houston, Jean. The Varieties of Psychedelic Experience. New York: Holt, Rinehart and Winston, 1966.

"Murder by LSD? Kessler Case," Newsweek, 67:29 (Apr. 25, 1966).

Newland, Constance A. My Self and I. New York: Coward-McCann, 1962.

Smith, Huston, "Do Drugs Have Religious Import?" The Journal of Philosophy, 61:517 (Oct. 1964).

Solomon, David, ed. LSD: The Consciousness-Expanding Drug. New York: G. P. Putnam's Sons, 1964. Containing:

Harrington, Alan, "A Visit to Inner Space," pp. 64-96.

Jackson, Donald D., "LSD, Transcendence, and the New Beginning," pp. 192-98.

Leary, Timothy, "How to Change Behavior," pp. 97-113.

Osmond, Humphrey, "A Review of the Clinical Effects of Psycho-mimetic Agents," pp. 128-51.

Wakefield, Dan, "The Hallucinogens: A Reporter's Objective View," pp. 40-63.

Watts, Alan, "A Psychedelic Experience: Fact or Fantasy?" pp. 114-27.

"Spread and Perils of LSD," Life, 60:28 (Mar. 25, 1966).

The selections illustrate the handling of quoted matter and footnotes. Observe also that the conclusion (p. 206) does not merely repeat or recapitulate what has already been said, but goes on to tell us what it means, what to make of it—in short, why the paper was worth reading.

FOOTNOTES

Common Abbreviations

In the footnotes and the bibliography of our LSD paper, we used the conventional abbreviations "ed.," "et al.," and "*ibid.*" The first stands for "editor," or more rarely for "edited by," as in "*The Complete Works of Shakespeare,* ed. George Lyman Kittredge"; in its meaning of "editor" it takes the plural "eds." Its most common use is to indicate a man who prepares for publication either an edition of another man's works (as Kittredge did Shakespeare's) or a work by many hands (like the Solomon book on LSD). As the preceding pages indicate, "ed." should be lower-cased and should not be enclosed in parentheses. The same abbreviation also stands for "edition," as in "3d ed." or "rev. ed."

"Et al." is an abbreviation of the Latin *et alii,* "and others"; it may be either roman or italic. The use of "and others" instead of "et al." is also perfectly acceptable. "*Ibid.*" is another abbreviation from the Latin; the full form is *ibidem,* "in the same place." (Purists object to "in *ibid.*" because this would translate "*in in* the same place," but most professional editors accept the expression anyway.) "*Ibid.*" is used to stand for as much of the immediately preceding citation as applies to the present one: thus if note 10 reads "*Paradise Lost,* Bk. 9, lines 115–121," note 11 might read simply "*Ibid.*" (meaning that the identical passage is being cited again), or "*Ibid.,* lines 122–123," or "*Ibid.,* Bk. 10, line 8."

Short Forms

In citing a book or article for the second time when the first citation does not immediately precede, some authorities recommend "*op. cit.,*" an abbreviation of the Latin *opere citato,* "in the work cited": thus "Smith, *op. cit.*, p. 89." Increasingly, however, writers and editors are abandoning *op. cit.* for a short-title system. Suppose Smith's book is the only work you cite by anyone named Smith; then your second citation (and any subsequent citation) need only read "Smith, p. 89." This is the style we recommend.

If you cite more than one work by Smith, say a book titled *The Situation in Southeast Asia* and a magazine article titled "The Hong Kong Refugees," you need give just enough of the title in your next citation to make it clear which of the two works you are citing: "Smith, *Situation,* p. 89," "Smith, 'Refugees,' p. 191." Finally, if you cite works by more than one Smith, you should distinguish between Smiths by adding first names or initials: "H. E. Smith, p. 89," "Margaret Chase Smith, pp. 10–12."

Checklist of Footnote Forms

Here is a brief checklist of the most common footnote forms:

Books

First reference to a book:

> [1] C. G. Jung, *The Archetypes and the Collective Unconscious,* trans. R. F. C. Hull (New York, 1959), p. 185.

> [2] Wilhelm Windelband, *A History of Philosophy* (New York, 1958), II, 447.

Immediately following reference to the same page of the Windelband book:

> [3] *Ibid.*

To a different page of the same volume:

> [4] *Ibid.,* p. 449.

To a different volume of the same work:

> [5] *Ibid.,* I, 25–26.

Later references to the Windelband book if it is the only work by this author cited:

⁶ Windelband, II, 450.

If other works by this author are cited:

⁷ Windelband, *History*, II, 450.

If a work by another author named Windelband is also cited:

⁸ W. Windelband, II, 450.

First reference to a book with two or three editors:

⁹ Cleanth Brooks, John Thibaut Purser, and Robert Penn Warren, eds., *An Approach to Literature*, 3d ed. (New York, 1952), p. 34.

Notice that "3d ed." is not included in the parenthesis; this is not parenthetical information, but an essential indication of which edition you are quoting from, since page 34 of the first or second edition might be very different from page 34 of the third. If there are four or more authors or editors, it becomes cumbersome to list all the names; it is conventional in this case to use the form "Cleanth Brooks and others," or "Cleanth Brooks et al."

Later references to the same book:

¹⁰ Brooks, Purser, and Warren, p. 80.

First reference to a chapter in a multiauthor volume:

¹¹ Joseph Frank, "Spatial Form in Modern Literature," in Robert Wooster Stallman, ed., *Critiques and Essays in Criticism, 1920–1948* (New York, 1949), p. 317.

Later reference to the same chapter:

¹² Frank, in Stallman, ed., pp. 323–25.

If there are many references to the Frank chapter in close succession, the citation can be abbreviated still further to "Frank, pp. 323–25," as was done in notes 6 and 7 of our LSD paper in citing Wakefield.

Reference to another chapter in the same book:

[13] Edmund Wilson, "Historical Criticism," in Stallman, ed., p. 457.

Reference to an edition of the works of a single author prepared by an editor:

[14] *The Works of Schopenhauer,* ed. Will Durant (New York, 1955), p. 456.

Even though your concern may be exclusively with what Schopenhauer says and Durant's name may mean nothing to you, it is customary to cite the editor's name so that knowledgeable readers will immediately understand that you are using the Durant edition of Schopenhauer rather than any of the other English-language editions.

Reference to an encyclopedia article:

[15] "Etruscan Pottery," *Enyclopedia of Crafts* (New York, 1923), IV, 239.

Reference to a quotation available to you only in a secondary source:

[16] Axel Munthe,*The Story of San Michele,* p. 245, as quoted in Karl Menninger, *Man Against Himself* (New York, 1938), p. 66.

Articles

First reference to an article in a periodical:

[17] Thomas S. Szasz, "Moral Conflict and Psychiatry," *Yale Review,* 69:564 (Summer 1960).

Alternatively, "LXIX (Summer 1960), 564" or "69 (Summer 1960), 564." Whichever of these forms you use, stick to it for all articles cited in your paper.

Later references to the same article:

[18] Szasz, p. 566.

This assumes that no other works by Szasz are cited in your paper. Otherwise use a short form: "Szasz, 'Moral Conflict,' p. 566." Reference to a book review:

[19] Joseph Frank, review of *Symbols and Civilization* by Ralph Ross, in *Sewanee Review*, 72:478 (Summer 1964).

Reference to an unsigned article in a newspaper:

[20] "Black Power vs. 'White Guilt,' " *San Francisco Chronicle*, Oct. 15, 1966, p. 6.

Note that a periodical's dates are in parentheses when they follow a volume number; that is because the volume number is enough to enable the reader to locate the periodical in a library and the date is accordingly extra information, given parenthetically for whatever interest it may be to the reader. Where no volume number is given, the date becomes essential to finding the reference; it accordingly appears between commas, like a volume number, e.g. "*New York Times*, May 11, 1967, p. 12."

What to Footnote

If you have trouble with footnoting and need a single central idea to get hold of, it should be the concept of *retrievability*. In the last analysis, the use of parentheses or commas, italics or quotation marks, is a matter of form, a convention to be learned for your own convenience and your reader's, but not the heart of the matter. The basic purpose of footnotes is to tell your reader where you got your information so that he can decide for himself how much faith to put in it. Did you get it from the *New York Times*, May 11, 1967, page 12? Well and good. Your reader can either accept the information as true, dismiss it as biased (if he feels, for example, that the *Times* is generally biased), or look it up for himself to see whether your source really says what you say it says and to find out what else it says at the same time. Had you not footnoted your information, your reader would not have had these options. He would have had to take you on faith or to dismiss you as talking through your hat. Given these alternatives, skeptical readers take the second.

In deciding what to footnote, it may help to imagine just such a skeptical reader, one disposed to question everything you say. He may ask, How do you know the Russian Navy is the world's third largest? Your footnote is your answer: " 'Red Sails in the Sunset,' editorial in the *Topeka News*, Dec. 10, 1965, p. 28." How do you know that President Kennedy was popular in Spain? "Letter from my brother, Lt. Eugene Hart, in Madrid, Sept. 20, 1962." Where did you learn that Mao Tse-tung was a lifelong champion of equal rights for women? "See Stuart Schram, *Mao Tse-tung* (Penguin Books, 1966), p. 43." Some sources are more trustworthy than others; your readers have the right to judge this matter for themselves.

Finally, make sure you include enough information in your footnote to take your reader straight to the right place if he wants to follow in your footsteps. "*Topeka News*, Dec. 10, 1965" is not enough; the reader may have to search through 50 pages of small type to find the passage you cite. "According to Stuart Schram" is not enough; Schram has written several books, each with several hundred pages, and dozens of articles. Even the citation of your brother's letter—not a recommended thing to do, by the way, but permissible where you have reliable information not readily accessible from more public sources—gains authority from the details. Your brother was a lieutenant, which means that he was not a child and probably not a mere tourist; and he was in Spain during President Kennedy's administration, which means that his information is firsthand. "Letter from my brother" alone would tell us none of this.

To repeat, the content of footnotes is more important than their form. Get your information down first. You can learn the conventions of punctuation, italicization, and so on later.

PLAGIARISM

Plagiarism is literary burglary. At its worst it involves an outright intent to deceive, to pass off another's work as one's own. More often, it is the result of carelessness or ignorance. But whether intentional or unintentional (the distinction is often hard to draw), plagiarism is always an error, and a serious one.

Whenever you borrow another writer's words or ideas, you must acknowledge the borrowing. The only exceptions are information in the public domain (Columbus landed in America in 1492; oxygen was orginally called phlogiston; oranges grow on trees) and opinions within anyone's range (*Hamlet* is a great play; time flies). Many undergraduates have trouble with this problem. Some react with an overnice conscience and footnote even dictionary definitions. Others change two or three words in a quotation and feel that they have somehow made it their own. The first practice is irritating, the second unethical. The right course is a generous and intelligent consideration of both the reader you are addressing (he will take 1492 on faith) and the writers you are using. When you use their words, their ideas, even their organization or sequence of ideas, say so—in a footnote or in the text. Claim as your own only what properly is your own.

The following examples may help to clarify the difference between legitimate and illegitimate borrowing. Here is part of the paragraph on Thoreau from Vernon Louis Parrington's *Main Currents in American Thought*:

> At Walden Pond and on the Merrimac River Thoreau's mind was serene as the open spaces; but this Greek serenity was rudely disturbed when he returned to Concord village and found his neighbors drilling for the Mexican War, and when authority in the person of the constable came to him with the demand that he pay a due share to the public funds. The war to him was a hateful thing, stupid and unjust, waged for the extension of the obscene system of Negro slavery; and Thoreau was brought sharply to consider his relations to the political state that presumed to demand his allegiance, willing or unwilling, to its acts. Under the stress of

such an emergency the transcendentalist was driven to examine the whole theory of the relation of the individual to the state.

The following examples will demonstrate some representative ways in which the passage, or parts of it, might be misused.[1]

Inadequate Acknowledgment: Outright Theft

When Thoreau was at Walden Pond or on the Merrimac River he knew considerable peace of mind, but when he returned to Concord this peace of mind was rudely disturbed. He came back to find his neighbors drilling for the Mexican War, a war he thought wrong, and when the constable came to him and demanded that he pay taxes to support that war, he balked. The war to him was a hateful thing, stupid and unjust, waged for the extension of the obscene system of Negro slavery; and Thoreau was brought sharply to consider his relations to the political state that presumed to demand his allegiance. In such an emergency, just how did the individual relate to the state?

In this example the writer has rephrased Parrington's first and last sentences, using some of his own words and some of Parrington's. He has made enough other minor modifications so that no full sentence of the original remains intact. But these trivial exceptions apart, he has copied the original word for word. His intent to deceive is clear, the more so from his inept camouflaging of the first and last sentences. Had the writer put the directly quoted portion in quotation marks (or made it a single-spaced inset quotation) and footnoted it, he would not be guilty of plagiarism. He would have made it clear that he was contributing nothing of his own to the discussion, but was simply inviting us to listen to Parrington. As it is, however, he is passing off

---

[1] For simplicity we omit footnotes from the following discussion. A truly adequate acknowledgment to Parrington would of course include a footnote giving his name in full, the title of his book, the city and date of publication, and the page number or numbers from which the writer's information is drawn.

Parrington's words as his own, pretending to a knowledge (and style) he doesn't have. This is an inexcusable moral error.

Inadequate Acknowledgment: Paraphase

At Walden Pond and on the Merrimac River Thoreau's mind was calm as the open spaces; but this serenity was rudely disrupted when he returned to Concord and discovered his neighbors drilling for the Mexican War, and when the constable, representing authority, came to him and demanded that he pay his share of taxes for the war. He regarded the war as hateful, stupid, and unjust, and waged to extend the slave system, which he opposed. This experience caused Thoreau to reconsider sharply the whole question of the relations between the individual and the state.

This example represents only a negligible improvement on the last. The writer has made more changes in wording than the outright plagiarist, but has contributed no more of his own thinking or wording. Every idea in his paragraph and most of the words and phrases are taken directly from Parrington without acknowledgment. Though the writer has avoided copying whole clauses word for word, he is plainly guilty of plagiarism.

But what is a writer to do in such a case? Clearly it is impossible to enclose a paraphrase in quotation marks, for quotation marks may be used only where an author's words are reproduced exactly and completely. How then can plagiarism be avoided here? The best way is by running acknowledgments in the text, as in the following example.

Adequate Acknowledgment: Paraphrase

According to Vernon L. Parrington, the "Greek serenity" of Thoreau's mind at Walden Pond and on the Merrimac River was rudely disturbed when he returned to Concord and found his neighbors drilling for the Mexican War, and when the town constable, representing authority, came to him asking that he pay his share of taxes for the war. Thoreau regarded the war as stupid, unjust, and designed to extend the slave system, which he opposed. Now his direct experience of its effects, says Parrington, caused Thoreau sharply to reconsider the whole question of the relation between the individual and the state.

In the two sentences in which Parrington's name appears, it is clear that the ideas are his. But what about the other sentence? Has the writer slipped in something of Parrington's as his own? An argument can be made either way; but since in general the writer is being straightforward about his debt, there can be little difficulty about giving him the benefit of the doubt.

Decisions like this are not always easy, since too many phrases like "Parrington says" or "Parrington goes on to point out" make writing graceless. If the claims of honesty and grace conflict, be honest first, but try also to be as graceful as you can. Every last comma need not be acknowledged. In the above passage, for example, only one phrase was placed in quotation marks even though other words—among them *stupid* and *unjust*—were used by Parrington. Since it was inconvenient to quote *stupid* and *unjust* in the exact phrasing used by Parrington, and since it would have seemed fussy to put *stupid* in one set of quotation marks and *unjust* in another, the writer decided that honesty was adequately served by his two general acknowledgments to Parrington. We think he was right.

Inadequate Acknowledgment: Forgetfulness

When Thoreau returned to Concord, he was shocked to find his neighbors drilling for the Mexican War. It was still worse when the government asked him to pay taxes for a war he didn't believe in, a war he considered hateful, stupid, and obscene. At Walden and on the Merrimac his thoughts had taken on an almost Greek serenity; now he was confronted with the dilemmas of real life. He did not hesitate. Putting aside his transcendental notions, he plunged into an examination of what the individual may legitimately be said to owe the state.

This writer has clearly mastered his material and knows what he wants to say. He has abandoned Parrington's sequence of ideas; he has added his own emphases; and his phrasing is largely his own. But in questions of acknowledgment, "largely" is not enough. Three bits of undigested Parrington remain: "his neigh bors drilling for the Mexican War," "hateful, stupid, and ob scene," and "Greek serenity." The first of these phrases is neutral enough to make its borrowing forgivable. The other two, and especially "Greek serenity," are not.

Given the writer's general performance, it seems likely that he has unconsciously drawn on his memory for the words in question, or perhaps that he has worked from slovenly note cards. He is nonetheless guilty of dishonest borrowing. At the very least he should have put "Greek serenity" in quotation marks and acknowledged a general indebtedness to Parrington.

Adequate Acknowledgment: Mature Borrowing

There was a time when writers paid no attention to plagiarism. Chaucer and Shakespeare, for example, borrowed incessantly from other writers without acknowledgment, and never gave the matter a thought. But in the last century or so Western writers have taken an increasingly proprietary attitude toward their own work, and it is now considered common decency to give a writer credit for the use of his ideas, his words, or even the sequence in which his ideas are presented.

Many people who do not write much themselves feel that there is something natural or inevitable in a writer's sequence of ideas— they might feel that Parrington, for example, starting with Walden Pond and ending with the state, was simply recording the sequence established by history. But of course he was doing no such thing. History is written by historians; the shape of past events is the shape of the minds that set down these events. And so it is with the Parrington passage: what makes it useful is not so much its individual ideas and phrases as Parrington's general authority and intelligence.

If, therefore, you begin with Walden Pond and end with the individual and the state—no matter what words you use in between—you must make a bow to Parrington somewhere along the line and thank him for his help. This is not only elementary honesty, but elementary courtesy. Here is such a passage:

Vernon Parrington pictures Thoreau at Walden as knowing a kind of "Greek serenity" that was rudely shaken when he returned to Concord and found his neighbors drilling for the Mexican War. Yet the more one studies Thoreau, the more one wonders whether this contrast between the serene recluse and the embattled citizen is a valid one. We are increasingly knowledgeable these days about the hostility implicit in an act, any act, of withdrawal. Parrington implies that Thoreau was driven by events to take a political position, and in a sense he is right. But was there no political content in his move to Walden?

Here the writer has used Parrington, but not exploited him; Parrington has helped him, and he admits as much in the very act of taking issue with one of Parrington's ideas. Such a writer doesn't want to steal and doesn't have to. The words of others are not some sort of mask or false identity that he puts on to deceive the world; they are elements in his search for truth. Why not honor those who have gone before and done good work? We need all the help we can get. In the search for truth we have too few ideas, not too many; if we are honest men, we should let the world know what lights we are following and who lit them.

INDEX TO CURRENT USAGE

The following alphabetical sequence mixes words (e.g. *overall*) and categories (e.g. ANTECEDENT PROBLEMS), following the precedent of the first and greatest dictionary of current usage, Henry Watson Fowler's *Modern English Usage* (1926). Owing to space limitations, the present sequence is necessarily superficial. It should be supplemented as necessary by reference to Fowler, preferably in the second edition (1965), which was thoroughly revised and updated by Sir Ernest Gowers; or to Wilson Follett's *Modern American Usage* (1966), the best of several efforts to compile an American Fowler.

a, an. (1) *A* should be omitted after *kind* and *sort*: not *What kind of a fool do you take me for?* but *What kind of fool*; not *This must be some sort of a trick,* but *some sort of trick.* (2) *A half a* is illiterate: either *a half dollar* or *half a dollar,* not *a half a dollar.* (3) *Historic, historical,* and *historian* are properly preceded by *a,* not *an*; the sames goes for *heroic* and *humble.* The use of *an* before these words is an affectation. (4) Distinctions of number often depend on the proper use of *a.* For example, *a secretary and treasurer* is one person who handles both jobs; *a secretary and a treasurer* are two people. Such locutions as *a man and woman* and *a hat, coat, and tie,* by leaving out articles after the first, make a false, unpleasing, and sometimes puzzling amalgam out of elements inherently separate.

acronyms. See INITIALS AND ACRONYMS.

actually. The use of *actually* as a mere intensifier in sentences like *I was actually afraid to speak* and *She actually begged him to stop* is rarely effective in making a description more vivid, and may lead to confusion with the proper use of *actually,* which is to contrast the facts with some incorrect prediction or version of them.

ADVERB CONFLICT.   When a sentence begins with an adverbial phrase, every verb in the predicate of the sentence proper (independent clause) is modified by that phrase. Thus in *When I am sick, I get moody and snap at people* the opening phrase properly modifies both *get* and *snap*. A problem arises when the second verb is incompatible with the opening phrase. This often happens when a conflicting adverb is introduced, e.g. *In 1966, he taught at Harvard and returned to Yale a year later*. Clearly the man cannot have returned to Yale simultaneously in 1966 and 1967. The solution here, and to adverb-conflict puzzles in general, is either to introduce a second subject (*In 1966, he taught at Harvard; he returned to Yale a year later*) or to subordinate the opening phrase clearly to the verb it belongs with (*He taught at Harvard in 1966, and returned to Yale a year later*). In *By and large Lewis's opinions strike the reader as reasonable and are invariably thought-provoking*, change to *reasonable, and they are*.

affect, effect.   The verb *affect* means to influence or concern; the verb *effect* means to bring about or cause. A decision may *affect* your future, or *effect* a change in your way of life; taking some pills may *affect* your blood pressure, or *effect* your recovery. The noun *affect* (pronounced *AFFect*), a technical term in psychology, is rarely encountered; for all noun meanings but this one, the word is *effect*.

aggravate.   This word, which for centuries meant to make worse or more burdensome, has come in recent years to mean exasperate, irritate, or annoy, as in *I find her very aggravating*. Purists shrink from this usage, but its triumph is no longer in doubt.

all right, alright, alrite.   The first form is correct. The second is a corruption of 50 years' standing but no status. The third is a cute spelling (see CUTE SPELLINGS) with no past or future.

allude.   An allusion is an indirect reference or hint; for example, you may allude to a raucous Christmas party by asking a participant if he is still full of Christmas cheer, or you may allude to love by invoking Venus or Cupid. *Allude* is misused when the reference is direct, as in *I allude to your speech of February 24* or *I do not understand your allusion to "No. 4 tacks."* Change to *refer* and *reference*.

along with takes the singular: *Mark, along with his two brothers, has been seeing Dr. Bennett regularly.*

although, though. These words are interchangeable except in such fixed expressions as *even though* and *as though*, and in inverted constructions like *Excellent though his performance was.*

among. See BETWEEN (1).

an. See A, AN.

ANACHRONISMS. One mark of a good writer is sensitivity to time and history in the choice of words. To say *Louis XIV was a teen-ager when he assumed full power* is technically correct but impossibly jarring: *teen-ager* is a twentieth-century word for a twentieth-century phenomenon. In *Here Donne uses a technique that is one of his trademarks* a great poet is diminished by the clatter of modern merchandising. Difficulties of this sort come down to a matter of connotation and denotation, on which see pp. 140–142.

and. (1) It is perfectly permissible to begin a sentence with *And*. (2) The precision of *and/or* may make it useful for legal documents, but its bizarre appearance and legalistic connotations make it unsuitable for any writing that aspires to please. Use *and* or *or*; if neither works, write *X or Y, or both*. (3) When a series of two or more elements is referred to by a plural noun, the proper conjunction is *and*, not *or*. *Or* should be *and* in the following rare lapse by Follett: "Others may be influenced by newspaper shortenings, which produce such unidiomatic phrases as *long-drawn recital, stave attack,* or *put in jail on charge he threatened president.*"

ANTECEDENT PROBLEMS. (1) An antecedent should be a clear noun, noun phrase, or noun clause, with the exception listed below for *which, this,* and *that*. An antecedent cannot be a verb: *The court tried to subpoena him but he would not ac-*

cept it should read *accept the subpoena.* An antecedent cannot be an adjective: the feature story headlined *feminine ideas on where they want to live* should have read *women's ideas.* This error is particularly common with adjectives of nationality: *a Japanese view of their attack on Pearl Harbor* should read *Japan's attack.* Finally, an antecedent cannot be negative: *Although nothing important happened, it impressed me deeply* should read *I was deeply impressed.* (2) *Which, this,* or *that* may refer to a preceding idea that is not grammatically a noun or noun clause, provided the idea is completely clear. In *She is beautiful, which is more than you can say for Ada,* the idea is clear and the construction is accordingly admissible. In *We needed a flagpole, which was a problem,* it is not clear what the problem was and the sentence should be rewritten. In *His mother was happy; that was all he cared about,* the idea is clear and *that* is correct; in *Eileen was often angry, and this irritated her friends,* it is not clear whether *this* stands for her anger or its frequency. (3) *Such* and *this* are not synonyms. *Such a man* means "a man of this sort"; *this man* means "the man just mentioned." *Such* should be *these* in *He would eat ice cream or sherbet, but even such desserts he did not really enjoy.* (4) A pronoun should not precede its antecedent unless its meaning is immediately clear and any other construction would be demonstrably awkward. In *When his first play was performed, Shakespeare was 28,* either reverse the sequence of clauses or change *his* to *Shakespeare's* and *Shakespeare* to *he.*

See also NEGATIVE PROBLEMS (2).

anymore is now one word, not two: *We cannot go there anymore.* This relatively recent change, which brings *anymore* into line with such long-standing one-word forms as *anywhere* and *anything,* applies only to the meaning "any longer"; in other conjunctions of *any* and *more* they remain separate words, e.g. *I could not ask for any more. Any time* remains two words in all uses.

as. (1) *As to* should be restricted so far as possible to emphatic constructions like *As to my so-called duplicity, I deny it.* (In this use *as to* is interchangeable with *as for.*) *As to* should be used most sparingly, if at all, as a straight preposition. *A clue as to* is an error for *a clue to*; *the question as to whether* should be *the question whether*; *doubts as to* might better be *doubts about*. Use *as to* only when you are convinced that no other preposition will serve your purpose as well.

(2) *As well as* takes the singular: *The doctor, as well as his nurse and his receptionist, is involved. As well as* cannot follow *both*: in *I invited both Henry as well as Ann and Bill*, delete *both*.

(3) Prepositional constructions in *as* must be properly related to the rest of the sentence. *As a man of experience, we would welcome your opinion* violates this rule by relating the *as* clause to *we*, an impossibility.

(4) Sentences requiring two *as*'s cannot get by with one. Technically speaking, an *as* has been swallowed at the indicated place in each of the following sentences: *"Old Foxy," as he referred to himself /, had won again. The cheese was as good / or better than Boursault. I thought of Mary not so much as my aunt / as my friend.* Since adding *as* at any of the slashes would be awkward, rewrite: *as he called himself, as good as Boursault or better, not as my aunt but as my friend.*

(5) Good writers do not use *as* to mean *because*. In *As Jane was ill, we did not go*, change *as* to *since* or *because*.

(6) *As* is not idiomatic with *consider, appoint, name, elect,* and *brand*. In *The senators considered the administration's behavior as an outrage*, delete *as* or change *considered* to *regarded*; in *He was appointed as district attorney in 1961* and *McCarthy branded him as a traitor*, delete *as*.

(7) *As* for the Latin *qua*, meaning in the capacity or character of, is overused by literary critics in such expressions as *Milton as polemicist* and even *Speaking as polemicist, Milton*. Since the shade of difference between *as* and *as a* in these phrases can rarely be discerned, the popularity of the newer and more jarring *as* construction is hard to understand.

On *like* and *as*, see the text, pp. 115–117.

based on. *Based on past experience, we expect a sellout crowd* is not an acceptable sentence. *Based on*—unlike *according to, seeing that,* and other participle compounds (see text,

p. 107)—has not made the full transition to prepositional status; when used as it is here, it must modify the first noun in the independent clause. Since this is rather a tall order, change *based on* to *on the basis of* or simply *from.*

because. *Because* can lead to puzzles when carelessly used with *not.* *She did not go because she was ill* could mean either that she was too ill to go, or that she went (e.g. to the hospital) not because she was ill but for some other reason. The first meaning can be brought out unmistakably by adding a comma before *because*; the second meaning requires rewording, e.g. *It was not because she was ill that she went.* See also REASON IS BECAUSE.

beside, besides. *Beside* is a preposition meaning by the side of and (by extension) apart or separated from, as in *beside oneself* and *beside the point.* *Besides* is a preposition meaning in addition to, as in *She needs something besides pills,* and an adverb meaning moreover, as in *Besides, the wench is dead.*

between. (1) *Between* properly takes as its object two elements, or any number of elements thought of as relating or interacting in pairs, e.g. *The Constitution regulates relations between the states.* *Among* properly takes as its object more than two elements not thought of as interacting in pairs, e.g. *The book is about his life among the savages.* This distinction is not always easily made; when in doubt, use *between.* (2) *Between* must be followed either by a plural noun or by a plural construction in *and.* In *Negro family earnings grew between 1960–1964,* change to *between 1960 and 1964.* In *Between 30 to 50 persons are killed annually in hunting accidents,* change to *Between 30 and 50* or *From 30 to 50.* In *The choice was between going to jail or incriminating Larry,* change to *and.* In *He soaked his foot in ice water between each act,* change to *between acts* or *after each act.* In *differences between the hospital in Akron and Canton,* the *and* is in the subordinate *in* phrase and does not make a true plural out of *hospital*; change to *and the one in Canton.*

biweekly, semiweekly. *Biweekly* means every two weeks, *semiweekly* twice a week. *Biweekly* is often misused for *semiweekly,* and some dictionaries, indifferent to the confusion they are authorizing, accord both meanings full status. The same is true of *bimonthly* and *semimonthly*. For years there are three words: *biennially* means every two years; *biannually* and *semiannually* both mean twice a year, with *semiannually* having the stronger suggestion of every six months. Our advice is to use the *bi-* forms for every two weeks, etc., and the *semi-* forms for twice a week, etc.; this means ignoring the newer meanings of *biweekly* and *bimonthly* and forgetting *biannually* altogether.

blond, blonde. Use *blonde* as the noun for a woman, *blond* as the noun for a man, and *blond* as the adjective always: *Her hair is blond.*

both . . . and. What follows *both* should be parallel and grammatically equivalent to what follows *and*; see the text, pp. 103–105. For *both . . . as well as,* see AS (2).

bureaucrat is not a neutral synonym for official. It is a disparaging word, implying narrowness, stuffiness, or rigidity.

case is often superfluous. *In Mary's case, there were two problems to be solved* might better read *Mary had two problems to solve,* and *In the case of the senior class gift, we tried hard to raise money* might better read simply *We tried hard to raise money for the senior class gift.* Use *case* when you must; avoid it when you can.

CLASHING VALUES. Avoid marrying words with no tolerance for each other's company. Three classes of such pairs may be distinguished: absolutes subjected to comparison or appraisal (*almost unique, more perfect, rather exhaustive*); absolutes with redundant modifiers (*sufficiently adequate, general consensus, dead corpse*); and words of great force qualified by tepid words (*slightly overwhelming, somewhat dreadful, a bit vile*). In the last class one sometimes finds the opposite phenomenon; thus a Japanese travel brochure describes Nikko as *unspeakably pleasant.* Combinations of opposites may occasionally be used deliberately to achieve a striking effect, as in the poetic device of oxymoron with its *sweet bitterness* and *harmonious discord*; but a little of this sort of thing goes a long way. See also ANACHRONISMS.

classic, classical.   Use *classical* to mean relating to ancient Greek and Roman history and literature, or the equivalent. Use *classic* for everything else: e.g. outstandingly important (*a classic battle*), authoritative (*Blackstone's classic pronouncement*), model (*a classic golf course*), memorable (*a classic blunder*), notably representative (*a classic case of mumps*).

CLICHÉS may be divided into four categories—stale metaphors, familiar pairs, vogue words, and jargon—but it should be understood that these categories are not easily distinguished from each other, and that many clichés put in one class for our purposes here might as readily have been put in another. Stale metaphors (*rolling stone, brass tacks*) are discussed in the text, pp. 53–54. Familiar pairs (*felt need, far and wide, tender mercies*) are discussed on pp. 147–148. For the other two categories, see JARGON and VOGUE WORDS.

COMMA PROBLEMS are discussed in the text, pp. 167–176.

COMMA SPLICE.   In *He did not shrink from the charge, he welcomed it,* the headlong effect attained in joining two independent clauses with a comma is unattainable by the period, the semicolon, or the conjunction. This being so, there can be no objection to the so-called comma splice when this effect is sought, and when the two clauses are relatively short and closely connected in meaning. The comma splice is justly condemned when either clause is long or complex, when the two clauses are not closely connected in meaning, or when the breathless effect is inappropriate or pointless. In *K. felt no inclination even to make a retort, the girl's intentions were no doubt good,* the comma should be a semicolon. Other examples are given in the text, pp. 166–167.

compare.   (1) To compare X *with* Y is to appraise or measure X in relation to Y: *I compared my notes with hers.* To compare X *to* Y is to assert a categorical similarity between the two: *You are wrong to compare Nkrumah to Nasser.* The distinction is not always clear; when in doubt, use *with.* (2) The quantities linked by *compare* should be comparable. In *My allowance was high compared with Sally,* they are not; change to *Sally's.*

COMPARISON OF ABSOLUTES. See CLASHING VALUES.

compose, comprise. Compose means to make up; *comprise* means to be made up of, to take in, to include or contain. The parts compose the whole; the whole comprises the parts. Since *comprise* is the rarer word and the harder to use correctly, and since its exact meaning is conveyed by the passive use of *compose*—i.e. *comprises = is composed of*—why not use *compose* in both senses and forget about *comprise?*

consensus. Thus spelled (not *-census*). A *consensus* is by definition general, and by definition has to do with matters of opinion or belief. Hence *general consensus* and *consensus of opinion* are redundant expressions. See CLASHING VALUES.

consider. See AS (6).

continuous, continual, constant. Continuous means uninterrupted: a string is continuous; the sound of an ambulance siren is continuous; a movie theater properly advertises "continuous performance." *Continual* means repeated at frequent short intervals: a bad cough may be continual; an executive may be continually interrupted by phone calls. *Constant* is a higher-voltage equivalent of *continual.*

convince. You do not convince a person *to* do something; you convince him *that* he should do it, or you convince him *of* its desirability. If the *to* construction is irresistible, use *persuade* or *prevail on.*

council, counsel; council(l)or, counsel(l)or. A council is a group of persons with administrative or other functions. A *counsel* is a lawyer, and *counsel* are lawyers collectively or anonymously (*on advice of counsel*); *counsel* also means advice in general, and *to counsel* means to advise. *Councillor* is preferred to *-ilor*, but *counselor* to *-ellor;* no one knows why. A *councillor* is a member of a council; a *counselor* is one who gives advice. The teen-ager at a children's summer camp, though he may be a member of a council, is a *counselor.*

crucial has a connotation of finality or decisiveness. It is an absolute word, not to be used either with such comparatives as *more, less,* and *rather* or for relatively trivial matters. Above all, *crucial* should not be overused, as it persistently is by sports writers and other journalists. See CLASHING VALUES; JOURNALESE.

CUTE SPELLINGS. Spelling reformers from the time of George Bernard Shaw and Theodore Roosevelt to the present day have affected such simplified spellings as *tho* and *thru;* advertisers have offered us *lo-cal* and *lo-fat* food and *hi-fi* sets; restaurants serve *donuts, ham 'n' eggs,* and *leg o' lamb;* teenage girls fill their letters and diaries with *'cause, thot* (thought), and *tonite.* What slight appeal these forms may have soon wears thin; only a few, e.g. *rock 'n' roll,* are acceptable in Standard English. See also SHORTENINGS.

DANGLING CONSTRUCTIONS are discussed in the text, pp. 105–107.

data is plural; the singular is *datum. This data is* is fairly common and gaining ground, but most good writers still write *these data are.*

de in French names and titles (*Guy de Maupassant, the Cardinal de Richelieu*) is omitted when the last name alone is used (*Maupassant,* not *de Maupassant; Richelieu,* not *de Richelieu*) except with names of one syllable (*de Gaulle,* not *Gaulle*) and names beginning with a vowel (*d'Alembert,* not *Alembert*). Names in *de La* drop *de* (*Jean de La Fontaine* becomes *La Fontaine*); but names in *des* and *du* retain them (e.g. the *Chevalier des Grieux* becomes *des Grieux*). When the particle is retained, the *d* should not be capitalized except at the beginning of a sentence. These rules apply to French names and titles only; English, Spanish, and Italian names in *de* and *De* invariably retain the particle.

dichotomy is a vogue word (see VOGUE WORDS). In logic, from which it was needlessly borrowed, it means a division of a whole for analytical purposes into two mutually exclusive parts, as opposed to two overlapping parts, three or more parts, a continuum, or what have you. It has been extended by its borrowers to mean any division into two parts, whether analytically precise or not (*The Negro-white dichot-*

omy is the only meaningful basis of discussion), and thence to other meanings of *division*, notably rift or discord: *The French Revolution, however, deepened the dichotomy between radical and conservative.* Good writers rarely use the word.

different than.   Fastidious writers go to great lengths to follow *different* with *from*, and Follett, among others, supports them. It is not clear why. *Different than*, by analogy with *other than*, has been a staple of American spoken English for at least a century, and sometimes offers a brevity that *different from* cannot match. In *He used the word in quite a different sense than he did yesterday*, to require *from* would mean to replace *than he did* with no fewer than eight words: *from the one in which he used it.* Use *different from* where you can; but where it does not work and *different than* does, take the plunge.

discreet, discrete.   *Discreet* means prudent; *discrete* means separate, or consisting of unconnected elements. The two words have nothing in common but their pronunciation.

disinterested means impartial, free of emotional interest in the issue at hand. A disinterested judge is not one who finds the case boring, but one who is well qualified to judge it fairly because he has no personal stake in the outcome. As Follett and others have remarked, the present tendency to equate *disinterested* with *uninterested* is not only depriving the world of an expressive word, but rendering less accessible a noble idea.

doubtful, dubious.   *Doubtful* may mean either doubting, full of doubt (said of a person), or of uncertain worth, character, or outcome (said of a person, a thing, or an event). *Dubious* has only the second meaning. In *Adam was dubious about joining*, change to *doubtful.*

doubtlessly.   There is no such word; use *doubtless.*

due to, like BASED ON, has not made the transition to full prepositional status (see text, p. 107), and must accordingly, as a participle, attach itself to a noun or pronoun. In *Due to illness, he could not attend*, change *due* to *owing.*

each, every.   *Each* as a noun takes a singular verb and a singular noun or pronoun: *Each of the boys has his own car,* not *have,* not *their own car,* not *their own cars. Each* and *every* as adjectives take the singular when they precede what they modify: *Every man is his own worst enemy,* not *their own worst enemy.* When *each* follows what it modifies, it takes the plural: *They each are wearing the hats they wore yesterday.* Usage is wearing down these distinctions, however, particularly in the first and second persons. *We each have our own cars* is nominally correct, but *car* is almost universal; *Each of you should write his congressman* is nominally correct, but *your* is far more common. The rule is by now so far eroded that these departures may be considered correct.

    Each and every, being simply an emphatic way of saying *each,* takes the singular despite the *and*: *Each and every one of you is guilty.* So do compounds of the form *Each (every) X and (each/every) Y: Every man and woman here has a college education.* The compounds *everybody, everyone, anybody,* and *anyone* take the singular: *Everybody thinks of himself first / Does anyone want his money refunded?*

each other, one another.   The two phrases are identical in meaning and use, except that some writers find it convenient to use *each other* for two and *one another* for three or more. Both phrases take singular possessives, and in the possessive take a singular noun: *We have read each other's diary,* not *others',* not *diaries.* Neither phrase can serve as the subject of a verb: change *They know what each other wants* to *Each knows what the other wants* (or *what the others want*).

effect.   See AFFECT, EFFECT.

e.g. stands for *exempli gratia,* "for example": *Shakespeare's comedies, e.g. "As You Like It."* It is never used parenthetically: in *There were reasons, e.g., to suspect George,* change to *for example.* It may be followed by a comma or not, at the writer's option. Being slightly pedantic in appearance and connotation, *e.g.* is better suited to footnotes and technical exposition than to the text of an essay. It should not be confused with *i.e.,* which stands for *id est,* "that is": in *the three triumvirs, e.g. Octavius, Antony, and Lepidus,* change to *i.e.*

either. (1) In constructions of the form *either . . . or,* what follows *either* should be parallel and grammatically equivalent to what follows *or;* see the text, pp. 103–105. (2) *Either . . . or* may be used of three or more alternatives: *Either you go, or I go, or he goes.* As an adjective, however (*Take either road*), and as a pronoun (*Either is all right with me*), *either* is properly confined to two alternatives.

employment, like *utilization,* is often simply a ponderous word for *use.* In *The engineers recommended the employment of heavy earth-moving equipment,* change to *the use of* or *using.*

enable is incomplete without a following infinitive, whether active (*His fortune enables him to live as he likes*) or passive (*The new law enabled major improvements to be made*), preferably active. In *The committee's proposal would enable several changes in the clubhouse rules,* the infinitive is lacking; either add it or change *enable* to *make possible.*

enhance is not an exact synonym of *increase.* When Governor Wallace spoke of going to Vietnam to "enhance my knowledge of the war," he meant *increase. Enhance* means specifically to increase in desirability, value, or attractiveness, and is properly said of something already to some extent desirable, valuable, or attractive. The word takes an abstract object: not *The simple tiara enhanced her,* but *The simple tiara enhanced her beauty.*

equally as. Equally cannot tolerate *as:* in *Her behavior was equally as foolish,* either delete *as* or change *equally* to *just.* In a complete *as . . . as* comparison there is no place for *equally:* delete it in *Her behavior was equally as foolish as his.* Constructions in between *equally X* and *as X as* should be resolved one way or the other: in *German wine is equally good, in its way, as French,* change *equally* to *as* or *just as.*

equate takes either *with* (*How can you equate Meyerbeer with Mozart?*) or *and* (*The new salary scale equates men and women*), or a plural resolvable into the equated compo- nents (*I equate the two sentiments*). Like BETWEEN, *equate* cannot take a singular: in *He appears to equate "democracy" in its American and Soviet senses,* either change to *equate the American and Soviet senses of "democracy"* or rewrite.

etc. is permissible in formal English to avoid a tedious and easily inferrable elaboration. Good writers, however, disliking its in- elegant appearance and lazy-careless connotations, tend to use it chiefly where elegance is no issue, as in footnotes, lists, and tables. Getting rid of *etc.* elsewhere is usually no great trick; many phrases of the form *Castroism, Maoism, etc.* can be simply changed to *such as Castroism and Maoism,* and in the rest *etc.* can almost always be replaced by *and so on* or *and the like.*

every, everybody.   See EACH, EVERY.

fabulous is the adjective form of *fable* and means legendary or fictitious. By extension it has come to mean amazing or mar- velous, in which sense it has been so badly overused, espe- cially by the young, as to have no force or credit left.

fact.   Novice writers overuse *the fact that.* They write, for exam- ple, *I accepted the fact that I could not learn French* and *His lameness was due to the fact that he had had an acci- dent* where they might better have written *I accepted my in- ability to learn French* and *His lameness was the result of an accident.* Use *the fact that* as sparingly as you can, and preferably where some fact as such is in question: *What I dispute is not the fact that he lied, but his motive in lying.*

farther, further.   *Farther* tends to be used of physical distance: *Chicago is farther from New York than from Washington. Further* tends to be used of abstract distance: *We will go into this further at some later date.* When in doubt, use *fur- ther.*

fewer, less.   *Fewer* is used of countable units: *fewer cows, fewer days, fewer cups of coffee. Less* is used of abstract or insep- arable quantities: *less air, less salt, less pain.* The same dis- tinction is made between *less than* and *fewer than,* except that *less than* is used with countable units considered as single quantities (*less than five dollars, less than three weeks*) and with countable units in large numbers, where the mass dominates the individual: *less than 10,000 armed guerrillas, less than a hundred hotel rooms.*

former, latter. *Former* and *latter* may be used, together or singly, only when immediately preceded by two explicit parallel antecedent nouns, pronouns, or noun phrases, and then only when it would be awkward to repeat the nouns themselves. The following sentences violate the successive conditions of this rule. *Of the grants made to Oklahoma, Texas, and Louisiana, the largest went to the latter.* (More than two antecedents.) *A notice was sent to the dead man's next of kin, and the latter supplied the information.* (Only one antecedent.) *When they would not recognize Lyman's immunity, the latter was forced to resign.* (Antecedents not explicit.) *German cooks may respect French cooking, but the former are poor cooks themselves.* (Antecedents not parallel.) *The judge and the court clerk had the same name; the former was apparently the latter's father.* (Better to repeat *judge* and *clerk.*) In general, avoid *former* and *latter;* good writers get along very well without them.

fortunate, fortuitous. *Fortunate* means lucky; *fortuitous* means accidental or unexpected. *Webster's Seventh* to the contrary, *fortuitous* should not be used as a fancy way of saying *fortunate.*

further. See FARTHER, FURTHER.

FUSED PARTICIPLES are discussed in the text, pp. 114–115.

gap. In 1958 a reporter coined the term "missile gap" to characterize an alleged American inferiority to the U.S.S.R. in the number of intercontinental missiles completed and under construction. Although this expression did some violence to the classic idea of a gap as a hiatus or break in continuity, it was apt enough to be given wide circulation. Inevitably there followed a large number of less apt imitations like *communications gap, import-export gap,* and *credibility gap,* in some of which the idea of a gap could barely be discerned. *Gap* is today a vogue word (see VOGUE WORDS); it is time to give it a rest.

GERUNDS. A gerund is the *-ing* form of a verb used as a noun: *Swimming is fun / I am tired of fooling around / How about frying some eggs?* (1) Gerunds, like participles, should be attached as closely as possible to their subject (if it appears in the sentence); in *By yelling at the top of their lungs, we finally heard them*, change to *they finally made us hear them*. (2) An infinitive is sometimes erroneously used where only a gerund is idiomatic. Instead of *The Navy was committed to support the program*, idiom requires *to supporting*; instead of *I confessed to have found the question pointless*, idiom requires *to having found*. Only someone with an excellent sense of idiom will have no difficulty on this point. When in doubt, use the gerund.

For the distinction between gerunds, participles, and fused participles, see the text, pp. 114–115.

got, gotten. *Got* is the past of *get*; the past participle is sometimes *got*, sometimes *gotten*. *Gotten* is now the usual choice when a sense of progression is involved: *You have gotten much more cautious lately / Grandma has gotten worse again / I have gotten to know her better*. In other senses *got* and *gotten* are interchangeable: *I have got to bed late every night this week / We had got our feet wet*. As an intensive of *have* (*I've got the tickets / George has got to help us*), *got* is the only choice. Purists still reject *got* in this sense as colloquial, and disallow *gotten* altogether; but neither position is now tenable.

graduate. Forty years ago, *I was graduated from high school* was the only wording teachers considered proper. Today, *was graduated*, though still acceptable, sounds stuffy; the natural wording is *I graduated from high school*. The newer wording *I graduated high school* is not Standard.

help. When *help* is used in the sense of *avoid* or *refrain from*, the correct form is *I cannot help liking her*, not *I cannot help but like her*. The incorrect form, though widely used in speech, is not acceptable in writing. Remember also that the subject of *help* in this sense must be animate: in *The book could not help becoming a best seller,* change to *was certain to become.*

historic, historical. *Historic* means historically important or famous (*a historic battle*); *historical* is the general adjective (*the historical record*). *History* and all its derivatives take *a*, not *an*.

home, house. A *house* is a building; a *home* is an abstraction. *Home* means the locus of family life (whether a building, a cave, or what have you), or the family itself, as in *a broken home.* Since *house* has neutral connotations and *home* favorable ones, advertisers have taken to advertising *homes, home furnishings, homewares,* and the like, and addressing themselves to *homeowners* and *homemakers.* The dictionaries have accepted—which is to say, recorded—these new locutions, but in good writing *home* remains inseparable from the idea of people. Any good writer will tell you that if *Dad sold our home in 1960,* Dad is a swine indeed.

hopefully means in a hopeful manner: *"Is there a part for me?"* *she asked hopefully.* Although many writers have deplored the recent extension of the word to mean *it is to be hoped that,* as in *Hopefully, the war will be over soon,* the usage seems warranted by the notable gain in conciseness. Other unattached adverbs of this form and derivation have long since proved their usefulness: e.g. *undoubtedly* for *it is not to be doubted that.*

house. See HOME, HOUSE.

however. (1) When *however* comes at the beginning of a sentence or clause, it can be either a conjunction meaning *but* (*However, the children may feel cheated*) or an adverb meaning in whatever way or to whatever degree (*However the children may feel, we must proceed*). So that the reader may distinguish immediately between these two very different constructions, good writers always use a comma in the first. (2) *However* should be placed early in the sentence if it is not to lose its force. In *The Secretary of Health, Education, and Welfare and two of his undersecretaries, however, maintained that the appropriation was insufficient,* move *however* to the beginning. (3) When *however* does not come at the beginning of a sentence or clause, it has the effect of emphasizing the word it follows, and this emphasis must accord with the meaning. In *There was no official reply from the White House; the President, however, unofficially praised the plan,* change to *speaking unofficially, however,* or to *however, the President.*

I, me. Although *I* is nominative and *me* objective, such technically correct expressions as *It is I* and *That was I* strike the American ear as prissy, with the result that *me* has all but replaced *I* in the predicate nominative: *It's me / Could it have been me that she saw? / The two people they forgot were you and me.* There is no opposing this development, and no reason to oppose it.

identify with, said of human beings, has two legitimate applications: to long and devoted service to a well-known cause or institution (*King has long been identified with the campaign for civil rights*), and, in psychiatry, to a close and continuing emotional orientation toward another person (*Boys often identify with their fathers*). The expression has of late been improperly and pointlessly extended to more casual connections (*Jones did not identify sufficiently with the company's aims / The Beatle I identify with is Paul*) and seems well on its way to becoming a mere vogue word for *like* or *admire.*

i.e. stands for *id est,* "that is," and may be used as a substitute for *that is* or *namely* in footnotes and wherever else elegance is not an issue. *I.e.* should be distinguished from *e.g.,* which has the very different meaning "for example." In *The most populous states, i.e. Illinois, are the richest,* change to *e.g.*

implement as a verb is a vogue word of some twenty years' standing (see VOGUE WORDS). It is especially beloved of big businessmen and government officials, perhaps because the scale and complexity of their operations make simple expressions like *carry out* and *put into effect* inappropriate, perhaps because *implement* suggests the sort of impersonal, deliberate, and orderly changeover that will disrupt things least, perhaps out of sheer pomposity. "With *implement*," as Follett says, "the layman can sound technical." Good writers use *implement* rarely, if at all.

imply, infer. *Imply* means to suggest or hint, *infer* to deduce or surmise. A politician who is unwilling to announce his candidacy might *imply* his willingness to run by winking at an interviewer, from which the interviewer might *infer* that the politician would announce his candidacy later.

in-. See UN-, IN-, NON-.

include, including. *Include* supposes the listing of some members, but not all, of the whole, as in *The jurors included two women.* In *Some of those arrested included schoolteachers,* either delete *some of* or change *included* to *were.* In *The guest list included General Curtis, General Watkins, and others,* change to *General Curtis and General Watkins.* In *The four countries to be considered include Syria, Lebanon, Jordan, and Iraq,* change *include* to *are.* What goes for *include* goes also for *including*: in *Twenty-one poems were read, including poems by Ginsberg, Patchen, and others,* change to *Ginsberg and Patchen.*

individual as a noun has only two legitimate uses of any interest: in biology, to designate the single organism as distinguished from the species; and in general, to designate the single human being as contrasted with a group, an institution, or the state. The use of *individual* as an exact synonym for *person,* as in *Harry is a well-meaning individual,* is a "colloquial vulgarism" (OED) and, in a memorable phrase quoted by Fowler, "one of the modern editor's shibboleths for detecting the unfit."

infer. See IMPLY, INFER.

INFINITIVES. For the split infinitive, see the text, pp. 113–114. For the misuse of the infinitive for the gerund, see GERUNDS (2).

INITIALS AND ACRONYMS. The burgeoning use of initials like *D.C.*, *GHQ*, and *U.S.S.R.*, and of acronyms like *UNESCO, Benelux,* and *scuba* (for *s*elf-*c*ontained *u*nderwater *b*reathing *ap*paratus), has greatly increased the efficiency of the language, though at some expense to its elegance. Three cautions are in order. First, use initials and acronyms only when you are sure your readers will know exactly what they stand for. Initials familiar to you may be Greek to others. When in doubt, spell out the initials the first time you use them: *the gross national product (GNP)*. Second, keep the incidence of initials down. Pages bespattered with clusters of capitals are uninviting. Write *electrocardiogram* rather than *EKG*; and before using *ICBM* for a second time, see whether plain *missile* will serve. Third, avoid headlinese. *LBJ* for *Lyndon B. Johnson, GOP* (Grand Old Party) for *Republican,* and *GM* for *General Motors,* however indispensable to headline writers, have no place in formal expository writing; the same goes for common-noun abbreviations like *P.O.* for *post office* and *C.O.* for *commanding officer* or *conscientious objector.*

irregardless is non-Standard, a bastard mixture of *irrespective* and *regardless.* Use one or the other of these two Standard words.

it's, its. The first stands for *it is* or *it has;* the second is the possessive. A memory device that some people find helpful is *It's its own excuse for being.*

-ize. (1) Some words ending in the sound *-ize* are spelled *-yze* (*analyze, paralyze*) or *-ise* (*advertise, exercise*). If you are not sure how such a word is spelled, look it up. (2) New words in *-ize* are the delight of the young and the despair of the old. Some are clearly here to stay: *winterize, Americanize, tranquilize.* Others—among them *finalize, personalize,* and *slenderize*—have been accepted by Webster but are not used in formal writing by educated people. Still others— *containerize, concertize, accessorize, moisturize*—are as yet too much even for Webster. A good rule for formal writing is to use only such words in this suffix as have no ready equivalent, and to coin no new ones.

JARGON is the name commonly given to writing that is ugly and hard to understand. Originally, *jargon* meant the lingo of a particular science or occupation (especially as viewed from outside), and this meaning is still current. Among the jargons of American academic writing today, for example, as seen by its detractors, are that of the social scientists, with their *societal needs, functional capability, variables associated with organizational effectiveness,* and the like; and that of the literary critics, which numbers among its current delights *ambience, dualism,* and *Yeatsian.* More often, however, *jargon* today refers to the general blend of pompous diction and imprecise reference that has become America's style for ceremonial speech and writing. The mark of jargon in this sense is long words, pat phrases, and lifeless verbs; its intent is not to communicate, but to impress or reassure.

JOURNALESE. Newspaper writing at its best has the great virtues of clarity and brevity. It also has certain defects that arise from the circumstances of its writing and printing. The newspaper writer has limited space, little time to reflect, and precious little a priori claim on the attention of his readers, who may be justly thought of as reading their newspapers hastily over breakfast or in the subway on the way to work. Neither subtlety nor complexity is possible in such circumstances, and the grays of truth give way to the facile blacks and whites of melodrama. The result of this process is journalese.

One mark of journalese is its heavy use of intensives: every difficulty is a *crisis,* every important decision *crucial,* every retrenchment *drastic,* every college student *brilliant,* every death *tragic,* everything impressive *great.* Another mark is gimmicky noun-verbs like *pinpoint, highlight,* and *trigger,* which give the most prosaic proceedings a factitious liveliness. Headlines, with their premium on short, vivid words, have the same effect: critics do not criticize, they *rap;* a political opponent is a *foe;* a disagreement, however mild, is a *clash.* Activity, conflict, crisis are everywhere. The routine investigation of a Soviet complaint about an American aircraft is rendered seemingly ominous by the headline

Red Charge Spurs Probe. This "tone of contrived excitement" (Follett) is the essence of journalese. Its characteristic exaggerations and oversimplifications have no place in serious writing.

See also TIMESTYLE.

latter. See FORMER, LATTER.

lay. See LIE, LAY.

leadership. See -SHIP (1).

lend, loan. Use *lend* as the verb, *loan* as the noun. *Loan* as a verb was formerly Standard, but is now colloquial.

less. See FEWER, LESS.

lie, lay. *Lie* means to recline, *lay* to place or put in place. The following sentences exhibit the correct use of *lie* and *lay* and their various forms:

	Lie	*Lay*
Present	I *lie* down.	I *lay* the carpet.
Past	I *lay* down.	I *laid* the carpet.
Perfect	I *have lain* down.	I *have laid* the carpet.
Present progressive	I *am lying* down.	I *am laying* the carpet.
Future	I *will lie* down.	I *will lay* the carpet.

like and *as* are discussed in the text, pp. 115–117.

-like as a suffix is conventionally hyphenated in ad hoc compounds when the root word is two or more syllables (*magnet-like, catapult-like*). The hyphen is omitted when the root word is only one syllable (*elflike, chromelike*), except when it ends in *l* (*snail-like, bell-like*). In familiar words with this suffix the hyphen is never used: *ladylike, businesslike, statesman-like.*

literally is not a mere intensive. *Bill literally broke his heart over Mary* implies that his heart is now, or was at some time, actually in two or more pieces. Since this is impossible, *lit-*

erally should be omitted. Note that *figuratively* here, though technically accurate, would be both redundant and inept, implying as it does the possibility of its impossible opposite.

loan. See LEND, LOAN.

-ly. (1) Avoid piling up adverbs in *-ly*: in *He acted completely honorably*, change *completely* to *altogether* to get rid of the singsong effect. (2) Avoid forming adverbs in *-lily* from adjectives in *-ly* for the same reason: instead of *He answered surlily*, write *He answered sullenly* or *His answer was surly*. (3) Avoid coining adverbs in *-edly* from participles in *-ed*. Some adverbs so formed have become unobjectionable by reason of manifest convenience and long use: *allegedly, repeatedly, undoubtedly*. But most tend to give the effect of a Germanic excess of syllables and components: *undisguisedly, animatedly, disappointedly*. Worst of all, and intolerable to good writers, are *-edly* words in which the *-ed* syllable cannot be given full weight: *satisfiedly, puzzledly, discouragedly*. If an *-edly* word cannot be confidently pronounced, it should not be written. (4) Do not hyphenate compounds formed by adverbs in *-ly* and participles or adjectives: *the newly married pair*, not *newly-married; the brightly lit room*, not *brightly-lit*.

majority. *The majority* is often an unnecessarily long way of saying *most*. In *The majority of my friends went to college*, change to *Most of my friends*.

masterful, masterly. *Masterful* means imperious or domineering; *masterly* means supremely skilled or talented. Webster now admits *masterful* in both senses, but careful writers observe the distinction made here.

me. See I, ME.

membership. See -SHIP (1).

militate, mitigate. *Militate* means to count or have weight, and is used exclusively with *against*: *Three things militated against our accepting the offer*. *Mitigate* means to lessen in severity: *Her pleasure mitigated his grief*. The combination *mitigate against* does not exist.

more can be ambiguous. What is meant, for example, by *The proposal called for more fully integrated restaurants?* More restaurants that were fully integrated, or restaurants that were more fully integrated? What is meant by *We need more unbiased reporting on Vietnam?* Only a more carefully chosen wording can tell us.

more than one. See ONE OR MORE.

most. The use of *most* for *almost,* as in *Most everybody was there* or *You can come most any time,* is a colloquialism that should never find its way into formal writing.

NEGATIVE PROBLEMS. (1) Few sentences can easily tolerate more than one or two negative words. In a sentence like *Cohen did not consider the chance of failure negligible,* at least some readers will have to pause and sort out the three negatives (*not, failure, negligible*) before they can be sure what Cohen thought. The writer should have done the sorting for them: *Cohen saw a significant chance of failure.* (2) A negative noun compound or pronoun is not an acceptable antecedent for a positive pronoun: in *No member could smoke in public, and they were not to wear short skirts,* change *they* to *members* or make some other change. In *Since no one was home, we left them a note,* omit *them* or change to *Since the Joneses were not home.* In *The police expected no trouble, but were prepared for it if it came,* change to *did not expect trouble.* (3) A negative noun compound or pronoun (e.g. *nobody*) cannot serve as the subject of a verb requiring a positive subject: in *Neither the Yankees nor the Mets gave up, but kept on playing to win,* change the comma to a semicolon and *but* to *both.* See also NEITHER; NOR.

Negro should be capitalized, whether as a noun or as an adjective. Sensitive Negroes take the lowercase form *negro* as a slight to their race.

neither. (1) Make sure that with *neither* you use *nor,* not *or.* (2) *Neither . . . nor* may be used of three or more elements, as in *Neither illness nor bad weather nor financial reverses ever dimmed his good spirits.* As an adjective, however (*Neither one is any good*), and as a pronoun (*Neither will do*), *neither* is properly confined to two elements. (3) Whatever part of speech follows *neither* should also follow *nor*; see the text, pp. 103–105.

NON-. See UN-, IN-, NON-.

none may take either a singular or a plural verb; see the text, p. 91.

nor. Poetic diction apart, *nor* has only two legitimate uses: as the second (or subsequent) element in the correlative pair *neither . . . nor,* and as a conjunction introducing a clause (*Nor do I agree with Senator Kennedy / There was nothing to say, nor was there anything Jean could do*). The correct word after *not* or *no* is not *nor* but *or.* In *The word does not occur at all in Shakespeare, nor in Marlowe,* change *nor* to *or*; make the same change in *No one sent a contribution, nor offered to help in any way.* In *No telegrams have come, nor any other messages,* change to *No telegrams or other messages have come*; alternatively, change *nor* to *and no.*

not only . . . but also. (1) *Also* is optional in this formula: it is commonly used when the second element is simply added to the first (*We will be seeing not only Dr. Shapley but also Uncle Bob*), and omitted when the second element is an intensification of the first (*She is not only the fattest girl I know, but the fattest girl I have ever seen / We drove not only to Southampton, but all the way to Plymouth*). When *also* is used, it need not immediately follow *but.* (2) The same part of speech that follows *not only* should also follow *but also*; see the text, pp. 103–105. (3) *Not only* may be used without *but* to get intensive effects, as in *He not only smelled, he reeked.* The comma splice here is intentional.

not un- is a construction that persists despite Orwell's celebrated suggestion that writers cure themselves of it "by memorizing this sentence: *A not unblack dog was chasing a not unsmall rabbit across a not ungreen field.*" The wording should be used, if at all, most sparingly, and only where the alternative (positive) wording has been considered and found wanting. In *I have not infrequently been bored to tears by his stories,* change to *frequently.*

NUMBER PROBLEMS are discussed in the text, pp. 88–94.

NUMBERS. (1) A good rule is to spell out numbers through twenty, and use figures beginning with 21. This rule has two major exceptions. First, in a series of numbers of which some are over twenty and others under, ignore the rule and make the series consistent in itself: *Sue was 19, Jane 21, and Martha 22.* Second, if a number over twenty is used as a round number or approximation rather than as a specific figure, feel free to spell it out: *We must have seen a hundred cathedrals.* (2) Write numbers of four or more figures with a comma, except dates and page numbers of long books. (3) Spell out numbers at the beginning of a sentence: *Thirty-eight men were wounded.* If possible, avoid beginning a sentence with a date, there being no such thing as a capital number. (4) Some words have arithmetical aspects that cannot be ignored. If a performance is given three times for example, we cannot say it was *repeated* three times, since *repeat* implies an initial performance preceding the ones it governs. Perhaps the trickiest words are *few* and *several,* which imply more than two but rarely as many as five or six. Here are two examples from the pen of a careless English professor: *We do have a few specifically female nouns: "actress," "alumna," "poetess," "Negress." Except for "actress," however, most of the other female forms are disappearing / Among the best of several good books in this class is Warren and Brooks, "Understanding Fiction."* In the first example, delete *most of* and *other;* in the second, delete either *Among* or *best of.*

O.K. and *okay* are colloquial and unacceptable in formal writing.

one . . . his. The pronoun *one* has two uses, the numeral (*One of them must be Michael*) and the impersonal (*One cannot please everybody*). In the numeral use, *one* is followed by *he, his, him,* etc.: *One had his dog with him; another had a parrot.* In the impersonal use, *one* is followed by *one, one's, oneself: One cannot take one's dog into a restaurant.* The common error is to follow the impersonal *one* with *he, his* etc.; in *One has a hard time keeping his temper in such cir cumstances*, change *his* to *one's* or *One* to *A man*.

one another. See EACH OTHER, ONE ANOTHER.

one or more takes the plural by convention: *One or more of you are going to be surprised / One or more waitresses have been hired.* Oddly enough, the more unambiguously plural *more than one* takes the singular by convention: *More than one example comes to mind / More than one has been found*

or. On number and gender problems in sentences having sub jects linked by *or*, see the text, pp. 88–90. See also AND (2) (3); EITHER; NOR.

oriented is a vogue word (see VOGUE WORDS), and like many vogue words is more sonorous than precise. When we call Western civilization *work-oriented* or Mr. Jones *family-oriented* or a large corporation *people-oriented*, what exactly do we mean? Are we saying, for example, that Jones puts his family above his job, or that he would rather play with his children than shoot pool with his friends, or simply that his family gives him a lot of pleasure? We need more and different words to begin to understand what Jones's family orientation amounts to. The adverb construction is even less precise. What in the world is meant, for example, by *Jack is visually, not typo graphically, oriented*?

overall is a vogue word (see VOGUE WORDS) for *whole, total, com prehensive, general*, etc.; good writers do not use it. *In over all terms the new gymnasium made sense* presumably means either *in general terms* or *in long-run terms;* if one of these phrases had been used, we would know which meaning was intended. In *The overall cost came to $650*, change *overall* to *total*. Sometimes *overall* is simply redundant, as in *Har vey's overall speed for the 100-yard dash was 10.0 seconds;* delete *overall*.

overly, once a perfectly acceptable word, has been displaced by the prefix *over-* (as in *overenthusiastic*) and now sounds bumpkinish to a fastidious ear. It is also superfluous, given the availability not only of the *over-* compounds but of *too* and *excessively.*

PARALLELISM.   See the text, pp. 101–105.

PARTICIPLES.   The participle is the adjective form of a verb. The present participle ends in *-ing: defeating, flying, proving.* The past participle is often the same form as the simple past (*defeated*), but may be a separate form (*flown* rather than *flew*); some verbs have two past participles (*proved, proven; burned, burnt*). The present participle should be distinguished from the GERUND: the first is always an adjective (*Walking away, he began to whistle*), the second a noun (*Walking is good exercise*).

The chief questions about participles fall under two headings: dangling or misattached participles (see the text, pp. 105–107) and fused participles (pp. 114–115).

PASSIVE PROBLEMS.   For a general discussion of the passive, see pp. 120–122. The two chief points to remember are that passive verbs are less forceful than active verbs (compare *I was made angry by what I heard* and *What I heard made me angry*); and that passive constructions without agents may tell the reader less than he has a right or need to know (compare *The invading force was repulsed* with *The Marines repulsed the invading force*). In a given case only a slight gain in force or clarity may come from switching to the active, but the cumulative gain from several such changes can be impressive.

per should be avoided except in heavily technical contexts. For *30 miles per hour,* say *30 miles an hour;* for *two new trainees per annum,* say *two new trainees every year;* for *1,800 calories per person,* say *1,800 calories each.* Such expressions as *information per central office memorandum of May 12* and *as per your request* are commercial jargon and have no place in formal writing.

percent, percentage, proportion.   Percent and *percentage* refer to degree or amount reckoned on a scale of 100: *What percentage of applicants are accepted? Between 70 and 80 per-*

cent. Proportion, as currently used, is a synonym for *percentage* except for the scale of 100: *What proportion of appli cants are accepted? Perhaps seven or eight out of ten.* Do not use *proportion* to mean nothing more than *part*; in *A large proportion of the beef was spoiled,* change *A large proportion* to *Much* or *Most.*

personal used to mean simply the opposite of *impersonal*; something personal involved a person, as contrasted, for example with a machine or a block of wood. In recent years, *personal* has increasingly been used to mean *individual* and even *private*: schools now offer *personal counseling,* not individual counseling, and where a man once spoke of his private life and his private secretary, he now speaks of his *personal life* and his *personal secretary.* A still further extension has made *personal* a mere intensive, in which sense it is unnecessary and virtually meaningless. More often than not, it should simply be eliminated from such expressions as *my personal opinion* and *my personal friend,* as should *personally* from such expressions as *I personally liked the play very much.* As for *personalized,* which rarely means more than imprinted or monogrammed and often means nothing whatever (*personalized cosmetic care*), leave it to Madison Avenue.

ploy, meaning a stratagem or gambit, was invented by the British humorist Stephen Potter in the late 1940's and is now solemnly admitted by Webster with the notation "[prob. fr. *employ*]." For all its jocular charm, *ploy* is unacceptable in formal writing.

PLURAL PROBLEMS are discussed in the text, pp. 88–94, 157.

possess should not be used as a fancy synonym for *have*. In *Bismarck possessed a keen intellect,* and in *That was all the money I possessed,* change to *had.*

POSSESSIVE PROBLEMS.   (1) For whether singular words and names ending in *-s* or *-x* take *-s* or apostrophe only in the possessive, see the text, p. 156. (2) For whether to write *George's* *and Harry's mother* or *George and Harry's mother,* see the text, p. 95. (3) When a name must be added in brackets to a quotation, avoid the intolerable forms *"George's [Baker] bat"* and *"George [Baker]'s bat"*; whatever the newspapers may say or do, the only acceptable solution to this problem is *"George's [George Baker's] bat."* (4) *Time* magazine, as part of its effort to minimize wordage, uses such possessive constructions as *at week's end* for *at the end of the week* and *London's Institute of Strategic Studies* for *the Institute of Strategic Studies in London.* Despite the efficiency of this construction, good writers eschew it, as they do TIMESTYLE in general.

PREPOSITIONS. It is no easy matter to choose a preposition in such sentences as *We succeeded (by) (through) sheer good luck* and *Many men go to pieces (in) (under) such conditions*; and it is too complex a matter to tackle here. The leading treatise on the subject is Frederick T. Wood's *English Prepositional Idioms* (New York: St Martin's, 1967). A useful list of 67 preposition choices that give many writers trouble appears in Follett, pp. 257–259.

pretty as an adverb meaning *somewhat* or *moderately* is still borderline-colloquial and should be used sparingly in writing. Use it when no suitable equivalent comes to mind, as in *We could do pretty much as we liked*; but replace it with *quite* or *rather* when you can, as in *a pretty presumptuous attitude.* Often it can be simply omitted, as from *a pretty good job* or *a pretty tall order.*

promote, when it means elevate in rank, requires *to.* In *He was promoted captain last May,* change to *promoted to captain.*

proportion. See PERCENT, PERCENTAGE, PROPORTION.

proved, proven. Most editors prefer to use *proved* as the past participle, restricting *proven* to a purely attributive use: thus *a case that has proved difficult, a man who has been proved guilty,* but *a proven criminal, a proven remedy.*

provided, providing. If you cannot make do with *if,* the word you want is *provided,* not *providing.* In *They agreed to support Johnson providing he honored his pledge,* change to *provided,* or better still to *if.* The full form *provided that* should be used only where omitting *that* would cause confusion.

rather is a halfhearted word and should never be used with all-out words like *spectacular* or *magnificent.* See CLASHING VALUES.

re-. To *reform* does not mean to form again; to convey this last meaning without confusion we must write *re-form.* Similarly we *re-solve* a recurring problem, *re-cover* our furniture, witness a *re-creation* of a historical event. Though correct, these hyphenated forms are irritatingly self-conscious; use an *again* construction if you can.

really is used by young writers either to persuade the reader of the intensity of their response (*I really loved that dog*) or to solicit his agreement to an argument for which no evidence is offered (*We really made a mistake at Yalta*). Invariably the strategy misfires and *really* comes through as a bankrupt effort to win the reader's respect or attention on the cheap. Good writers do not make this mistake. It takes more than an adverb to convey intensity of feeling or persuade the unpersuaded; it takes honest thinking and good writing.

reason is because. Generations of grammarians have deplored this construction: in *The reason I phoned was because she asked me to,* they say, *because* must be changed to *that.* The grammatical argument for *that* is impeccable, yet *because* persists and may someday become accepted usage, as it has in the reverse syntax: *Just because Mother likes parties is no reason why Tom should.* Until that putative someday, use *that.*

REDUNDANCY. See CLASHING VALUES.

respectively is used to relate the individual components of one sequence to their proper counterparts in another sequence: *Jane, Lois, and Greta married a soldier, a sailor, and a Marine, respectively.* The word is obtrusive and should be used only where it is absolutely necessary. In *With people like my father and mother, poker parties and bridge clubs are a way of life*, it would be gratuitous to add *respectively*; the reader can sort things out for himself.

-self, -selves. (1) *Ourself*, not *ourselves*, is the reflexive pronoun for the imperial or editorial *we*: *We found ourself last week at a party for Mae West.* (2) The forms *themself, theirself*, and *theirselves* do not exist. (3) Never use the reflexive pronoun where the simple pronoun will serve as well. In *My sister and myself arrived early*, change *myself* to *I*.

semiweekly.   See BIWEEKLY, SEMIWEEKLY.

SENTENCE FRAGMENT.   A sentence fragment is any word or combination of words that is preceded and followed by a full stop (period, question mark, exclamation point) and that does not contain an independent subject and predicate: for example, the second, third, and fourth elements in *What did Scott need? A guide who knew the country. What else? Money.* Sentence fragments are perfectly legitimate in expository writing, if used with proper respect for three caveats. First, do not use many; the repeated use of sentence fragments, as in some humorous newspaper columns, marks the writer as committed to striving for cheap effects. Second, do not use them in highly formal or abstract writing, where their informality would be out of place, or in passages of routine exposition, to which their abrupt, emphatic quality would be unsuited. Third, do not separate them unnaturally from a preceding or following sentence of which they logically form part; in *He must have meant Truman. Because Roosevelt would never have said that*, change to *Truman, because.*

SERIES.   (1) In a series of three or more elements linked by *and* or *or*, put a comma before the conjunction: not *red, white and blue* but *red, white, and blue.* (2) On parallelism in series see the text, pp. 102–103.

shall, will.   In American usage *shall* is now for the most part restricted to the first person interrogative, and then only when a decision or recommendation is requested: *Shall we go? /*

Shall I tell him or will you? In all other uses *will* is idiomatic: *I will be 21 in March / We will be lucky to escape alive / Will you want a picnic lunch? / Will I be the only girl there?* To be sure, *shall* remains permissible in the classic uses: simple future in the first person, determination in the second and third. It is simply that *will* is equally idiomatic in these uses, and far more widely used. In general, you will not go wrong by writing whatever you would say.

-ship. (1) One of the best-known entries in Fowler bears the title "Love of the Long Word." It is hard to imagine any other motive for the present-day practice of saying *leadership* for *leaders, membership* for *members,* and *readership* for *readers.* The *X-ship* form is properly used to indicate the quality or state of being an X (*courses in leadership, an application for membership*), or the body of X's considered as a quantity (*a larger membership, a readership of over 20,000*); it is improperly extended to mean some or all X's as people. In *The party's leadership was discredited,* change to *leaders were;* in *Many of the membership disapproved,* change to *members.* (2) *Gamesmanship* and *oneupmanship* were coined by Stephen Potter, who also gave us PLOY; they should be used only in a jocular or ironic context.

SHORTENINGS is Follett's term for words like *quote* (for *quotation*), *recap* (for *recapitulate*), *photo, exam, psycho, grad,* and *prof,* which he properly considers unsuitable for formal writing. In speech and informal writing words of this form have not only a certain charm, but also an undoubted convenience (as opposed to full forms), especially for those who must use them frequently in writing: *photographs,* for example, takes twice as long to write as *photos,* and *photos* twice as long as *pix.* Some shortenings have become Standard: thus we no longer think of *bus* as a shortening of *omnibus,* or *taxicab* of *taximeter cabriolet,* or *coonskin* of *raccoon skin.* But most shortenings, including all those in the first sentence of this entry, are no more suitable for serious writing than slang or the simplifications listed under CUTE SPELLINGS.

should, would. In American usage *should* means *ought to.* In the conditional, *would* is proper with the first person as well as the second and third: *I would be glad to call on her / Would we be welcome in that case?*

SIMPLIFIED SPELLINGS.   See CUTE SPELLINGS.

situation has the combination of vagueness and polysyllabic weight that insecure writers love, presumably because they think it makes them sound impressive. Sometimes the word can be simply dropped: in *It is an awkward situation when no one understands English,* change to *It is awkward when.* Almost always some less pretentious equivalent can be found: in *The situation called for prompt action,* for example, we could change to *They had to act promptly,* and in *if I were in John's situation* to *if I were John.*

so.   Some writers, chiefly women, mistakenly use *so* and *such* as synonyms for *very* in sentences like *Ireland is such a lovely country* and *We were so glad to get home.* This feminine intensive is essentially a conversational gambit, designed to evoke a routine assent: "Lydia is *so* beautiful tonight, don't you think, Mr. Palmer?" It has no place in writing.

SPLIT INFINITIVES are discussed in the text, pp. 113–114.

structure as a verb, meaning to organize or arrange, is social science jargon, and should be restricted to social science uses: e.g., one might contrast a structured psychiatric counseling session with one carried out by the technique of free association. Beyond this domain, *structure* tends to be vague. What is meant, for example, by *Miss Jones works best in a highly structured situation?* That she needs supervision? That she like clear rules? That she feels more comfortable in a highly stratified or bureaucratic office than in a more informal work setting?

substitute as a verb means to put in place of, and *substitution* means putting in place of; they are not synonyms for *replace* and *replacement. Substitute* takes *for* (*They had substituted a Chevrolet for my Ford*); *replace* takes *by* or *with* (*I replaced my old Ford by/with a new Chevrolet*). In *The wartime board was substituted by a new nine-member board,* either change *substituted* to *replaced* or turn the sentence around: *A new nine-member board was substituted for the wartime board.* In *The substitution of Ed's plan by Harry's seems unwise,* change to *The substitution of Harry's plan for Ed's.*

such. See ANTECEDENT PROBLEMS (3); SO; SUCH AS . . . AND OTHERS.

such as . . . and others, like *including . . . and others,* is a redundant construction. *Such as* selects one or more items from a class; *and others* asserts that the items selected do not constitute the whole class. Since *and others* tells us nothing that *such as* has not told us already, it is pointless to use both expressions; we should choose one or the other. Change *Confederate generals such as Lee, Jackson, and others* either to *Confederate generals such as Lee and Jackson* or to *Lee, Jackson, and other Confederate generals.*

sufficiently should be followed either by the infinitive *to* (*sufficiently reassuring to allay Nancy's fears*) or by *for* (*sufficiently equipped for an emergency operation*). It should not be followed by *as to, so that,* or *that.* In *sufficiently naïve as to believe him,* delete *as;* in *sufficiently rare so that a real one would bring a high price,* change to *so rare that;* in *sufficiently experienced that they hired her as a supervisor,* change to *to be hired as.* What goes for *sufficiently* goes also for *enough,* which should be preferred (as shorter and more familiar) wherever the two words are equivalent.

teen-ager and *teen-age* are relatively new words, dating only from about 1942; for better or for worse, they have strong connotations of the social concerns and commercial preferences of young middle-class Americans of the present era. Their use should accordingly be restricted to where these connotations are more or less appropriate: e.g., it would not be appropriate to refer to Keats's early poems as the work of a teen-ager.

than. (1) On *different than,* see DIFFERENT THAN. (2) Good writers do not admit the constructions *hardly . . . than* and *scarcely . . . than.* In *Scarcely had I finished than Father Wolofsky started complaining,* change *than* to *when;* alternatively, change *scarcely* to *no sooner,* which properly takes *than* and not *when.* (3) *Prefer . . . than* is an unacceptable construction. In *I prefer doing things right away than letting them pile up,* change *than* to *to;* in *He preferred to leave than stay and face the charge,* change *than* to *rather than.* (4) A few sentences of the form *I like Mary better than Bob* need an extra verb to be clear: is it *than Bob does* or *than I like Bob?* Most such sentences, however, are clear enough in context to get by without elaboration: *The state chairmen liked Taft better than Eisenhower / The Senate committee was more courteous to Budenz than the House committee.* Don't add the clarifying verb unless you have to. If you have to, add it after its subject, not before: *than Bob does,* not *than does Bob,* which has the artificial ring of something never heard in speech.

that. For when to use *that* and when *which,* see the text, pp. 109–112. For the double-*that* construction and how to repair it, see pp. 131–132. See also ANTECEDENT PROBLEMS (2).

the. (1) The unidiomatic omission of *the* before abstract nouns followed by *of* is brilliantly analyzed and justly deplored in Follett, pp. 37–41. Instead of *The discussion of politics was forbidden,* we now often find the truncated *Discussion of politics was forbidden;* instead of *Meyers opposed the extension of the draft,* we find *opposed extension of the draft.* The effect of this development, as Follett says, is to create a kind of new pidgin English, in which phrases arbitrarily shorn of *the* and *a* "arouse no sense of incompleteness." The trend in this direction is at once too powerful to oppose and too destructive to the present beauties and rhythms of English to welcome. In the circumstances the rule must be to follow your ear, and when in doubt add *the.*

(2) A special case of the unidiomatic elimination of *the* before *of* occurs in course names and the names of academic disciplines: *John did especially well in philosophy of science / I am majoring in history of art.* Whatever the formal name

of the course or the department, these subjects as subjects require the article: *the philosophy of science, the history of art.*

(3) When a possessive precedes a book title (or the equivalent) beginning with *The*, it is permissible to omit *The*: thus "Hardy's *Mayor of Casterbridge*," "Jonson's *Alchemist* and Shakespeare's *Tempest*."

(4) In writing the names of magazines and newspapers beginning with *The*, it is permissible to omit *The* for convenience: "his *New Yorker* articles," "a *New York Times* reporter." When *the* is retained, it should be lowercased and roman rather than capitalized and italic: "as the *San Francisco Chronicle* says," "the *New Republic's* coverage." The lowercased, roman form is of course inevitable when *the* attaches not to the title but to a following noun, as in "the *Reporter* editorial."

thereof, therein, thereto, etc. are sometimes substituted for the rhetorically weak *of it, in it, to it,* etc., especially at the end of a sentence: *The book was tedious, and he longed to get to the end thereof / Morgan knew of the plot but not of Nye's part therein.* However serious the *of it* disease may seem, the pompous and archaic *thereof* cure is fifty times worse. If no other cure can be found, live with the disease.

this. See ANTECEDENT PROBLEMS (2), (3).

though. See ALTHOUGH, THOUGH.

TIMEstyle is a word made up by an exasperated rival editor to denote the unique style of writing created and purveyed by the magazine *Time*. The word is on target: with its ironic bow to the magazine's ritual capitalization of TIME, its echo of such lunatic *Time* amalgams as *cinemactor,* and its hollow and tinny ring, it comes as close as any single word can to capturing *Time's* distinctive spirit, which may be described briefly as self-important, verbally daring, but ultimately without substance. TIMEstyle is one of the great influences on present-day American English. A student reads words like *kooky* and *pad* in *Time* and presumes that they are suitable for an essay on Charles Lamb; another student confidently uses TIMEstyle possessives like *at week's end* and *California's Senator Thomas H. Kuchel* (see POSSESSIVE PROBLEMS); a third achieves a bogus briskness by dropping *and*'s; a fourth piles up human-interest adjectives before his nouns (*genial, balding, 48-year-old Colonel Possiel*); a fifth becomes addicted to sentence fragments, a sixth to facetious asides, a seventh to impudent global pronouncements (*Every so often an art needs to go a little crazy*). To be sure, such devices make for lively writing, writing that will tell people something interesting in only four minutes about Vietnam or the stock market or the newest Italian movie—writing, in short, that will sell magazines. But that is all that can be said for TIMEstyle. What it cannot do is examine serious questions seriously or subtle questions subtly; chained as its writers are to the proven commercial negotiability of the short and snappy, they are as likely to produce an eloquent statement on Christianity or civil rights or war as Hollywood is to produce a genuine Abraham Lincoln. If *Time's* inventiveness and editorial discipline are to be admired—and they surely are—it must be for their contribution to journalism, not to English.

together with.   A singular noun followed by a phrase beginning *together with* takes a singular verb. In *The emperor, together with his ministers and his household, were exiled,* change *were* to *was.*

too.   It is colloquial to use *not too* for *not very* in such sentences as *I was not feeling too good that morning* and *Fuentes was not too pleased with the verdict.* A number of alternatives are available, among them omitting *too,* changing *too* to *very,* and switching to the Standard idiom *none too.*

total.   *A total of X* takes the singular or the plural according to whether *X* in the context would take the singular or the plural. Thus *Five hundred signatures was their goal / A total of 500 signatures was their goal;* but *Five hundred signatures were obtained / A total of 500 signatures were obtained.*

-type, in such expressions as *hose-type apparatus* and *California-type sunglasses,* should be restricted to dealers' catalogues, parts lists, the patois of supply sergeants and commercial travelers, and jocular evocations of the preceding. Good writers shun the construction as vulgar; bad ones embrace it as a way of sounding authoritative without the labor of fully articulating their meaning. The loser, as usual, is the reader, who is left to imagine what the hose-type apparatus looks like and how it works, and to wonder in what way the sunglasses are related to California.

The noun *type* is overused to mean *kind* or *sort.* Properly used, *type* implies a strong and clearly marked relationship to a more or less formal class of objects. Where the relationship is less clear or the class less formal, as in *He is the type of person who hates old ladies,* change to *kind* or *sort.*

un-, in-, non-. *In-* and *un-* are the classic negative prefixes. Since there is no clear difference between the two—no reason, for example, why we should say *ineligible* and *unacceptable* rather than *uneligible* and *inacceptable*—there is no way to resolve uncertainty about which prefix is right except with a dictionary. *Non-,* a more recent arrival, may be distinguished from *in-* and *un-* by its strong connotation of a division of the whole range of possibilities into two opposite categories, the X and the *non-X:* the smokers and the *nonsmokers,* fattening foods and *nonfattening* foods.

When you need a negative prefix for a new word, or for an old word for which the dictionary gives no negative form, the choice is between *un-* and *non-.* Use *un-* for informal negatives of participles (*unbearded*) and adjectives (*unfacetious*), and for ad hoc negatives of verbs (*unsimplify*). Use *non-* for nouns (*nonpeasant, noncompeter*); for formal or scientific negatives (*nonhostile, nonpsychedelic*), especially where the two-part-division connotation is very strong; and for negatives of compounds; (*non-smoke-abating, non-zero-sum*). The hyphenation of *non-* compounds is a matter of dispute; most editors follow Webster's principle of hyphenating only proper compounds (*non-Euclidean*) and compounds of three or more elements (*non-self-governing*).

underway is an adjective only, and occurs exclusively in the attributive position in such seldom-used technical compounds as *underway refueling*; the adverb is two words, *under way*. In *We had a hard time getting the project underway*, change to *under way*.

unique should not be compared or qualified. Something unique is the only one of its kind. A thing is accordingly either unique or not; it cannot be *almost unique, rather unique*, or *more unique* (*less unique*) than something else; nor can it be the *most unique* member of its class. See CLASHING VALUES.

unlike is subject to the same rules as *like*; in *Unlike Sunday, the weather yesterday was pleasant*, change to *Unlike Sunday's weather, yesterday's*. For other examples, see the text, pp. 116–117.

utilize and *utilization* are ugly and unnecessary synonyms for the verb and noun forms of *use*. In *The committee praised our utilization of Russian and Spanish materials*, change *utilization* to *use*.

very is overused by young writers. Four times out of five it can be eliminated without either changing the meaning of a sentence or weakening its force, e.g. in *George's father drives a very big truck* and *I was very sorry to hear of her illness*.

VOGUE WORDS are words or short phrases that have achieved prominence from their association with a public event or pronouncement, their conspicuous use by some arbiter of taste, or their capacity for solving certain problems faced by large numbers of speakers or writers, notably how to sound impressive at the least expense of time and thought. Some characteristic vogue words of the 1950's and 1960's are the low-level metaphors *framework* and *ceiling* and the noun-derived verbs *fault, trigger,* and *structure*; half a dozen others (e.g. GAP, OVERALL) are discussed in the preceding pages. A few vogue words go on to become permanent parts of the language in their vogue sense, but most soon lose whatever aptness may have initially commended them and linger on as clichés, overused by the hasty and misused by the uninformed. Everyone uses some vogue words, but good writers keep the number small by their habit of scrutinizing all but the simplest of the words they use for wrong connotations or shades of meaning. Must this reconsideration, they ask, be called an *agonizing reappraisal,* this difficulty a *gap,* this rise in costs or productivity a case of *escalation?* Hasn't the time come to give up *ceiling* and go back to *upper limit,* to give up *fault* and go back to *find fault with?* The handful of vogue words that survive this kind of scrutiny may be given safe-conduct; they have earned their place in the story.

we, editorial. The editorial *we,* as used, for example, in the "Talk of the Town" section of the *New Yorker,* has a persistent fascination for young writers, who see it as the very hallmark of the light touch. As it happens, however, few constructions are more difficult to master, and not one in a thousand college writers can achieve and sustain the sought-after tone of modest, twinkling urbanity; the usual effects range from arch to cloying to intolerably self-conscious. Our advice is to experiment with the editorial *we,* if experiment you must, in your extracurricular writing; use *I* in your themes.

which. For when to use *which* and when *that,* see the text, pp. 110–112. See also ANTECEDENT PROBLEMS (2); WHOSE.

while has two meanings: the temporal (at the same time that) and the concessive (despite the fact that). Many good writers do not use *while* in the second sense, preferring *although* or *whereas;* and nearly all would change *while* to *although* in a sentence like *While Lincoln was a great leader, Woodrow Wilson was equally great,* in which *while* carries the misleading suggestion that Lincoln and Wilson were contemporaries. Another doubtful use of *while* is as a fancy synonym for *and;* in *Some were playing cards, while others were reading,* change *while* to *and* or replace it with a semicolon.

who, whom. For a discussion of the impact of usage on the classic case distinctions in such sentences as *Who are you looking for?* and *He chose men whom he knew would be loyal,* see pp. 95–96.

whose may be freely used as the possessive of *which*; whether the antecedent is animate or inanimate makes no difference, so long as it is clear. *Caves for the treasures of which men have given their lives* is clumsy; change to *caves for whose treasures.*

will. See SHALL, WILL.

-wise. Like the reckless addition of -TYPE to nouns to form adjectives and of *-ize* to nouns or adjectives to form verbs, the reckless addition of *-wise* to nouns to form adverbs (*saleswise, percentagewise, footballwise*) is an affectation of the slovenly and the tin-eared, in whose keeping it may safely be left. What is to be will be, and if the language is to be Germanized it will be Germanized; but that time is not yet, and resistance may defer it.

would. See SHOULD, WOULD.

INDEX

INDEX